Connected

INTELLIGENCE

D0064320

Praise for **Connected Intelligence**

"His first few chapters sent a rocket into my thinking certainly, about the connected intelligence now mediated by the Web."
Boyd Neil, Vice President, *Hill & Knowlton Canada, The Globe & Mail*

"An engaging application of McLuhanesque theory to the Web ... Most of the writing in *Connected Intelligence* is very good – erudite but clear and accessible to the average reader."
ID Magazine

"In *Connected Intelligence* ... Derrick de Kerckhove outlines a framework for discussion about this emerging networked, wired world with an eye for creating a just technological society that will actually make good of its utopian promises ... *Connected Intelligence* is an intellectual gunshot across the bow of collective consciousness with the eye on the ultimate prize: a healthy republic of connected, engaged and enfranchised humans."
Bilbert Bouchard, The Edmonton Journal

"*Connected Intelligence* wonderfully explores the implications of externalized central nervous systems melding together on a global scale ... de Kerckhove has written an important book with fresh and thoughtful insight. The world needed him to carry forward the ideas of McLuhan into the next century."
Mark McNeil, Computer Column, The Hamilton Spectator

"De Kerckhove's voice is as valuable as McLuhan's was in predicting the impact that media will have on our lifestyle, economy, and the collective consciousness of the world."
Ingrid Hein, The Montreal Gazette

"The writing in *Connected Intelligence* is intelligent and pithy."
The Quill & Quire

Connected
INTELLIGENCE

THE ARRIVAL OF
THE WEB SOCIETY

DERRICK DE KERCKHOVE

EDITED BY
WADE ROWLAND

**KOGAN
PAGE**

YOURS TO HAVE AND TO HOLD

BUT NOT TO COPY

First published in Canada by Somerville House, 1997
First published in the UK by Kogan Page, 1998

Kogan Page Limited
120 Pentonville Road
London N1 9JN

British Library Cataloguing in Publication Data

A CIP record for this book is available from the British Library.

ISBN 0 7494 2780 9

Printed and bound in Great Britain by Biddles Ltd, Guildford and King's Lynn

For Marnie and Jan

CONTENTS

COMMUNICATUS
INTERRUPTUS

I CELEBRATE November 5 as the day when, in 1988, something ridiculous and grandiose happened to me and to fifty of Canada and France's most innovative artists and telecom engineers. We were performing one of the world's first video conferences for the arts in front of 1000 people (600 in Toronto and 400 in Paris). There were two huge video screens, one at the Ontario Science Centre and the other at the Centre français du commerce extérieur. Doug Hamburg, in Paris, was dancing with Eve Lenczner in Toronto. Hardly into the first thirty seconds of this "transinteractive pas de deux," appropriately called "The Dawn of the New Age," Doug's arm stretched from Paris to Eve Lenczner in Toronto became frozen into the characteristic patterns of jittering pixels which clearly indicates that you have just lost your connection to the satellite. We learned later that a drunken driver had hit a pylon carrying power to us Sprint's uplink earth station in Staten. We lost our satellite signal only thirty seconds into a two-hour show.

Two years of preparation wasted, over $100,000 down the drain and a cast of a hundred artists, engineers, and technicians stranded on both sides of the Atlantic. Well not quite. The show went on. The seventeen transinteractive performances turned out to be just as interesting in their simpler local interactive mode as if they had been performed across the ocean. The overflowing audience at both sites remained in their seats until the end, as if the fact that the connection across the Atlantic did not work, didn't matter. It was the poetry of the idea that counted. I, personally, was shattered by the whole thing, but, in spite of serving me with the most painful verification of Murphy's Law ("if it can break down, it will at the worst possible time . . ."), my disaster turned out to be a blessing.

As Eckart Wintzen, the celebrated founder of BSO, a Dutch System Integration Company now restructured under the name Origin, recounted to me, Joel de Rosnay, one of the main sponsors of the event on the French side, and a guest of the 1989 Infolutie, called it a "gallant failure." Eckart, with his typically visionary approach to technology, saw something interestingly "communicational" in Transinteractivity and invited me to the 1990 Infolutie on Communications. For the 1991 Infolutie, Eckart asked me to write *Brainframes*. It was my first book for Origin.

Willy Melgert, who was then Vice-President, Public Relations, of BSO/Origin, asked me to write the second, this one. He suggested that I collect all the papers of the talks I had given in connection with Origin and its clients and put them in a book. So this book is a reflection of my enduring relationship to the Netherlands and to the people and the organizations who helped me to write it by stimulating my thinking. I would like to thank all the persons and organizations who put me on the track of new thoughts and the audiences who patiently listened to me thinking aloud. As each chapter reflects different influences, just like the poet François Villon used to dedicate each strophe to different people, I would like to dedicate each chapter to those who were my inspiration.

The introduction is dedicated to Willy Melgert who helped me shape the whole book, but I also remember fondly my students at the McLuhan Program who taught me about the Net and my undergraduates in the Department of French at the University of Toronto, who make me think about their future which is so evidently tied to technology and culture.

I began to focus on the theme of interactivity to estimate the future of television, partly thanks to the invitation of Stefano Marzano, Vice-President of Design at Philips (Eindhoven). Stefano asked me to imagine what would become of television once it went "interactive." "The Biology of Interactivity," was inspired by all the artists I mention in the chapter and many more, but especially by the vibrant Dutch art and technology scene. For example, I gave several talks and wrote papers for the v2 Organisatie which was first located in 's-Hertogenbosch, and is now in Rotterdam. It is also in Rotterdam that ISEA, the International Symposium for the Electronic Arts, and DEAF, the Dutch Electronic Arts Foundation, were created and I am grateful to Alex Adriaansens, v2's director, who, along with people such as Caroline Nevejan and Marlene Stikker, at the famous Paradiso, and De Balie, and now at the Wang (Society for Old and New Media), and also René Coelho at the Montevideo Gallery in Amsterdam, who continue for Holland what they have done for me, that is to accelerate the understanding of what is happening at the edge of technology, through the study of the arts. At the same time I would like to recall here, among many other outstanding and deeply inspiring art and biology events in Holland, the beautiful and ephemeral "Brain, Internal Affairs" at the Beatrixziekenhuis in Gorinchem, a show that was placed in the older building of the hospital destined for demolition and which lasted until the old building came down. This was another great idea by Suzanne Oxenaar, founder-creator of the celebrated Supper Club, and of the Aha! group. The McLuhan Program's video-conferencing participation to the events surrounding this epoch-making show were superbly assisted by my friend Louis Molnar.

Chapter 3, "Person, Real and Virtual," is dedicated to Pier Bosscher and Marije Dippe from the Dutch Congress Buro who got me going on comparing human and technological networks. Chapter 4, on telepresence has to be dedicated to Geke van Dijk and her magnificent team, from the Amsterdam Cultural Studies Interactive. In collaboration with the Netherlands Design Institute in Amsterdam and the McLuhan Program and with the support of BSO/Origin and Telindus, among others, ACS-interactive organized "The World Series in Culture and Technology" during the fall of 1995. A video-conferencing link with Toronto (the McLuhan Program) enabled the audience at three different Dutch universities (Amsterdam, Delft and Groningen) to "attend." The guest speakers had the opportunity to exchange their thoughts and ideas on the various themes by way of presentations from the different locations. These presentations were followed by a debate in which members of the audiences were invited to engage. Each week an artist was invited to perform an experiment using the video-conferencing link. My warmest thanks to Geke and also her able assistants Karl Koch and Bas Rijmakers, and to the chairman Patrice Riemans, to Gertjan Broekman, who ran the Delft end of the operation, and to Eric Kluitenberg who took charge of the Groningen end.

For all of Part 2, I want to thank Wolter's Kluwer's CEO, Cornelius Brakel, Joost Kist, and Jeff van Gool from the Nederlands Bibliotheek en Laktuur Centrum who, in the course of a few months directed my attention squarely on the future of books. Another constant source of inspiration for its many experimental forays into CD-ROM and Web sites is Mediamatic and its Balzacian director, William Velthoven. To him and to the remarkable team of vpro, the Netherlands most innovative independent television production team, I dedicated the chapter on the future of news.

Chapter 8, on the future of museums, is dedicated to my Dutch-Canadian colleague at the McLuhan Program, Professor Kim H. Veltman, a Friesen in fact (an origin which, apparently explains everything in the Netherlands), who, by working untiringly on finding ways to put the contents of museums and galleries on line, has kept me and the program abreast of the most cutting edge on-line technologies.

I learned about connectedness by watching Marlene Stikker and Felipe Rodriguez demonstrate Digitale Stad, Amsterdam on-line, the first virtual city on-line, a full year before the Web made its public appearance. "The Connected Economy" is dedicated to John Thackara, and to the Netherlands Design Institute where I discovered the real art of brainstorming with Caroline Nevejan, Helen and Loes Vreedeveld, and Conny Bakker, as well as Josephine Grieve, Jill Scott, Ross Harley, who along with Chris Ryan, Catherine Murphy, and other Australian friends later in Melbourne, first taught me the rudiments of applied connected intelligence.

The next chapter goes to Eckart Wintzen whose series of Infolutie conferences for BSO, and later Origin, revealed to me the Intelligence of Business. I am indebted to Eric Kluitenberg for inviting me to Groningen and introducing me to SCAN and to its director. This visit led me to write the chapter on Planetization. I must also thank here Patrice Riemans for a tonic reminder of not letting my overly positive approach carry me away.

The last chapter, "Thinking the Earth" is dedicated to Holland where that kind of thinking has been going on for centuries, and to Canada too.

During the time I wrote the book, I had much help and support first from the publishing team, Wim de Ridder and Ms. Elizabeth Jonkman, of SMO, and from a lengthy and rich discussion with two of the three translators, Eli ten Lohuis and René Wezel. At the Origin office, I received help as well from Yvette Schuyl and Keejet Philippens. At the Toronto end I would like to recognize first, my publisher, Patrick Crean, from Somerville House Books, who has supported my work for a long time and my editor, Wade Rowland who generously shares his writing skills and expertise in communication technologies with me. I want to thank as well, my research assistants Derek Robinson and the two junior McLuhan Fellows from Cologne, Oliver Brink and Henrik Greisner. I would also like to thank for their administrative support Kathryn Carveth and Roger Bannister. Many people have made suggestions in conversation or have commented on different parts of the book; among these, I would like to thank Chris Neal, Sally Grande, Takeshi Amano, Wade Rowland again, Brian Alger, who e-mailed lengthy and valuable observations, Cattle Ken, the McLuhan Program Webmaster, Kaja Kruus (a graduate student who introduced me to the Internet), Amanda Brown, Henriette Gezundhajt, Diana Platts, Susan Fast, Johanne Besnard, Tom Strong, and José Mourao whose paper on hypertextual literature written while he was at the program as a Senior McLuhan Fellow, was an inspiration to my own chapter on the same theme. Another Senior McLuhan Fellow, Bob McIlwraith, developed the notion of the "feelings economy" from his association with the Program. And then, there is my wife, Marnie, to whom I dedicate the whole book, because without her, I would not be in the position to write a book at all.

Toronto, March 13, 1997

INTRODUCTION

BY WADE ROWLAND

T HE BOOK you have in your hands (so much more convenient than a laptop!) is an informed, highly creative, and wholly credible exercise in near-term prophecy; an argument for, and a poetic proclamation of, the existence of an emergent property called connected intelligence. It is also a call to action, because as Derrick de Kerckhove writes:

> With the common nervous system and senses of the world population now in the care of satellites, and with machines approximating the condition of mind and the minds of humans connecting across time and space, the future can and should be more a matter of choice than of destiny.

The notion of emergent properties is one that comes from the new science of Chaos Theory, which in turn has been made possible by our recently acquired ability to examine the inner workings of seemingly random or chaotic systems, using the formidable calculating power of electronic computers. The classical science of Newton was initially constructed on linear equations and predictable, clockwork systems because that was how science believed the universe worked. Increasingly, though, it became evident that chaotic systems—in which equations were nonlinear and in which the relationship between cause and effect could be wildly disproportionate, allowing for many surprising things to happen—were the rule in nature, rather than the exception. Science had been looking for the keys to the universe beneath the street lamp of linear equations and static, predictable systems because that was where the light was best, where the tools available to them worked. But the keys were to be found elsewhere.

The physics of quantum mechanics, now nearly a century old and still unshaken, tells us that nothing happens in the universe without in some way affecting everything else. It also tells us that the fundamental constituent of the universe is something closely akin to information; an insubstantial force-field out of which the material world is distilled in the form of dense concentrations, or focal nodes of the field. "We may therefore regard matter as being constituted by the regions of space in which the field is extremely intense," said Dr. Einstein. Physicist David Bohm has added, "There is a similarity between thought and matter. All matter, including ourselves, is determined by 'information'." Modern Information Theory equates information with unpredictability: if you already know the answer to a question, the answer contains no information. If the answer is a surprise, it is also information. Chaotic systems, full of surprises, are information generators. Out of the chaotic dynamics of the information-rich universe emerge phenomena that are self-organizing and can be self-perpetuating. One such emergent property is life. Life, it is now understood, could not be a product of a static, Newtonian universe. It takes the randomness of a chaotic system to produce surprises: like life; like a thunderstorm; like a black hole; like a supernova; like a genius. Like consciousness. It takes a chaotic system to produce a miracle.

Computers are our window on this world of nonlinear systems, for they are information processors without equal. With their gargantuan computational capacities, they have allowed us to begin to see the patterns, the logic, the recurrent themes behind apparent randomness in nature.

A computer is a wonderful thing, all the more marvelous because it is the product of human minds. It is a machine that can simulate the workings of any other machine. In fact, it can simulate the workings of any other rule-based *system* whatsoever. If you can figure out what makes something tick, you can get a computer to replicate it. The levels of complexity that the computer can replicate are limited only by the machine's memory and processing power, each of which has expanded a millionfold since the first "electronic brains" of fifty years ago, and continue their explosive development with no end in sight. And now, tens of millions of computers are being linked by the global Internet, which doubles in size (and computing capacity) every ten months. As it doubles, its potential power is squared, by the law of networks.

Some researchers think the stand-alone computer will eventually be capable of simulating the functioning of the human mind to a degree that will force us to admit the existence of machine intelligence; others find the idea preposterous and abhorrent. But what if a computer *can* be intelligent: what does that mean for the worldwide network of these machines? What does it mean for *us*?

The rules a computer follows in manipulating information are called algorithms. An algorithm is simply a list of the step-by-step processes that must be followed to execute a given procedure. Algorithms can be simple or they can be enormously complex, and they may have buried within them other algorithms which in turn contain further algorithms and so on. But no matter how complex or multilayered they may be, the digital computer can execute them flawlessly, because it follows them step-by-step with infinite patience and because it shares with all digital systems the ability to perform such operations flawlessly.

Whatever intelligence may be, we know that it is a product of a complex, self-contained, rule-based system, namely the mind. Unfortunately no one, despite two thousand years of focused inquiry, can say what a mind is. But we can, now, produce self-contained, rule-based systems inside computers to virtually any degree of complexity. Complex in their algorithmic rules, certainly, but complex in another important way as well.

Computers run on binary, machine language (1's and 0's), but very soon after they were invented, programmers had devised "assembly languages" which were easier for humans to deal with and which the computer itself could translate back into machine language. Then "compiler languages" were created, in which programmers could use scraps of ordinary English in composing their programs. The computer would translate that back into assembly language and from there into machine language.

There is no practical limit to the number of layers of language that can be used by programmers in feeding information to computers. Indeed, ordinary speech is being used more and more: the computer translates it, stage by stage—flawlessly, within the limits of its evolving algorithms—back down to machine language of 1's and 0's. It is not impossible to imagine that in the process of designing ever more complexity into the language we use to communicate with ever more powerful computers, we may reach a level at which it becomes clear that in its dealings with us, the machine is indistinguishable from an intelligent entity. At that point, we will have to concede the reality of machine intelligence.

Some of us may seek what cold comfort is offered by a belief that human intelligence is in some way innately superior to other forms of intelligence. It will be a perilous position to defend. The human brain, with its awesome electrical networks of billions of neurons and synapses, may be demonstrably superior in processing capacity to any foreseeable computerized artifact, but in what way would the intelligence that emerges from the brain's networks be intrinsically superior to the intelligence that emerges from a silicon-based entity? More sophisticated perhaps, or broader or deeper, or different—but better? The same laws of physics that govern our enigmatic universe apply to both brain and machine. "A rose is a rose is a rose."

The very earliest electronic computers, thirty-ton monsters with thousands upon thousands of vacuum tubes, were so powerful, so staggeringly fast in their internal processes (and so expensive), that their designers thought that perhaps a dozen or so would serve the foreseeable needs of the entire world. Today the capacity of one of those computers is likely be contained in a child's video game. Any one of the millions of computers now connected to the Internet and its World Wide Web contains more computing horsepower than existed in the entire world until the mid-1950s.

The question (among others) that Prof. De Kerckhove is asking, and in important ways answering in this book, is what happens when all of that computer capacity gets wired up in a worldwide web of high-speed, high-bandwidth data lines? What happens when the amplified and accelerated intelligence of humans equipped with high-powered computers in the tens of millions connects on the Net? Other highly complex systems we are familiar with exhibit an ability to throw off emergent behaviors; what might we expect from all of this networked intelligence?

No generation of humanity has lived in a more fascinating, portentous time. When Marshall McLuhan began writing the diary of this new era of information, the personal computer had scarcely been launched: he died the year Apple went public, in 1980. Derrick De Kerckhove, as a student, collaborator, translator, and co-author of McLuhan, and head of the McLuhan Program on Culture and Technology at the University of Toronto, in this work is carrying on a brilliant tradition of scholarship and imagination that allowed us to see clearly for the first time the meaning of media in our lives, and to ask where they might be leading us.

PROLOGUE

I T TOOK ME A WHILE to get on the Net. It cost me many hours of nail biting just to learn how to send e-mail. And then I needed more time to overcome a reluctance to read my incoming mail for fear of having to answer it. I couldn't handle yet another information stream pouring into the office. At the minuscule coach house headquarters of the McLuhan Program on Culture and Technology, besides the routine torture of three telephone lines ("Should call-waiting be on or off?"), we have a fax landing every ten minutes, snail mail twice a day, students, staff, and visitors coming and going through three doors (sometimes simultaneously), three TV sets (one often on), three radios (one almost always on), and three times a week on average, we do video conferencing with somewhere in the world.

For years, people had gently warned me that this situation simply couldn't continue and that, if I didn't rationalize activities, time, and resources, the program was heading for disaster. I have learned, however, that if you are at the center of things, chaos turns out to be just fine. It is only at the edges that chaos frays focus and dissipates energy. In fact, chaos may be the only answer when you are really interested in knowing what is going on *right now*. Chaos works for me like a kaleidoscope, with information churning and turning, tumbling into patterns which make sense. Nowadays I can't let a day go by without getting on-line, and our cluttered little office boasts seven PCs connected to a ten-megabit backbone. Anywhere from three to twenty people can be found there at work—or at play—anytime from 9 A.M. to midnight every day of the week (except some Sundays). There will always be some madness in my methods.

I can still recall the precise moment when I bought into the idea of the Net. During a seminar, one of my students showed us a video of a museum's World Wide Web site and told us—we had to believe her because audio recording hadn't been possible—that when you clicked on a button *there* you could hear the song of *that* bird in the photograph. I thought: This is it! Interactive CD-ROMs on-line, in real time! Now we're talking! It was not long after that that I realized to my own surprise that I was using e-mail routinely and beginning to develop a new kind of compulsion, the hunger to get to the next log after ever-shorter lapses of time.

None of this should be taken to mean that I am an avid surfer, anymore than I am an avid TV watcher. I keep my distance from all media except the telephone and the computer. However, I find that I keep looking into the direction of the Web, almost in spite of myself. There are any number of things about the Web that I actively dislike: first, the waiting; then the lifeless colors of Windows and Netscape; the primitive clumsiness of so much of the design; the occasional stupidity of the contents, and, of course, the hype surrounding it all. Nevertheless I can't avoid the growing conviction that something genuinely revolutionary is taking shape there, that it will affect all of us, and that we ought to get to know it better. That is what this book is about.

While I was at work on these pages, from time to time I referred back to my previous book, *The Skin of Culture,* to measure my current thoughts against what I had written earlier. I found that my understanding had evolved in several areas. One of my biggest surprises was to read the following: "Not long ago, the world was dumb and we were clever. But the computer-assisted world is becoming very clever and faster than we are. Very soon our collective technological intelligence will outperform the individual organic ones both in speed and integration. It will be interesting to know how this unified cognitive organization will take care of the environment and poverty, and what criteria it will dictate for genetic engineering. For the time being, relax. We are not there yet."[1]

Since writing those lines I have revised my thinking in two important respects. The first is that our commonly shared technological intelligence is not really "collective" but more precisely "connected"*. The other is that we *are* in fact there, and while we should keep our cool, this is no time to relax.

Indeed, the present book is driven by a new sense of urgency. While *The Skin of Culture* was about electronic media seen separately, this book shows how they are converging and tries to discover what it is they are converging towards. While *Skin* is basically on the mark, what it lacks is a discussion of the implications of *networked* digital communications.

Whether we call it the Net, the Internet, or the Information Highway, the growing synergy of networked communications is, with the exception of language itself, the communication medium par excellence—the most comprehensive, the most innovative, and the most complex of them all. It is also the most interesting. In the mega-convergence of hypertext, multimedia, virtual reality, neural networks, digital agents, and even artificial life, each medium is changing different parts of our lives—our modes of communication, entertainment, and work—but the Net potentially changes all of that and more, all at once. The Internet gives us access to a live, quasi-organic environment of millions of human intelligences perpetually at work on anything and everything with potential relevance to anyone and everybody. It is a new cognitive condition I call "webness."

By webness, I mean the essence of any network. The word is derived from the World Wide Web. During the summer of 1991,

---

* I owe this change to a suggestion made by Australian technology artist Ross Harley, who kindly rescued me from my embarrassment with the negative, potentially fascist connotations of the word *collective*. Readers of my previous book would do me a great favor if they replaced, at least mentally, each occurrence of the word *collective* in connection with intelligence with the word *connective*.

Tim Berners-Lee and his colleagues at the CERN (Centre Européen de Recherches Nucléaires) released the World Wide Web computer communications protocol to allow researchers to address the specific contents of databases directly, without having to search each one separately. In effect, this amounted to linking all the contents of any server anywhere in the world to any other computer on-line. You could now access the world's memory just as you access your own. Within five years there were thirty million users of the Web, with the number growing exponentially, and there was every indication that a new sector of the economy, if not the economy as a whole, was converging there.

And if, as Esther Dyson et al. have recommended[2], you added to this new phenomenon all telecommunications, wired or cabled; all broadcast and narrowcast via satellite or cellular relays; all the thousands of radio and TV stations busily sorting out the daily reality of the planet for everybody more or less at once, you were confronted by the sudden realization that a giant transformation is underway.

The main technological thrusts behind this convergence are the digitization of all content, the interconnection of all networks, the humanizing of interface hardware and software, and the globalizing effects of satellites.

Digitization is smashing everything to bits and placing the rebuilding of matter, life, and reality in the hands of people like you and me. A defining phenomenon of our time, it is moving commerce and industry from the realm of atoms to that of bits. At a more fundamental level it is moving objects from the realm of the material to that of thought. Bits make matter more malleable than atoms. Digital data is making shapes, substances, and identities mutually compatible, the way ideas and images are in our minds. Things are being digitized to enter the realm of the mind.

Interface technology, pushed by an unlikely combination of pressures from art and military aviation engineering, is getting closer and closer to direct access hardware-software combinations which will allow thought to control computers directly. Every step taken in that direction—from joystick, keyboard, and mouse, to voice, to direct mental command—is making our relationships with machines more intuitive, one might say more human.

Networks support the extension of what we know as mind into new, connected (not collective!), associations. They are providing the operating environment for convergence of all data. Such mind as we can still call our own is spilling into the networks as we engage them more interactively, more intimately, more sensorially than ever before.

The three main underlying conditions of the new ecology of networks, by which I mean both the economy of related industries and the new social and personal cognitive habits that support them, are:

1. Interactivity, the physical linking of people, or communication-based industries (the industries of the body)
2. Hypertextuality, the linking of contents or knowledge-based industries (the industries of memory)
3. Connectedness, or webness, the mental linking of people, or the industries of networks (the industries of intelligence)

Satellites figure importantly in the equation in that they give humanity the agency and the image of the new planetary scale of its reach; the new proportions of its collective body image. As individuals and as a species, we can begin to see the growing connections between our selves, our bodies, and our minds on the one hand and the planet on the other.

Together, interactivity, hypertextuality, and connectedness constitute the basis for the planetization of ordinary people as well as organizations, nations, and continents, by a permanent, self-updating synergy of local computers, global networks, and satellites.

INTERACTIVITY

The word *interactivity* was a lexicographer's curiosity ten years ago. Now it's on everybody's lips. What does it really mean? Interactivity is the relationship between the person and the digital environment as defined by the hardware that connects the two. There is rapid progress being made in military and artistic research into mind-machine direct access interfaces. However the bulk of human interventions in both the material and the virtual environments will remain grounded in the human body. It is no surprise that one of the most interesting areas of research in virtual reality (VR) today is in tactile feedback. *Interactivity is touch.*

VR, multimedia, and interactive systems are multisensory projections. Within the rich electronic environment that we have created for ourselves, we often entertain unconscious proprioceptive relationships, that is, responses activated by stimuli so deeply embedded in the media that we are scarcely aware of them.

Networks, too, are extensions of touch. Interactive networks like the telephone and video conferencing are all the more tactile in that they allow instant feedback. What constitutes "presence" in this kind of "telepresence"? If you can be "here" and "there" simultaneously by telephone or by video conferencing, and if "there" is seven thousand kilometers away, you have become either very fast or very large. Proper communications require feedback to confirm that the message has been received, even if it is just the return information on a data string—that is the truly "tactile" dimension of the relationship, and the essence of presence.

From the time of the telegraph to that of the Web, the population of the world has continuously increased the density of its network connections. New forms of concentrations of human energy happen on-line in these networks and they do not necessarily coincide with physical population centers. On the Web, ancient cities such as Pompeii, Monte Alban, Çatal Huyuc, Karnak, and others, rise ghost-like in digital replication. Real twentieth-century cities such as Berlin, Florence, and San Francisco are being recreated in databases and readied to connect with real-time information, on-line. Three-dimensional worlds, complete with virtual architecture, reliable news and weather services, age-old social and antisocial behaviors ranging from the disposal of virtual dog droppings to virtual vandalism, are beginning to appear and to attract thousands of "residents." Virtual malls are opening up at Web sites, URLs (Universal Resource Locator, the protocol for assigning addresses on the World Wide Web) with walls to make you feel better about shopping in virtuality. Very soon, "virtual offices" will have replaced many of their material counterparts, as communities learn to dispense with some of the trappings of real estate. Because it is increasingly possible for people to assume real presence in their virtual environments, it seems highly likely that they will transfer many of their current "real space" activities to these virtual environments.

It should come as no surprise that artists vie with military researchers to be at the cutting edge of technological investigation in all of this. Both have a vested interest in understanding and exploiting the impact of the technology on the human sensorium. And each is involved in his or her own way with issues of aggression—the military for obvious reasons and artists due to their special sensitivity to the destructive potential of new technologies invading the established social order. The paradox, of course, is that society grants the military lavish funding for its R&D and the art world lives on crusts. Moreover, the military works in secrecy, while art tries at every opportunity to claw its way out of obscurity. Having no access to military secrets, I have opted to go to the art of our time to learn about where we are going, trusting McLuhan's perceptive recommendation:

If men were able to be convinced that art is precise advance knowledge of how to cope with the psychic and social consequences of the next technology, would they all become artists? Or would they begin a careful translation of new art forms into social navigation charts? I am curious to know what would happen if art were suddenly seen for what it is, namely, exact information of how to rearrange one's psyche in order to anticipate the next blow from our own extended faculties.[3]

The privileged realm of the new art is the world of interfaces, not only because it is an accessible field for exploration but because it is the technological metaphor for the senses. With our hands, ears, eyes, and other conduits for action and sensation, we are constantly relating to or interacting with the world: those are the relationships to which artists have devoted most of their attention since the beginning of art. It is therefore quite logical and predictable that they would now turn to the modulation of these interactions through the new technological environment. Though most (but not all) artists choose to look at patterns in phenomena—sounds, images, thoughts, processes—the new breed is not afraid to get intimately acquainted with the digitized substitute.

HYPERTEXTUALITY

Hypertextuality means interactive access to anything from anywhere. Just as digitization is the new condition of content production, hypertextuality is the new condition of content storage and delivery. By itself, hypertext might be thought of as a very clever, text-based, automated indexing and referencing system. But the big news of the implementation of the principles of hypertextuality in the World Wide Web is precisely that the search-space is worldwide. The World Wide Web is the paradigm for what happens to hypertext when it emigrates from a stand-alone system, or a local area network (LAN), to the worldwide network. It changes the rules of the content game.

Hypertextuality is invading the traditional realms of content provision in data, text, sound, and video. It is changing the rules of space-based storage, distribution, and delivery of books, records, tapes, video, and film. Because it is becoming ubiquitous and because it responds much better to the instant delivery requirements of the market, it is replacing older methods of news delivery wherever the existing networks permit. Countries such as Canada and the Netherlands that are endowed with a good network infrastructure*

---

* For example, cable penetration in both countries is well over 90 percent.

stand to gain immediate economic advantage over their neighbors, if their governments and industries will only allow themselves to be persuaded to facilitate the hypertextualization of their economies. There is, of course, some resistance to such a move. First, because it rocks established patterns of commerce; second, because corporations tend to focus on short-term profit rather than longer-term opportunities; and finally, because it takes both vision and skill to implement hypertextual access across the board, and the first of these requirements, in particular, is generally in short supply.

Nevertheless, digitization has already "zapped" or dematerialized traditional memory-support devices such as books, tapes, and records. The opportunity to incorporate hypertextuality is also a powerful motivating force behind changes in the modes of production and access from linear (analogue) to nonlinear (digital) media. Thanks to the ease of reconfiguring data, news is now shifting from mass distribution to customized delivery. The information economy is moving away from concrete storage technologies such as analog video, audio, and print towards intelligent machines which produce the information on demand. In other words, while the technologies of information of the past are aids to memory or storage (books, tapes, records, films, videos, photographs), the main technologies of today's information systems are aids to processing; that is, aids to intelligence. This shift is a reflection of a much broader permutation of the culture from memory-based to intelligence-based production. We are moving from the era of "replay" to that of "remake." We are developing computer-assisted cognitive habits and computer-assisted forms of collaboration—new forms, in fact, of connectedness.

CONNECTEDNESS

Connectedness is a human status or state just as surely as collectivity or individuality. It is that fleeting condition comprised of at least two persons in touch with one another, for example, in conversation or in collaboration. The Web, the connected medium par excellence, is the technology that makes explicit and tangible this natural condition of human interaction. The only other connected media we have known are the telegraph and the telephone, one-on-one, point-to-point affairs; extensions of the vocal exchange. The Internet, by combining the two and adding point-to-multipoint (broadcast) potential, much increased useful connectedness among people. The World Wide Web added another dimension of connectedness, with hypertext linking the stored content of their communication. Then, as if to achieve critical mass, Marc Andreessen threw in the kicker with the launch of Mosaic.* In making the Web colorful and sensual as well as useful, he made it irresistible.

What is "connected" about the Web is that it allows and encourages the input of individuals within a "collective" medium. The result is that the information processes and the social organization arising out of it are both connected and individual at the same time. Books, by comparison, fostered individualism only, isolating people from each other even as they made human communication silent. The effect of books was to accelerate the growth of individual minds and of individualism within those minds. (Books are not at all connected because they do not allow individual input.) Radio and TV are truly collective, addressing, as they do, everybody at the same time: like books, they are not connected because they do not allow or invite real-time individual input. The exception to the rule is the phone-in talk show on radio. These, however, are tightly formatted, heavily screened, and strictly moderated. Computers are unparalleled as accelerators of individual human information processing. And once they became networked, the connected became an alternative to both the individual and the collective. Connectedness is

---

* Mosaic was the first "browser" for navigation on the World Wide Web. A young programmer named Marc Andreessen working then with the NSCA (National Super Computer Association) developed it and launched it in the summer of 1993. Almost overnight, the Web, as it soon became known, was invaded by newcomers. Since then Mosaic and Andreessen have become associated with Jim Clark, founder and ex-CEO of Silicon Graphics, to create and launched the current market-leading browser, Netscape.

one of mankind's most powerful resources. It is a condition for the accelerated growth of human intellectual production.

Satellites have led to a formidable enhancement and change of scale in our connected environment. It is possible right now, for anyone with access to the Web, to download almost-real-time images of planet Earth from a weather satellite. It is not quite like standing atop a mountain, and the experience may not always generate the mountaineer's sense of pride of ownership, but what you see on your screen is unquestionably really there, and it is your *personal* access to the worldwide world. You can guide a cursor to change the angle of vision. You can see the sunlight to one side of the planet. With time-lapse imaging, you can watch the development of cloud formations and follow the course of hurricanes.

The extraordinary change of scale brought to ordinary humans by direct access to their total ecological environment is making room for new varieties of psychological structures. How tiny, by comparison, is the Renaissance model of man!

We might reasonably expect a connected sensibility, a new psychology, to emerge from the number and speed of network connections and that is what much of the rest of this book is about.

There is a growing need, perhaps repressed as a result of our century's sorry experience of shattered ideals, to believe in something that might yet have a pleasant outcome. While there is abroad in the world an increased religiosity rife with all the usual contradictions, and violent clashes between local and global cultures living in different time warps and different time zones, there is at the same a growing awareness, even among warring factions, of creative ways to make accommodations and find solutions.* With the common nervous system and senses of the world population now in the care of satellites, and with machines approximating the condition of mind and the minds of humans connecting across time and space, the future can and should be more a matter of choice than of destiny. It's

---

* Considering that it is also about the issue of survival, could ecology, as the vehicle that brings all agendas together, become the next religion?

much less difficult to make up one's mind when one understands the context.

Connected Intelligence is a book, not a hypertext. However, I have kept in mind that different people with different agendas might find some parts more pertinent than others. Each chapter can stand on its own. Parts one, two and three, entitled respectively, "Interactivity," "Hypertextuality," and "Connectedness," reflect each other and the whole book. I have tried to integrate interactivity, hypertextuality, and connectedness in each chapter as I believe these principles operate across the board in all concerns involving technology and culture. For those who enjoy the continuity of an argument, I have ordered the chapters in such a way that they reflect the one I support, namely that if indeed our technology is precipitating us in a new order of reality, it had better be informed by care and attention for everybody.

PART 1

INTERACTIVITY

CHAPTER ONE

THE BUSINESS
OF INTERACTIVITY

W HEN I WAS TRYING, between November 1986 and
October 1988, to raise money for that "gallant failure"
called Transinteractivity, all I could raise were eyebrows,
and polite refusals from business executives. Today, there's been
an about-face in attitude and it's turning industry and governments
around. "Interactive" has become a byword for a projected multi-
billion-dollar business in the media, and especially television. Industries involved in content delivery by satellite, cable, telephone, and
even some electric power companies, are champing at the bit to
deliver "fully interactive services," in the form of programming on
demand, home shopping, and financial services. On the retail end,
there is a huge market for interactive games, a healthy industry in
multimedia hardware and software, and a steady stream of "hit
CD-ROMs" that get hyped as the latest and greatest in interactivity.
Both the cultural and the entertainment sectors are investing in
interactivity as a lure to patrons. Interactivity has penetrated displays in museums and galleries. Virtual reality, the *summum* of interactive applications, after being a trade show curiosity for selling
cigarettes and motorcycles, is finding its way in to media parks and
arcades with a full complement of shoot-'em-ups and Jurassic ter-
rors. And the upshot of this frenzy of "interactivity" is that people
still don't get it.

Take the most common example—CD-ROMs, the core of the retail interactive business. These can hardly be deemed interactive, if one means by the word that the medium responds in some way to the input of the user, other than by bringing up the desired display. Most CD-ROMs are less interactive than a dictionary. The fact that QuickTime video gives you an illustrating low-definition motion picture instead of an illustrating high-definition still photograph can scarcely be classified as qualitative progress in interactivity. It may be fun for a while to see Mick Jagger strut in slo-mo, choppy, impressionistic splashes of pixelated colors, but you soon tire of it. Video games are more seriously interactive and I will get back to them in due course, but by and large today's so-called interactive systems, or installations, are a steady source of disappointment.

I have tried. As a judge for several interactive media festivals and prizes for government and educational instructional media, and as a member of the Interactive Digital Media Association in Toronto, I have been subjected to hours of explorations into Peter Gabriel's *Xplora, Myst, Johnny Mnemonic, Burn Cycle*, and many more. What kept echoing in my mind was the stern interdiction of one of Toronto's top CD-ROM experts: "Always remember that your client has five times less patience than you do when waiting for the next screen to show up!"

Let's face it: the finest CDs—and there are quite a few—and the best VR are so slow and clunky, and the image definition is usually so poor as to dispel forever the fears of journalists and media commentators, that we might someday take them for the real thing. These facts are plain to see, yet they don't seem to lessen our fascination with the lures of interactivity. Even the ubiquitous spread of self-help, interactive instruction kiosks is not abated by the fact that they tend to be ugly, dirty, clumsy, and broken. So what's the attraction? Why do people part with small fortunes to upgrade their already pricey platforms to six-times sampling speed CD players and surround their computers (and now their TV sets) with cumbersome multimedia peripherals? The answer, in a word, is television.

In spite of all the talk about how "passive" it is supposed to make us, TV* has been implicitly interactive from the start. With its seductive influence over the viewer, television is like a siren.[1] The desire to cozy up to the screen seems to begin at an early age: preschool children tend to huddle with their nose to the set as if they wanted to immerse themselves in the stream of electrons. The current trend towards interactivity is an entirely predictable outgrowth of our involvement with a medium that, in a manner of speaking, sucks its user in. Indeed, while we are watching TV, the stuff of our imagination is not confined to the privacy of our mind, but is happening out there on the screen in full motion and color with a high sensory content which contributes directly to the elaboration of meaning. TV's auditory, visual, and kinesthetic stimulations address the spectator directly, without the kind of detached, secondary elaboration which is a feature of the decoding of a printed text by turning it into mental images. TV thus unavoidably evokes multisensory responses which summon our whole body into play. With its carefully crafted audio levels, visual features, and, especially, camera movement and editing rhythms which call for proprioceptive or kinesthetic reactions, TV acts very much like real-life events in evoking multisensory, integrated responses. Of course, the significant difference is that while real life usually brings about a direct physical as well as mental and emotional participation in the situation, TV's symbolic content does not lead to action, but only to interpretation.

As TV becomes explicitly interactive, first via remote control and now with CD-ROMs and video game controllers, the elaboration of one's mental images must continue to be conducted on a screen outside the body, only now with the body's active, voluntary participation in the process of making sense of the world. This has led to three related, largely unconscious, drives in the culture of television: the recovery of touch, a need for telepresence, and a

---

* By TV, I mean the appliance or delivery vehicle rather than the content provided for it by the conventional television producers at Fox, CBC, Televisa, and the rest.

reversal of the relationship between man and screen in virtual reality.

The technological search for ways to realize these unconscious drives has taken many forms, some more naive than others. But since the invention of the zapper, TV's potential for interactivity has been growing by leaps and bounds. If so-called passive TV was the ultimate step in the evolution of frontal and detached media, the zapper may have been the first step towards a radical reversal in our relationship with the information we process: I zap, therefore I think. While I zap, I am in control of the screen. As for VR, it reverses another aspect of our relationship to TV: while books allowed people to introduce information in their heads, virtual reality allows them to introduce their heads into information.

It is no surprise that the television industry, after some initial hesitation, has tried to move in on the interactive business in a big way. But what exactly is "interactive television"? Is it technologies like Montreal and Quebec City's Videoway and UBI, two reasonably successful though now defunct cable-based experiments with asymmetrical, two-way interactive services? The secret behind this system was to split a single channel's content four ways, giving an illusion of control to the user by permitting him to choose among the four with his zapper. Do we include "full service" trials such as Time-Warner's Orlando experiments or Viacom's Castro Valley test of Video-on-Demand (VOD), or Intercom Ontario's high-bandwidth, wired community test? Other trials have been conducted in Chicago, Cambridge (U.K.), and Queen's (New York), but none has succeeded in capturing the imagination, not to mention the wallets, of consumers. Perhaps the true destiny of interactive television is better represented by NTN Communications, the very successful U.S. network that for eleven years has been broadcasting interactive video games to restaurants, bars, and hotels in the U.S., Canada, South Africa, and Australia.

One of the reasons why the broadcasting industry is finding it difficult to get at the real meaning of interactivity is that its vision is still, understandably, blinkered by the broadcasting model of the audiovisual economy. At its root, the broadcasting model is simply the extension to radio and TV of the top-down industrial or factory system for production and distribution of goods and services. The paradox of the business of interactive TV is that while it is perfectly true that conventional television with its universal presence provides an ideal means of introducing interactive media into most homes, real interactivity is available only through digital media, another technological universe altogether.

Digitization all but eliminates the technological boundaries separating communications media and reduces their essence to binary data, the new common denominator of all information. By eliminating their material differences, digital convergence brings together in a unified environment the previously distinct industries of telephone, radio, television, computers, and print publishing. The television industry's primary response to the promise of digital technology has been High Definition Television (HDTV), still in the development stage. With its emphasis on image definition instead of technical flexibility, HDTV demonstrates once again how little the television industry has understood the message of computers. The real value of HDTV—and its only real hope of commercial success— lies not in its high-definition screen display, but in the fact that it will put television squarely in the digital domain. Television will then enjoy the same level of intelligent and adaptable processing as exists on a computer screen, closing the loop of convergence between the digital and analogue worlds of information processing. Much, if not most, behind-the-scenes production in television has already migrated to digital technology: when HDTV makes the final delivery system digital as well, TV will be solidly in the digital camp, with all that implies for the medium's message. If the TV industry is uncomfortable with the interactive capability implicit in digital media, it has every reason to be, because interactivity spells the end of corporate control of the erstwhile "mass culture."

What we are seeing, as many commentators have observed (Jaron Lanier, George Gilder, John Perry Barlow, and others), is indeed an end to television as we've known it, though not its demise.

TV will go on doing what it is good at for a long time to come. It will continue, as well, to hold a prominent place in the mass cultures of the catching-up societies. TV's role has always been to provide shared experience and values in society. Far from being the alienating medium its critics have described, television is in fact a community builder, a socializer of our kids, a purveyor of community news and gossip. Thus the real identity of TV is "public" regardless of whether this or that particular station happens to be run by the state.

In some respects, people in the postindustrial societies have been interactive ever since they learned to get their money from Automatic Teller Machines (ATMs) instead of from bank clerks. In France, the Minitel has taught a whole generation the ABCs of interactivity. While the interactive society is not quite a palpable reality, it is creeping up on us from the periphery to the center, from the grassroots upwards, from the bottom up. The i-people are the grandchildren of TV. They have been trained by the video game both to run their parent's VCR and to get on the Net.

Television viewers, once putty in the hands of TV programmers, began to recover their lost autonomy the moment they were entrusted with zappers. The rapid distribution of the apparently innocuous remote-control interfaces in the middle 1970s marked the beginning of the end of top-down control of television production. The first effect of putting this crude form of instant "editing" power in the hands of the average consumer was to allow him to skip boring dramatic sequences and hackneyed advertising spots. In response, program producers learned to "zap the zapper" before he had the chance to zap the channel. This tug-of-war between producers and consumers of programs helped to accelerate the pace of programming, and later its structure, so that particular attention was paid to the opening moments. The average length of commercials soon shrunk from the original sixty seconds to thirty and fifteen seconds. Quick editing and "jolts-per-minute" strategies were implemented in programming to help maintain the zapper's attention.

No sooner was this battle joined than VCRs made their appearance in the early 1970s, allowing the more discriminating viewers to store one program while watching another, or to "time shift" a program from its scheduled airing to a time more convenient to the viewer. The mere notion that you could actually record and replay, and with the right equipment even reedit your own programming, put a new bug in the television system even as it was preparing mass culture for a future of shared responsibility for content delivery and use.

Meanwhile, home video cameras and editing decks were improving at warp speed, thanks to the application of digital technologies. The dividing line between professional quality and consumer equipment blurred to the point of disappearing altogether. As a result, the late seventies and the eighties witnessed an unprecedented growth in small, quality-conscious independent video production companies.

THE USER AS CONTENT

Understanding the potential of all of this digital technology, with its latent potential for interactivity, demands a fundamental shift in point of view. To look at interactivity from the traditional broadcaster's perspective is about as helpful as looking through the wrong end of a telescope: the user's point of view should be the critical one. The First Law of Interactivity is that the user shapes or provides the content, either by taking advantage of nonlinear access to make program selections, or by actually taking full responsibility for the content as a bona fide content provider. This is by no means a trivial distinction: Marshall McLuhan once quipped, "If the medium is the message, then the user, really, is the content." In other words, the message of any medium may be thought of as the way it shapes the user merely by engaging him or her in connecting with the medium. Television, radio, books, interactive media, each in their own way condition media-specific responses from their users, be they consumers or producers, or interactive "prosumers." Media, seen this way, are complete environments which contain their users as their content. This observation may have seemed obscure, not to say flippant, in

McLuhan's heyday when broadcast television was king. Today, however, with the proliferation of home pages on the Web, his aphorism takes on a more direct and pertinent significance. Home pages are, for their creators, instant "station identification devices." The fact that the viewer needs to actively seek out content makes *both* the addressors and the addressees of any digital, networked communication the principal providers, and thus the real content, of the communication. This should be kept in mind by the content quota watchdogs in national broadcast regulatory bodies. Any national user of the networked structure becomes, *ipso facto*, "national content."

Interactivity has also changed the processes by which we design content. While design used to be the prerogative of the producer imposing his or her vision on the service or the product to be sold (the "broadcast" model of design), the availability of new hardware and software tools to assist individuals in designing their own products is pushing the limits of design to the level of "meta-design." Meta-design is the design of tools, parameters, and operating conditions that allow the end-user to take charge of the final design. This is the "network model" of design. In a truly interactive environment, the advantages of meta-design are handed over to the end-user, with support and coaching from the provider. This makes the client of any on-line industry a partner in that industry.

Meta-design is affecting not only audiovisual software, but also the hardware-based industries, allowing end-users to take control of major design decisions in anything from a desktop publication to such products as shoes, clothing, and furniture produced by computer-assisted tools for pattern-creation, cutting, manufacturing, packaging, and even distribution. Thanks to the efficiencies in time, labor, and cost and the run-control abilities of software-supported meta-design (warehousing becomes a thing of the past), the once battered textile industries of Canada, the U.S., and Europe are beginning to beat back the low wage, labor-intensive competition from the world's sweatshops.

In this new context, the true destiny of interactivity is clearly not to stand alone, but to go on-line. For example, by itself, the CD-ROM industry is hardly more than a glorified adjunct to the book, record, and tape markets. Their "read-only" nature defines them as part of the old industrial order, that is, one-way or broadcast distribution of self-contained, mass-produced, packaged objects. However, just as books are useful only if they are read, understood, and reused in other contexts by literal or thematic quoting and elaboration, the CD-ROM's real providence is to be used and reused on-line in ever changing contexts. Indeed, the most positive aspect of interactivity in CD-ROMs is that, on-line, the content of interactive programming may enjoy a much longer shelf life than conventional, linear TV and video content. Most, if not all, television programming, whether interactive or not, is destined to become the content of network-accessible databases which will bring revenue to the producers on the basis of on-demand use. At that point the broadcasting and CD-ROM industries will merge.

ADAPTING TO INTERACTIVITY

Critics are prompt to take big business to task for overhyping interactivity. For example, the Finnish social critic Erkki Huhtamo makes the following comment in recording his disappointment with a demonstration of the Time-Warner's Orlando "full-service TV" experiment:

> The concept of interactivity seems to have been hijacked by corporate interests to sell more of the same in a newly designed package. . . . Many seem to believe that the existence of interactive gadgets, from teller machines to home computers, automatically implies a change in the human-machine relationship. However, interactive technology provides no more than a frame of opportunities, which is always filled by specific applications and ideological ideas. These may have little to do with "interactivity."

Among the most severe condemnations of the whole trend to the computerization of culture is one by Clifford Stoll:

Today's Internet hustlers invade our communities with computers, not concrete. By pushing the Internet as a universal panacea,
they offer a tempting escape from all this all-too-mundane
world. They tell us that we need not get along with our neigh-
bours—heck, we needn't even interact with them. Won't need
to travel to a library either; those books will come right to my
desk. Interactive multimedia will solve classroom problems. Fat
paychecks and lifelong employment await those who master
computers.

They're well-meaning, of course. They truly believe in virtual
communities and electronic classrooms. They'll tell you how the
computer is a tool to be used, not abused. Because clearly, the
computer is the key to the future.

The key ingredient of their silicon snake oil is a technocratic
belief that computers and networks will make a better society.[2]

And for critic Stephen Talbot, "by means of the computer, concrete human activity itself is invited towards passivity, automatism,
and lowered consciousness":

The sleight of hand in the argument about interactivity is
repeated on many fronts. To cite one example: the informality of
much computer-mediated communication is often seen as a
recovery of the direct, the personal, the participatory, the emo-
tionally expressive. Many observers, contrasting this "new orality" with formal or "literate" communication, see the computer
carrying us back to earlier, more vivid and personalized forms of
human exchange.

But the relevant comparison is not between oral and literate.
It is between the genuinely oral communication that once took
place face-to-face, and the "secondary orality" now electronically
replacing that communication. Here we see the computer's
influence running exactly counter to the usual thesis: informal
communication is tending towards the abstract, disengaged, and
remote, with feeling conveyed indirectly through the artifice of

written expression, and participation unavoidably constrained by the narrower channel.

I should add that the ease with which this sleight of hand succeeds—and anyone willing to spend time perusing a selection of Net discussion groups can quickly verify the success—is itself testimony to an idealism loosed from reality.[3]

On all these points, I have to say that I agree. But only because they are so obvious. Yes, it is true, and everybody knows it—for business, interactivity is just another delivery mechanism, a way to get people to buy more stuff; for the mass consumer, an interactive device is a toy with which to play with more toys. And yes, behind all the hype, you will uncover a singularly primitive model of man-machine relations based on the humble joystick. The way interactivity is hyped, one might be forgiven for thinking that the whole culture is going through an adolescent fixation on a video game. But perhaps that is precisely what is happening.

If, as a society, we didn't want silicon snake oil, we didn't know it until it was too late. We should have gotten rid of television, as Jerry Mander recommended.[4] Of course, that was a ludicrous proposition—like suggesting that we pull the plug on all electrical power. Electricity is here to stay and interactivity is stage two of mankind's large-scale adaptation to it. Stage one was television.

Interactivity has become the leading edge of a comprehensive biotechnological interplay which no doubt began with the invention of the wheel, but has fully flowered only with electricity. This is because electricity is coextensive with the human nervous system. In every interaction with our new technologies, electricity comes in and out of the human body as impulses and currents affecting nerve cells and electronic relays, synapses and semiconductors. Interactive systems, in creating a new continuity between the body and the machine, clearly help to reinforce the network of connections that expand our central nervous systems beyond our bodies to the exterior world.

Until now, practically all our technologies fell under the general category of *extension,* described by Mumford, Leroy-Gourhan,

McLuhan, Giedion, and many others as a continuation or an outering of the body. The glove extends and protects the skin, the shovel extends the hand to allow it to dig the ground. The alphabet and the computer extend the mind to process language, itself a complex extension of the brain. With the interactive technologies, two very significant changes are taking place: firstly, the machine is developing a rudimentary will of its own as it becomes more and more adept at storing and analyzing the patterns of the interactions. Transcending its original status of extension, it now becomes more and more a projection. This means that it becomes separate from the body, more like a domestic animal than a car or a bulldozer. It is a robot. And it can develop an attitude. Indeed, the various aspects of research into interactive interfaces are coming together in the science of robotics in the attempt to build a completely synthetic body. This is autonomation, and it can be mechanical, or digitally virtual.

At the same time as they are "going digital," the extensions and projections of man developed by today's technological revolution are also going on-line. Hence a second, more comprehensive order of integration is occurring, well beyond the personal limits of the body and the self. We are about to be invaded by populations of "agents" and "avatars." Nicholas Negroponte predicts that:

> What we today call "agent-based interfaces" will emerge as the dominant means by which computers and people talk with one another. There will be specific points in space and time where bits get converted into atoms and the reverse. Whether that is the transmission of a liquid crystal (display screen) or the reverberation of a speech generator, the interface will need size, shape, color, tone of voice, and all the other sensory paraphernalia.[5]

As more "virtual communities" take hold and more telepresent technologies develop and spread through the economy and the culture, the meaning of interactivity may become transitive (and transparent) and designate not the primitive concept of the "man-machine interaction," but a more fulfilling—and "adult"—sense of person-to-person, computer-assisted interaction.

Telepresence, or virtual presence, for example, is fast developing into an indispensable industry, and, if we believe media critic Peter Weibel, will become more so in the future under the pressure of ever more limited physical and material resources:

> We need technology to survive. The scarcer the space, the larger the population, the more vital is the overlapping and simulation of spaces, times and bodies, so that more objects and subjects can be present at the same time. Technology must therefore develop further towards teletechnology. The tools must become teleoperators and telefactors, society must become a teletech-notronic civilization.[6]

For the moment, interactivity, whether transitive or not, is still mostly fun and games. But there are enough portents of reality reproducing itself in virtuality that we should pay keen attention. While I do not expect for a moment that we will "escape" to cyber-space, as my friend Pierre Lévy fears, I am certain that it will be the way in which as individuals we connect in these virtual environments, that will decide what kinds of people we and, especially, our children will become. These developments raise, as Sherry Turkle observed with keen attention in her recent book *Life on the Screen*, some serious issues about identity, personhood, presence, and, of course, that old standby, reality.

CHAPTER TWO

THE BIOLOGY
OF INTERACTIVITY

I T HAS OFTEN BEEN OBSERVED that playing and learning are born genetically intertwined in us, only to be artificially unraveled at school. Today, high-technology marketers have spliced them back together, with uneven results, in what is known as "edutainment." More hand-held video games sets are sold each year than TV sets, and this simple economic indicator underlines a major sociocultural transition. Sega, Nintendo, and other video game makers are the driving force behind a large-scale retooling of our educational practices.

Educators and toy marketers agree that games and sports can have as much educational as recreational value. But they often have no clear idea of why that is the case. The reason is that games and sports tune the nervous system. Like sports, games stretch personal limits by providing the right level of motivation and by rewiring the body, or the mind, for better performance. What these activities do for the individual, they also do for the culture at large. As Don Tapscott observes:

The new technology is penetrating our lives; much of this is happening through our children. Over one-quarter of American homes have a computer, but for many adults the machine is a mystery, or it is used for word processing, accounting, or home business applications. Children, on the other hand, are using machines for games, homework, communications, art, music, reference, and a host of emerging applications on the Internet.[1]

The main role and purpose of games in our technological culture may be normative, that is, to help introduce the technology into everyday use. The younger generation is addressed largely because their nervous system is still malleable and capable of integrating new structures.

Many video arcade games and their domestic versions in Nintendo, Sega, and Lynx-based platforms combine mental and hand-eye coordination skills in aggressive postures. In spite of their often simplistic scenarios and low-grade imagery, such computer games are successful to the extent that they integrate more complex syntheses of sensory-motor involvement, mental acuity, and reflexes. They work the body and the mind of users into new configurations, conditioning them for later professional use of computer-based technologies.

Video games are successful precisely because they respond to a need in growing children to externalize and monitor the growth of their own nervous systems. Games are to the central nervous system, what sports are to the neuromuscular system. Because they involve physical contact with a joystick, keyboard, mouse, or other instant-feedback interface, they address the nervous system directly. Thus, they are able to retrain the nervous system directly. On a purely physical plane, games generally accelerate reaction time and hand-eye-ear coordination but, more pertinently, they allow the children to form and improve schemata in their minds, installing, like new software, the required physical and mental approaches to deal with computers and the Internet.

Getting on-line or playing video games or trying virtual reality or experimenting in interactive arts each involve strategies to map and remap the user's nervous system at the psychological as well as the physiological level. The effect of video games, for example, with respect to the television industry, is to train ordinary people from childhood to take control and responsibility for the content of the screen. Douglas Rushkoff explains how children learn to integrate the schemata of the controlled screen:

> Thanks to their experience with video games, kids have a fundamentally different appreciation of the television image than their parents. They know it's up for grabs. While their parents sit in the living-room passively absorbing network programming, the kids are down in the playroom zapping the Sega aliens on their own TV screen. The parents' underlying appetite is for easy entertainment or, at best, prepackaged information. Meanwhile, they bemoan the fact that their kids don't have an attention span long enough to endure such programming. The kids, on the other hand, rather than simply receiving media, are actively changing the image on that screen.[2]

Video games are often condemned out of hand as onanistic, narcissistic devices that create antisocial dunces out of nice, clean kids. But video game critics fail to see the larger picture of the video game industry. There are indeed a plethora of solitary, not to say solipsist, games such as Gameboys, Lynxes, etc.; the solitary games tend to be used largely by boys, but often in the context of one-upmanship with other teens. Video arcades provide yet another cultural configuration, usually involving groups rather than individuals, and there are also the games designed to be played on home TV sets, some now offered on-line, via cable, or even by telephone or wireless transmission.

All these varieties of games perform different social and biological functions. Solitary game systems act as bio-accelerators and adrenaline-boosting mechanisms; in fact, they can be thought of as computer-assisted neurotransmitters. Whether hand-held or TV-linked, they put the user into an artificial "alert" mode. The group-oriented games for video arcades probably respond to genetically programmed self-assertion biases, and, like bodily sports, provide a limited range of survival-based competitive skills. They have already generated their own subculture and are training the cyber generation. The cyber culture surrounding them is best expressed in the gamers from all over the world who get on-line to play together. Here connection, not destruction, is the keyword. Some of the games, such as Simgraphics's *Combat Zone* and other paramilitary groupware products are of the old-fashioned aggression-based variety, but others, such as Carl Loeffler's *Virtual Polis,* and *Habitat,* are based on meeting, connecting, and relating—on cooperation rather than competition. Such connected games offer an enticement to get on the Net, and education as to how to excel at using it. They also give us a clear indication of where some of the most lucrative businesses of the forthcoming Infobahn are going to be.

Many critics have complained that a large proportion of the video games, especially those designed for arcades, are violent, ghoulish, and vulgar. (The same criticisms are often heard of TV.) I would argue, however, that there is redeeming social purpose in these games, as symbolic release valves for the larvae of our dreams and imagination. As well, the physical involvement burns off excess energy. There is a momentous social change going on right now and video games are an important part of the necessary adaptive process. That, I would argue, is their principal role and the explanation for their phenomenal popularity. Of course their distribution is driven by market priorities, but that does not fully account for the phenomenon. The less obvious motivation for their appearance may be hidden in our own unconscious drives, which regularly produce masses of cultural icons via the marketplace and its associated media. Board games like Monopoly and Clue were an epiphenomenon of the print world. Video games are closer to the psychological conditions that produce all games: they may be spontaneous expressions of a technology exploring new modalities of being and making them available to large numbers of people.

They may appear to be no more than the Trojan gifts of a mighty industrial-cognitive complex, but video games actually respond to real needs in the user. Anyone who has tried a well-designed video or computer game for more than two minutes knows that the experience is totally absorbing, and removes all other concerns from the mind. The game provides a perfect loop with one's own reactions.

Games like Lynx's BMX or Broderbund's *Loderunner* or Patrick Buckland's *Crystal Quest* put you in touch with your body in a paradoxical way. The hand-eye-ear coordination is quite specialized, of course, reducing one's proprioceptive connection to a single array of sensations, all geared to increase efficiency. However, what is lost in complexity of experience is made up for in the intensity of the feeling. Games cater to purely physical needs created by a social environment now irrevocably invaded by machines, and at the same time they help manage emotional stress by offering the opportunity to remove oneself completely from any other preoccupation.

The sportive aspect of computer and video games includes motor control, which is what makes them so involving in the first place. There may be a cathartic effect in the realignment of one's nervous energies in the engagement with the game. At any rate, there is recreational value for the whole person, body and mind together, as opposed to a process such as reading or watching television, which favor mostly mental relationships. These video "neurosports" are usually practiced at the time when the children need it most, that is, when their nervous system is still growing and pining for experience. After a couple of years of obsessive practice, video games are put aside when other, more adult concerns begin to emerge.*

THE JOB OF ART

If the purpose of computer and video games is to update nervous systems, the function of interactive art is more subtle and less direct. Interactive art, like interactive games, works directly on the body and the nervous system, but its function is primarily to update the

---

* As it is mediated by a screen-based event, the physiological and cognitive expression of the user is "outered" partly. The person moves out of the confines of the skin, if only for a very short distance, but often for a long while. Escapism, if you will, but of a different sort than that provided by passive entertainment such as cinema or television.

culture's psychology and sensibility. Technology is a significant source of dis-ease in the culture because it threatens the status quo. New technologies such as computers or networked environments change the behavior of the social constructs created by earlier technologies such as television, radio, or print. The main function of art in this context is not merely to entertain or to decorate, but to revise the standard psychological interpretation of reality in a way that accommodates the consequences of technological innovations.

In interactive art installations, as in games, the sensory-motor component is very high as it is in video games. But the goal is not to master something simplistic and well known, rather it is to enjoy something new. The art installation carries the exploration of the technology to new levels, attempting to generate new combinations of sensory-motor interactions. Thus there is an overt neuro-cultural function to new art forms which has always been present in older ones, though it has gone unrecognized within the strict limitations of our literate mental categories. This role of this neuro-cultural function is to position the body and mind of the human subject in relation to the environment as altered by the mediation of the latest technology. Interactive systems are essentially expanded biofeedback systems. What they teach is how to adapt to new sensory syntheses, new speeds, and new perceptions.

Christa Sommerer and Laurent Mignonneau's installation, *Interactive Plant Growing*, is a case in point. In front of you is a huge video screen where you see stalks and leaves and shoots of many different kinds of complex and richly colored plants. As you get closer you can see that some of the plants are growing in a kind of time-lapse, accelerated effect. They grow when someone approaches or gently touches one of five real plants which are on a stage in front of the screen. The real plants are very sensitive to human presence. Depending on how relaxed or tense you are, they create different kinds of shoots on the screen in front of you. The fact that the interface or the medium provided for the interaction in this installation is a plant, emphasizes the continuity between the human and the botanical. The combined output of a number of patrons can also represent the general mood of the crowd. *Interactive Plant Growing* could be a model for how to arrange a new kind of cocktail party where plants and flowers give instant, public feedback of the party-goers' state of mind on video-walls!

Within this installation, two simultaneous experiments on the connections between the human nervous system and the technocultural environment are being conducted. The first one is internal to the user, namely how to adjust, by trial and error using instant feedback, one's overall state of mind as it is expressed externally. The second experiment is how to integrate the nonbiological or technical elements of the whole experience within the realm of one's absolutely and irrevocably personal experience. Both experiments relate directly to the mapping and remapping of one's overall psychosensory experience.

Interactive arts, like games and sports, are directly tied to the human learning process. The mimetic function in higher animals as well as in humans serves to integrate new information in a sensory-motor and neuromuscular way. New synaptic connections are made in the nervous system to include and order new experiences. There is nothing inherently "natural" about human beings in any given historical period, and all media, whether interactive or not, have always been internalized by the central nervous system. This is done either directly, as favored routings of nerve impulses, or as schema of mental and gestural projections. This process applies to technologies from the wheel through to the computer, and most notably to writing, perhaps the most "desensitizing" of all the information-processing devices invented by humans.*

All the technological extensions we add to ourselves require strategies of integration. Just before you step into your car, from the

---

* Art only became a recognized human reality when the Greek alphabet shattered the human senses by reducing the rich sensoriality of oral language to a series of abstract squiggles. The job of art, then as now, was to take each sense and reconstitute a world around it in terms of drama, painting, music, dance, fine food, etc.

time you open the door to the moment you turn the key, you condition your whole physiology in preparation for a car-driving experience. Thus the role of the body as an interpreter and integrator of information and behavior is paramount. Meaning is achieved by the combination of verbal and sensory inputs. The meaning of what we see and hear is the result of the synthesis of sensory components, semiosis, and contextualized data-processing. We make sense of the world and of our role in it by finding the most focused and the most comprehensive configuration of images and words which are relevant to whatever situation is at hand. We can achieve this either in our mind or through the use of our body in context, or by a combination of both.*

It is clear from even a cursory analysis of how our sensory apparatus works that the senses are far from being hard-wired genetically, but rather include a generous supply of context-sensitive adaptation mechanisms. Many technological and artistic innovations address the physiological response of the performer or the user as an essential partner in sense-making and meaning creation. Interactive art installations play the role of connectors. They invite users to internalize what they are experiencing, to make new connections, in other words, to remap their own nervous system. This process usually involves sensory remapping, that is, restructuring our sensory responses according to the culturally and technologically grounded inputs that are experienced.

---

* However, in the wake of alphabetic literacy, Western cultures have tended to separate the psychological and the physiological levels and modalities of learning. One can, after all, learn new things without the use of one's body, simply rehearsing mentally, that is, by interiorizing the content of what one is reading. Westerners have thus lost touch, literally, with the physical component of learning, except in sports, which also carry the mark of mimesis. In a literate culture that has commonly practiced the radical separation, even the abstraction, of logos from bios, art was perhaps developed to recover for and from the body what had been lost to the exclusive cultivation of the mind. The art of the West has been characterized by presenting our main sensory experiences isolated from one another, as spectacles abstracted from the immediate context of living, for the purpose of contemplation and the achievement of meaning.

A longtime expert in surgical and psychological remapping of self-perception, Allucquère Rosanne Stone, makes the following keen observation:

> For me prosthetic communication and the things it creates, specifically interactive entertainment software, the Internet, cyberspace, and virtual reality, are not a question of market share or even of content. In a fundamental McLuhanesque sense these things are part of ourselves. As with all powerful discourses, their very existence shapes us. Since in a deep sense they are languages, it's hard to see what they do, because what they do is to structure seeing. They act on the systems—social, cultural, neurological—by which we make meaning. Their implicit message changes us.[3]

Tamas Walicksky's *The Garden* is without a doubt one of the most beautiful virtual reality environments ever created by an artist. But it is not really interactive, nor is it really "virtual." In its present state, it is just a plain old video of an animated computer graphic, but it contains much of what one needs to know about virtual reality and about the job of the artist within it. Walicksky wanted to get a sense of how a child sees the world. He simply took a video of his three-year-old daughter in a nice but ordinary garden, with flowers and trees, and birds and bees. Then he digitized the video in a computer so that he could work on all the figure/ground relationships between his daughter and her surroundings. He first separated the figure of the child from the ground of the garden. Then he mapped out the various shots of the garden into flexible frame structures that could be made to respond and adjust automatically and smoothly to the presence of another object in the image. He reinserted the images of the child into the new context-sensitive backgrounds and obtained what he readily admits are his own interpretations of how his daughter would see the world. What you see on the video is how the objects in the garden react to the child's presence. As she leans against the tree, it bends slightly to accommodate her back. As she goes up the ladder of a toy slide, the rungs expand and contract with her passage. As she rubs her eyes, the whole scene disappears. As a big dragonfly appears in her field of vision, the entire scene except for the insect turns blank, as if to show that the child's attention, at that precise moment, is entirely focused on the insect. As the child walks among flowers taller than herself, they seem to just glide by her without shrinking as they would in an adult's standard interpretation of perspective.

The Garden gives us a very strong conceptual tool for exploring not just the psychosensory synthesis of a child's world, but the perceptual environments of all of us. The historic film *La dame du lac* was edited entirely from the protagonist's eye-level point of view. It didn't do very well because the technology was not flexible enough to translate believably the subjectivity of the protagonist into that of the spectator. A recent film, *Strange Days,* has tried this again with greater success. VR is an ideal medium for a new genre in entertainment based on the substitution of subjectivities. It would enable us to experience in detail completely different psychosensory syntheses, even those of different animals. We know enough about horses, rabbits, and dogs, for example, to be able, at some point in the not-too-distant future, to simulate what they see and hear.

Another gentle and delightful way to remap our psychosensory synthesis is provided by David Rokeby's interactive art installation, *Very Nervous System (VNS).** *VNS* allows you to create a musical reflection of your presence within the installation. You dance—or just walk, if you feel shy—in front of a camera and sounds are instantaneously created by your movements. These are not the random sounds which are generated by so many early—and boring—

---

* Rokeby is a Toronto composer. *VNS* is an interactive total surround sound creation system, an installation which involves the linking of a set of video cameras, a computer, and a synthesizer. The performer's movements are recorded by a camera and are directly digitized into a computer as live data sources. I should say that the video stream from the camera is really "rokebytized" because, when Rokeby conceived of his instrument, there was no digitizing system available and he had to build his own; over the years, he refined the system in such a way that it is capable of many operations that are not available on standard systems.

so-called interactive music installations. In *VNS*, the music is the controlled interpretation of the movements of your whole body. Rokeby is a composer as well as a brilliant programmer. His installation allows for very flexible variables. Each body part, each gesture can create a different sound, and you can verify that this or that gesture makes this or that sound simply by repeating the gesture. The sounds do not clash with each other, but flow into one another with increasing levels of complexity depending on how fast you move or how close to the camera you are. You can thus create not just noise, but real music. You become simultaneously the composer, the performer, and the audience of your own musical environment. All the while, your body movements and your gestures, something undoubtedly very physical, are being translated into something quite ethereal and beautiful, not to mention limitlessly variable.

At the opening of Origin's Multimedia Center in Baarn, in October 1992, I had occasion to watch two professional dancers explore *Very Nervous System* for the first time. They were so taken by this novel experience that they danced nonstop for twelve hours. They couldn't get over the fact that, for once, they were calling the tune. It seemed as if they were rediscovering their own space, sharpening the perception of their own presence in the world. Rokeby explains that his work uses machines to give us back some of the intimacy that they normally rob from us. The experience is extraordinary: it is as if your body is pushing some melodious medium around you, or as if everything around you reverberates with the sounds of your presence. The effect is one of controlled improvisation.

Through the computer, the rokebytizer sends the real-time data to a MIDI (Musical Instrument Digital Interface), a special connector devised to allow a sound synthesizer to receive and execute commands from a computer. Depending upon the level of sophistication of the synthesizer, it is possible to introduce previously sampled sounds to generate the basic structures of the sounds used in the installation. Theoretically, it would be possible to record and sample piano music played by Glenn Gould or Keith Jarett, and use their exceptionally fine "touch" to characterize all the sounds coming from the performer's movements.

The whole experience creates an intimate involvement with space, at least with that part of space that is at the limit between sound and touch. That boundary is potentially the most important component of the sensory interface between man and the environment which is created by electronic communication technologies. It is an image of our unfolding relationship with that environment and it mimics some of the new physical and psychological dimensions given us by our extended electronic reach. That is why interactive artists are exploring that limit so intently.

Charles Davies' magnificent VR installation, *Osmosis*, is remarkable not only for the beauty of its imagery and the complexity of the many levels of exploration it affords the audience, but especially for the interface that was developed for it. The decor is a secluded spot in a forest, with a brook and foliage. You can go underground, through a dead tree down to the roots of life—at least to the roots of computer calculations!—and up into the sphere of the mind where you will encounter sound bites or quotations from famous thinkers. In *Osmosis*, you don the goggles and gloves that are standard VR paraphernalia. But you also wear a light, brassiere-like vest which enables you to move just by controlling your breathing. If you breathe in, you rise, if you breathe out, you sink. If you breathe normally, you stay on the same level. The symbolic implications of *Osmosis* are many, but the most powerful for me is that it reminds us that even in the immateriality of the virtual, breathing is still the mark of one's presence in life.*

People interact with machines with the help of interfaces: tools, handles, buttons, mice, keyboards—even Davies' brassiere; systems that allow them access to the machine's capabilities. The desire to

---

* Another, much earlier and equally poetic use of breathing is *La plume* by Edmond Couchot and Marie-Hélène Tramus, developed at the University of Paris VIII computer lab. In this installation, you simply breathe on what looks like a small microphone. A feather on a computer monitor reacts to your blowing in perfect simulation of how a real feather would react. The effect is eerie. Couchot explained that he wanted to find a precise interface between the virtual and the real.

improve interactivity is prompting the exploration and interpretation of all the possible technological interstices, all the modalities of
exchange and relationships available, from the fingers pressing buttons to gesture, voice, and breath control, and now to thought control. Explorations into the different ways people relate to their
environments and among themselves seem to be limited only by the
varieties of expression humans can produce with their minds and
their bodies. Interfaces emerge into the worlds of art and industrial
production as material precipitates or formalizations of our gestures.
However, thanks to the remapping process, these interfaces are
themselves internalized within the body.

In interactive art, as with interactive technology, the research on
interfaces can take at least two radical directions: the first one is
when the interface invades the body and physically penetrates the
human nervous system. I call this bionism, but it is also referred to
as cyborgism. In the second case, it is not the interface that invades
the body, but the mind that becomes its own interface. From the
humble keyboard to sophisticated eye-tracking devices and brain-
waves scanners, the pursuit of this ultimate goal in the development
of interfaces has been relentless. It will not end until we can command our own electronic extensions by thought alone.

The notion of bionism, cyborgism, is taken quite literally by the
Australian Stelarc, who in my opinion is one of the most important
artists of our day. Stelarc combines biological and technological sensors and effecters in his work. Using transponders taped to his arms,
legs, and chest, he commands the manipulation of huge industrial
robots directly from his own nerve impulses. In his work, we find
one of the most extreme explorations of bionism, or the new social
contract between biology and technology. His performances are
spectacular, verging on the repulsive. To make his statements about
the obsolescence of the flesh-based body and the bionic integration
of the organic and the technological, he has allowed himself to hang
150 feet above ground, in Manhattan, supported by an industrial
crane and attached by hooks attached to the skin of his back. Stelarc
practiced this novel form of the ancient ascesis for decades as if to

"punish" the skin for being so limited and weak, before getting into neuro-robotics. He never says "my body" when speaking about himself; he says "the body."*

When he exhibits on a large public screen the meanderings of his own digestive system as seen in real time from a tiny endoscopic video camera, Stelarc is demonstrating that electronic technologies, by emulating and extending our body functions, are turning us inside out and projecting our bodies on the outer world. Furthermore, by combining electronic with biological nerve-endings and even, in other performances, by affecting the neural controls of the body of another person with the help of an impulse simulator, Stelarc is co-opting medical technology for its metaphorical implications.

Relentlessly, Stelarc pushes both his own limits and those of the technological environment even as it expands around us. As the thrust of technology now goes to the networks, there goes Stelarc. At the first Telepolis conference (Luxembourg, November 4–11, 1995), Stelarc was "downloading" his nerve impulses onto the Internet to cause gestures in someone else's body in London. Sensors connected to his arms and legs picked up the impulses of his nervous system and transmitted them on-line to London so that somebody else's arms and legs, connected through the appropriate interface, could execute a dance neurophysiologically willed in Paris. Stelarc is saying that we have to get ready for new sensory configurations which will include their technological supports and infrastructures in a

---

* Stelarc is fond of saying both in private and in public that "the body —his, or anyone else's for that matter—is obsolete." One day, in Melbourne, Stelarc had arranged for me and a few friends to attend an Australian football match between the Tigers and the Bombers. He got so involved in the game, jumping up and down every time the Tigers scored a goal, that I kept wondering how long his body would remain obsolete. . . . As for his "self," where it is may be a moot point. He says that it is a distributed, self-organizing complex of different functions called forward by different situations at different times—postmodern attitude with enough grounds in formal biology and psychology to merit serious examination.

biotechnical totality, and that this new body is just as critical for information processing as our minds. We are invited by Stelarc to take the adaptation of the whole human nervous system, its techno- logical extensions and its cultural adaptability, as seriously as we have taken the often difficult but necessary remapping of our ideas, assumptions, and concepts, whenever we have been challenged by new paradigms.

The electronic extensions of the human body allow rapid crossover back and forth between hardware and software, between thought, flesh, electricity, and the outside environment. With the interactive arts, we are beginning to graduate from a passive, one- way relationship to our screens to an interactive one. We have shared our minds with TV for four decades. With TV often substituting for our own imagination, much of our visualization was already occur- ring on the screen. With the interactive systems, our psychotechno- logical development is taking us one step further. The video screen is often becoming a necessary intermediary not only for our imagina- tion, but also for our thinking processes. It serves as a display not only for the programs themselves, but also for the effects of the pro- grams on our minds and bodies. What we can do now that we couldn't do with one-way TV is "computer-assisted thinking." The contact between thinking and visualizing that is automatic in our inner imagination is currently assisted in most cases by our hands through physical interfaces, but there is also clearly a trend towards direct interaction between thought and screen. We are about to rec- ognize the fact that we wish to enjoy the same freedom of mental action on our screens that we can experience in our brains. Here is the progression from looking to thinking to doing in three quick steps:

- *Step one: Looking.* Joachim Sauter and Dirk Lüsebrink's *Zerse- her* allows its audience to change the structure and the texture of a painting simply by looking at it. You stand in front of a painting scanned onto a computer monitor and placed at eye level as it would be on a wall in a gallery. After a short time, you begin to notice that the surface of the painting becomes slightly blurred, distorted precisely at the point where your gaze is directed. Wherever you look, you find the same effect of destruction. A hidden, eye-tracking device is in fact following the movements of your eye to connect, in a quasi-tactile fashion, the end point of your gaze to the computer screen. The effect is to give a startling power to the art critic's eye, not merely to look at the artwork, but to modify it. One possible interpretation of this very postmodern piece is that it is a sardonic statement about beauty and truth being quite literally "in the eye of the beholder." Radical art criticism.

There is a problem with *Zerseher* in that it only works if the observer, like the classical art patron of the great masters of perspective and trompe l'oeil, is positioned at a rather precise point in the museum environment. Another eye-tracking interactive system invented by a group of Californian artists, collectively named Biomuse, is based not on following eye movements by a camera, but in the use of sensors which pick up and interpret the movements of the motor-control muscles surrounding the eyes. The Biomuse interactive device allows someone to direct precisely and deliberately his or her gaze as a pointer on a screen. The execution command is achieved either by pressing on a mouse-like device, or for disabled people who can only move their eyes, simply by blinking.*

- *Step two: Thinking.* While the systems so far described involve the use of one's eyes exclusively, they also use the eyes as the extension of the hand. We could say that it is really nothing

---

* An interesting fact about Biomuse research is that this group was not looking primarily to develop this particular system, but it grew out of previous work on connecting voluntary muscle contraction to various musical devices to create music directly from the body movements. Thus the literal touch involving the hardware materiality of muscular control led very quickly to another fundamental aspect of touching, which is to handle intervals.

more than a kind of "sleight of eye." But the eye is a lot closer to the mind than the hand. It is, in biological fact, an extension, or an outering, of the brain. Looking and thinking are almost coextensive. In advanced systems developed by military aviation, the visual interface is bypassed altogether, as if to complete a perfect symbiosis between mind and machine. The pilot, connected to command mechanisms by sensors placed on his skull inside his helmet, can order certain simple operations by thought alone. The basic technical principle is quite simple: all that is needed is access to a "yes" or "no," an on or off command, just like the basic language of the computer itself. Everything else can follow from there.

In the art world, there is a new generation of biofeedback systems, such as Masaaki Kahata's "Interactive Brainwave Visual Analyzer" (IBVA) system, which allow people to identify, select, and control some of their own brain waves. A headband containing two or three sensors is placed on the user's forehead. The surface electrical potential generated by the brain is picked up by the sensors and processed through a computer. It is possible to see on the screen, and hence presumably to monitor and affect—by thinking differently or by thinking about different things—the graphical rendering of brain waves. Even though the transmitted data is only a very loose and generalized rendering of what is in reality a much more complex series of psychophysiological events, the end result is a workable approximation of mind-controlled operations.

- *Step three: Doing.* The young German artist Ulrike Gabriel uses IBVA for her stunning installation, *Terrain 01.* I experienced *Terrain 01* as presented at the Landesmuseum in Linz for the 1993 Ars Electronica. Wearing the IBVA headband, I was seated in front of a computer screen and I saw what I was told was the almost instantaneous feedback of my mental state. I was asked to relax and the feedback information appearing as changing graphs on the screen helped me to quickly shift from an agitated, slightly anxious state to a more relaxed condition. Fairly soon, I realized that the more relaxed I felt, the more light there was in the room. This light came from a large reflector attached to the ceiling of the room. After the light reached a visibly higher level of intensity, I heard a curious rumbling coming from the floor area where I saw a few dozen big cockroach-like objects moving at first rather slowly and then gradually faster. These strange looking objects, about the size of a hand, were in fact light-sensitive robots bearing photoelectric cells on their backs. The robots are programmed to move smoothly within the performance area without banging into each other; even as they move, the rumbling sound created by their wheels is picked up and amplified to provide yet another feedback mechanism to the source of all this activity, the user. Thus the loop is completed between the power of thought and the technological extensions of this complex but unified biological activity.

Ulrike Gabriel's installation is one of the most striking and simplest demonstrations of the endlessly controversial "mind-body" interactions. The deconstruction of various stages of transformations of a single input go from the highly complex realm of the mind to the physics of acoustics via data processing in the computer for biofeedback, to pure electrical energy in the light-well, to electromechanical conversion with the photoelectric cells, to pure mechanical dynamics in the robots' motors, to computerized behavior-programming in the movements of the robots, and finally to a mechanical energy-to-sound conversion with the help of a pressure-sensitive surface upon which the robots travel.

Another artist, Seisuke Oki, has adapted the IBVA interface to create semidirect interactions between thought and electromechanical environments. Oki's *Digital Therapy* is a biofeedback system that allows a user to generate sight, sounds, and vibrations as feedback loops arising from his or her own brain waves as fed through filters and interfaces. First, you ease yourself into one of those automated self-administered massage chairs the Japanese are so fond of. Then you put on a helmet with VR goggles and earphones which also contains the sensors from the IBVA system. After a few seconds of adjustments during which you are asked to relax—not unexpectedly, since you happen to be in a La-Z-boy—you begin to hear buzzing sounds and see indeterminate shapes and colors in the eyephones' video screens. Nothing is happening yet while in the chair. Only after a little while do you begin to suspect that there is a potential connection between what and how you think and the changes in the patterns of light and sound. You find yourself straining to smooth out the sounds and the events in the VR world. This sets you back again. After much patience and appropriate goodwill, you eventually begin to succeed in stabilizing an image of what seems to be a landscape seen from a low-flying airplane. At that point I think I felt a vague vibration coming from the chair, but I will never know for sure because I don't think that in spite of my earnestness—or perhaps because of it—I ever made it past first base in the system.

Digital Therapy is akin to a neurosport, ready for the video game market. But with a little more technosavvy, it could become what its prophetic name says it is. We can imagine people easing into their electronic armchair for a quick zap into harmonious sensory-motor conditioning. The need to provoke a fully externalized response by the power of the mind alone in all likelihood invites a reordering of certain normal mental sequences and the temporary restructuring of one's body image.

Terrain 01 and *Digital Therapy* are the first tangible evidence of what may become routine in the near future: out-of-body physical events commanded by thought alone. To help technology reach that point, artists are leading the way, but the message of their work lies not in the technology, but in the psychological implications. The artwork is metaphorical; it is meant to help people feel and understand the new connections. What follows the artistic research is the technological development, in other words, a literal application of the remapped configuration of our psychosensory synthesis. Just as Nintendo picked up the data glove from another brilliant team of computer artists, Tom Zimmerman and Jaron Lanier, when Nintendo or another game producer picks up Ulrike Gabriel's or Oki's installations, the art form will turn into a game and the heuristic will lead into the normative.

Luciana Heill's project is perhaps one of the most ambitious, complex, and intimate of all the uses of Kahata's interface: she plans to use an improved version of IBVA to download her brain-wave patterns on the Net and mix them up in an orderly fashion with other participants' patterns so as to generate an interactive display that would be the combination of hers and the other people's thinking. When we begin to do that wirelessly—as we undoubtedly will—we will call it extrasensory perception and we will forget that ESP was once the object of incredulity.

From such installations, a whole new level of philosophical speculations about person-machine, person-environment, mental-physical, electrical-mechanical, biological-technical relationships can be reached. We may find, one day, that one of the most vexing philosophical and scientific problems, which is to know how the mind connects to the brain and the spirit to the body, is something relatively simple . . . a trick already performed for us by some of our machines.

CHAPTER THREE

PERSON, REAL AND VIRTUAL

E ACH YEAR in Canada and the United States, more than a million people voluntarily throw themselves off 150-foot-high structures. Most, if not all of them, are attached by the ankles to elastic bands which are measured precisely so as to arrest their free-fall just before it terminates in contact with the earth. This is called bungee jumping. It is hard to say whether it is a sport or a form of therapy, or both, or neither. Culture watchers are baffled. What drives people to subject themselves to such a bizarre experience?

THE BODY IN QUESTION

For me, the thought of leaping off a cliff or out of a plane is not a comfortable one. Even with the absolute assurance that all mishap will be avoided, the mere idea evokes in me a gut-wrenching sensation, a generalized panic, a vertigo that begins in my stomach and quickly expands to the tips of my fingers and toes. Perhaps this is the clue: the experience of bungee jumping surely must arouse every cell in the body, like an unspeakably violent and generalized blow, or like the slap the doctor gave us when we were newborns.

With the ephemeralization of interfaces, the distribution of human nerve impulses—one's flesh, even—across man-machine boundaries, we have good reason both to wake up and question what's happening to our sense of self and to try to redefine the boundaries of identity and personhood. Here is a quick sampling of the kinds of impact interactive technologies can have on one's body image and psychological envelope:

Teleception: Interactive technologies, at least to the extent that they give us a telesensory reach, add a new dimension to our biological sensory life, which I call teleception. That means, the remote perception of things outside the body, or, alternately, the perception of things approaching or touching the body in some way from a distance. A teleceptive sensibility might be expected to be found developing on networks.

Expansion: At the same time, there may arise a sense of loss of one's precise personal boundaries. Yes, we still have our skin and we can trust it to a certain degree to tell us who (and where) we are, but as we project ourselves outward digitally, occasionally without intermediaries, what else should we know about ourselves and where can we find out? The whole planet is up for grabs.

Multiple personality: As A. R. Stone says, "Multiple Personality [MP without the stigmatizing final D for 'disorder'] is a mode that resonates throughout the virtual communities." Networks present another challenge to the notion of personhood because they distribute self, thus greatly extending the body's reach and range. They do this either in broadcast mode, or in a distributed way that is partly self-organizing and partly agent-assisted.

There is no horizon on the Net, only expansions and contractions, and our relationship to it begins with a formidable expansion of psychological size. The loss of a clear sense of boundaries, the expansion of our mental frameworks by satellite, the on-line redistribution of our powers of action, all of these add up to a confused body image. We can't be absolutely sure anymore where we begin and where we end.

Proprioception: The apparent need people have to get back in touch with their bodies is expressed in ways calculated to increase their access to physical sensations, just to know where they stand. People appear to be testing the limits of their physical identity. They do different things to achieve the same result: many stop smoking, some run, others play squash. Every year in Pamplona, the bulls are let out of the ring and into the streets. The hardiest spectators try to get as close to the horns as they can without getting gored. In Calgary during the Stampede, some people ride wild horses. On the cable sports networks, so-called extreme sports of all kinds are proliferating: extreme skiing, extreme boxing, even extreme cycling. They share the characteristic of being dangerous to life and limb. All these people appear to be trying to remember that they have a body. I propose the theory that bungee jumping is an arguably desperate but reasonably safe attempt at recovering or awakening proprioception. By proprioception, I mean the sense of one's own body "being there"; the awareness of internal events. Proprioception is primarily a tactile perception both of one's own internal sensation and of events and sensations in one's immediate or electronically extended surroundings.

We are given little choice by electronic technologies but to include in the intimate recesses of our sensory apparatus larger, more distant, more complex, and more diffuse realms of experience. Electricity blurs the boundaries between our inner and outer experiences by being at the same time in the body as nerve impulses, and out of it as the energy supporting our technological interactions. Simultaneously, as labor-saving devices and automated processes transmute so many of the hardware realities of life into software processes, those of us who remain unaware of our proprioceptive sensations become angel-like, minds without bodies, and we may experience a growing sense of yearning for real feeling, for something substantial, like the panic of free-falling, like bungee jumping. Thus, bungee jumping may be the nineties' update on the sixties' trend of "dropping out to get back in touch": people trying to recover the immediacy and the urgency of proprioceptive information.

This is a line of argument that could be used in support of McLuhan and other critics who point to the dematerialization of human activities by electricity. In the Hegelian vision of matter transmuted into spirit by technology, one might experience a sense of loss, of disembodiment amounting to a latent feeling of vertigo. However, I am equally attracted to the opposite view expressed here by Katherine Hayles:

> Cyberspace, we are often told, is a disembodied medium. Testimonies to this effect are everywhere, from William Gibson's fictional representation of the "bodiless exultation of cyberspace" to John Perry Barlow's description of his virtual reality (VR) experience as "my everything has been amputated." In a sense, these testimonies are correct; the body remains in front of the screen rather than within it. In another sense, however, they are deeply misleading, for they obscure the crucial role that the body plays in constructing cyberspace. In fact, we are never disembodied. As anyone who designs VR simulations knows, the specificities of our embodiments matter in all kinds of ways, from determining the precise configurations of a VR interface to influencing the speed with which we can read a CRT [computer] screen. Far from being left behind when we enter cyberspace, our bodies are no less actively involved in the construction of virtuality than in the construction of real life.[1]

Propriodeception: The question is: "How much can we trust those extended senses?" Hayles concludes her brilliant essay by addressing the work of Canadian artist and critic Catherine Richards. In her video *Spectral Bodies,* Richards, who first came to public attention for a landmark exhibit on computer arts called *The Artist as a Young Machine* at the Ontario Science Centre in 1984, shows how different combinations of VR technologies supported by tactile simulators can fool one's proprioception. The basic notion Richards explores in her experiments with blindfolded subjects is how a technology as banal as a vibrator can invade the human body in its most intimate recesses to remap our body image. Is propriodeception the hidden wages of technology?

Neo-Puritanism: The most extreme position with respect to the transfer of human characteristics to software is the "who needs a body, anyway?" position adopted by Hans Moravec, director of the Carnegie-Mellon Mobile Robot Laboratory. He outdoes even Stelarc by suggesting that, in the future, we will not need a body at all, as long as we can download our brain into a computer. I heard him profess this and many other related notions in Essen, in 1993, an experience that convinced me that I was in the presence of a classic mad scientist. This is what Katherine Hayles, more soberly, has to say about him:

> Traditionally the dream of transcending the body to achieve immortality has been expressed through certain kinds of spiritualities. Dust to dust, but the soul ascends to heaven. Moravec's vision represents a remapping of that dream onto cyberspace, with an important difference: reversing a long-standing opposition between science and religion, he enlists technoscience as the ally of out-of-body transcendence. To achieve this apotheosis one does not need spiritual discipline, only a good robot surgeon. Such a vision is nurtured by a cultural tradition that has long dreamed of mind as separate from body.[2]

THE PERSON IN QUESTION

Musing about evolution in *Out of Control,* Kevin Kelly writes: "Out of nothing, nature makes something. I'd like to be able to do that. First a hunk of metal; then a robot. First some wires; then a mind. First some old genes; then a dinosaur."

Speaking of old genes, I once found myself making a wild connection between the work genetic engineering scientists were doing on DNA taken from an Egyptian mummy, and a computer scan of another mummy at the Royal Ontario Museum. The scan allowed the archeologists to penetrate the many layers of the mummy from the outer sarcophagus right through to the skin and bones, without breaking anything. The results of the analysis were so precise that it was possible not only to determine the gender of the body, a woman, but also her age, thirty-four, and the cause of her death, a large facial tumor which had received an unsuccessful treatment. What struck me was that, because the computer can reconstitute the whole from the parts, just as it is possible to rebuild a living cell from a sample of DNA, it is now theoretically possible to reconstitute a mummy into a person, combining the unique genetic material of the individual with a reasonably good estimation of its shape at maturity. When it comes to resurrection, perhaps the Egyptians were not so far off the mark after all.

Artist Chico McMurtrie has a life-size companion called "Tumbling Man" which he made with scrap metal articulated by hydraulic systems. As in the Simon Says children's game, whatever Chico does, Tumbling Man does too, and reasonably well. For example, if Chico decides to paint a picture on one side of a board, Tumbling Man can make another one on the other side. If you compare Chico and Tumbling Man's pictures, you might allow yourself to prefer the latter's. . . .

In some respects, Tumbling Man is the archetypal robot; man-size, man-like, mechanically articulated and serviceable. In others, it is not. For one thing, Tumbling Man is not autonomous. It is tied to its maker by a rather cumbersome umbilicus of tubes, wires, and relay boxes. The value of Tumbling Man is that it proposes a theory of robotics in action, so to speak. Robots are semiautonomous projections of human gestures. Tumbling Man's gestures are still attached to its human controller. The willpower is still completely in the head of the human. Tumbling Man is like all machines from the wheel to the rocket or the nuclear power plant—an extension of the human person. Their job is not to take over from humans, but to amplify or multiply human energy.

From the legend of the Golem, through to the story of Frankenstein's monster and all the way to Cyril Kapec who invented the word, the concept of "robot" has been applied to hardware. Robots have been conceived as being made of clay (like Adam), wood (like Pinocchio), steel (like Tumbling Man), or any substantial material deemed convenient. The issue, much fantasized over since Mary Shelley wrote *Frankenstein* in 1818, has always been how much autonomy to concede to robots.

When Tumbling Man is detached from Chico, it goes limp. At that point, it is somewhat less impressive as a piece of machinery than a bicycle, because a bicycle doesn't need to be plugged in to be ready to do its job. But autonomous robots are different. To go beyond Tumbling Man and achieve autonomy, they have to take two steps, one small, the other, huge.

The small step is simply to get detached from the human, and become self-powered, something achieved by any electric toy with fresh batteries. The bigger step is to engage in autonomous activity of some kind. Mark Tilden, an independent researcher attached to the University of Waterloo in Ontario, is world-renowned for the autonomous robots he makes out of computer chips he finds in discarded greeting cards. One of his many critters, for example, is trained to seek light to charge its minute battery. It has tiny, clumsy little legs, more lever than leg in fact. If Mark places the light-seeking robot in shadow, it will summon whatever energy it has stored to get to the light. Once it gets there, it stops and recharges. Tilden, Rodney Brooks at MIT, and others have created hundreds of these robots which respond automatically, in a lifelike way, to specific conditions of their environment. Robotic tinkering has in fact become a worldwide new discipline somewhere between art and engineering with "Robot Olympics" taking place every year. One thing achieved by this level of robotics is to bring technology out of the *extension* into the *projection* mode. When technology leaves the condition of extension to become an autonomous projection, it begins a new cycle which one could call "autonomation," a combination of *automation* and *autonomy*, a coinage which is useful in characterizing this new generation of robots.

Not all robots are hardware. A brilliant example of autonomy of the digital, ephemeral variety of robotic creatures is Christa Sommerer and Laurent Mignonneau's hauntingly beautiful installation called *A-Volve.** In this piece, you are invited to design a fish, tracing its rough shape with your finger on a computer screen. You can thus, in a few seconds, define in an approximate way its hydrodynamic profile and basic speed and size characteristics. Then you press the "send" button on the same screen. Within seconds, you will see your fish appear in a video-tank, in 3-D and spectacular color, swimming about according to the profile you have given it. Its lifespan is very short, about a minute and a half or so. To extend that duration it can opt between two strategies, either to gobble up any other fish already in the tank, or mate with another fish. In the first instance, it will increase its energy by the amount left in the creature it swallows—excluding what is spent in battle—and in the second case, it will not survive individually but will leave an offspring bearing the combined characteristics of shape, color, and profile of its parents. You can watch the offspring grow while the parents gently die by fading away.**

---

* Exhibit Catalogue of *Mimesis, Ars Electronica Festival 1996,* September 2–6, Linz, Austria,14. Sommerer and Mignonneau's latest work is called *Genma.* As they describe it in the catalogue of the exhibit: "*Genma* is a kind of a dream machine that allows us to 'play scientist' and enables us to manipulate nature. Nature exemplary is represented as artificial nature on a micro scale. Principles of artificial life and genetic programming are implemented in 'creatures,' allowing the visitor to manipulate their virtual genes in real time. The visitors to the installation themselves function as randomizing factors, giving the artwork a particular form and development. Their frequency of movement, body tension or pulse are linked to image events on the screen and guarantee a great variety of non-predictable image penetration."

** In his penetrating analysis of A-life and genetic arts, Kevin Kelly describes El-Fish, a software program developed by the Russian team who produced Tetris, now available commercially which allows the construction of fish from a total of fifty-six genes defining eight hundred parameters. Kelly writes: "The colorful fish swim in a virtual underwater world realistically, turning with the flick of a fin as fish do. They weave between strands of kelp (also bred by the program). They pace back and forth endlessly. They school around food when you 'feed' them. They never die. When I first saw an El-Fish aquarium from ten paces away, I took it to be a video of a real aquarium." In Kelly, op. cit., 277.

These little virtual creatures have motivation (to survive and pro-create). That's just a step away from having emotions. And it is emotion that interests Patti Maes, working out of MIT on virtual creatures which respond to the user's interactions with them. The setup is a large screen which brings the image of the user together with that of the digital creature. In her words:

> In the style of Myron Krueger's Videoplace system,* the ALIVE system offers an unencumbered, full-body interface to a virtual world. The ALIVE user moves around in a space of approximately sixteen by sixteen feet. A video camera captures the user's image, which is composited into a 3-D graphical world after the user's image has been isolated from the background.

There, the user is surrounded by virtual objects and can interact with "Hamsterdamer," the virtual hamster:

> The Hamster avoids objects, follows the user around and begs for food. The Hamster rolls over to have its stomach scratched if the user bends over and pats it. If the user has been patting the Hamster for a while, its need for attention is fulfilled and some other activity takes precedence (e.g., looking for food).[3]

---

* Long before interactivity had become the rather fuzzy buzzword it is today, an artist called Myron Krueger, as far back as the late sixties, had been hacking away at his Video Place system, perhaps the earliest and among the most aesthetically satisfying of the interactive works of art. Krueger's special universe consists in digitizing the image of the user and projecting it live into the screen environment where, by entering into contact with different kinds of dynamic designs, it interacts with them. You stand in front of the computer screen, at the center of the field of a camera which is pointed at you. The camera brings your image right into the screen, but before it gets there, it has been digitized. This means that it is not an ordinary video image anymore, it has become a movable icon, like the pointer on any computer screen. Then, by moving your arms, your hands, or your whole body, you can get the images on the screen to follow your movements, dance with you, or make amusing or beautiful sounds. There is the magic of childhood regained in experiencing this kind of power-at-a-distance.

Our machines are becoming intelligent and before long they will also acquire a self. We don't know a lot about "self," but we do know that it's not very difficult to program one. Some of these personality simulation machines have neural networks. I saw in Linz the ugly but interesting "Neuro Baby," programmed by Japanese artist Naoko Tosa to learn to speak in the same time scale as a human baby. This is an electronic creature appearing on a screen: you talk to it and it talks back to you. Within the next three years Tosa is hoping to be able to have a conversation with him. She calls her creatures "digital pets" and thinks that there will eventually be one in every family. Neither from a graphic nor an acoustic design nor an educational point of view could Neuro Baby be deemed a resounding success. The point, however, is that the artist illuminates the future.

"Helpless Robot" by Norman White, a biologist by training, also tests our propensity to grant human qualities to objects that behave in some ways like ourselves. Helpless Robot talks to you. It asks for your help. It wants you to move it around because it is helpless. But as soon as you have begun to help, it starts insulting you. So you move away. Then it calls you back, wheedling and begging your forgiveness. As the artist confesses: "I have devised this silly scenario so that I can experiment with the attractive, if probably impossible, notion of simulating a human personality." The robot raises another question: how much independence and how much complexity of thought do we need to put into our machines before we grant them personhood? I once knew a Catholic priest who wanted to baptize computers.

Many people, when asked how "real" is the communication between them and the computerized machine, answer that, of course they know it's not real, but it sure *feels* real. Author Sherry Turkle, in her book *The Second Self: Computers and the Human Spirit*, reports that many very young children who use computers think that the machines are "alive." In her latest book, *Life on the Screen*, Turkle observes that simply giving a name to a computer or a hard disk is enough to start the process of personalizing—attributing a "self"—

to the inanimate object. It is not unlike the medieval poet's practice of allegorization, of giving a human name, and personality, to abstract notions like love, death, or peace.

The more sophisticated the machine or the system, the more complex our interaction is likely to be, and hence the more "intelligent" its response will appear. We now recognize the possibility that it is not just humans who interact. Those strange new technological creatures in the world out there are also capable of intelligence. "*L'Autre*" ("The Other"), by Catherine Ikam, is indeed another presence, eerily *there*. The interface is almost transparent: as you move into the room, your presence is "observed" by a huge face on a screen. It seems to be looking right at you. As you move, it appears to follow your path through the room, watching you. It has a tender expression. A dreamy disposition. However if your movements get a bit abrupt, it will become agitated and show fear or anger. You may come out of the experience wondering what really constitutes the "otherness" of others. Ikam remarks, "Since antiquity, there have been hybrid beings that fall into a category between humans and gods. The nature of such beings changes with time, yet chimeras, automata, and androids still reveal our other faces to us."

We are about to step up the level of control—or "self-control"— among robots from automation to autonomation; that is, the power of autonomous selection among potentially vast arrays of environmental variables. We will achieve forms of intelligence that will require very exacting guidance and extreme reliability. True, the "self" within these creations will be rather crude at first, responding to simple criteria and making uncomplicated choices. But this experimentation will lead very quickly to embryonic forms of consciousness, which will arrive via the weight and seduction of sheer complexity. The quest for more complex interactions is an irresistible technological drive nowadays. Soon enough, the political problems attending the applications of complex neural networks in industry, medicine, business, banking, education, and government services, will bring about enough contradictions to require a fundamental psychological restructuring of our connected and personal minds.

AVATARS AND AGENTS

The development of robotics is also an emerging facet of life on the Internet, but with an interesting new wrinkle: the robots are connected, as well as being autonomous. As much as standard digital computers can operate on strings of data in the absence of any other form of context, the advanced neural networks supporting these network robots will require—and get—massive inputs of contextualized information, simply by being on the Web. The issue of identity or self is made more complex when robots go on-line equipped with the formidable powers of digital technology. So much so, in fact, that the critters are renamed "agents," implying that they are capable of agency, or autonomous action. A closely related species of digital robot found on the Net is the "avatar," a software package that you put on-line to represent you in the virtual world.

Both agents and avatars have a huge technological and commercial future, but the boundary between them is not distinct. Given enough autonomy, avatars can quickly turn into agents. It is not always easy to decide which is which.*

According to the description given on the Web by the Media Lab at MIT:

> An autonomous agent is a computational system that inhabits a
> complex, dynamic environment. The agent can sense, and act
> on, its environment, and have a set of goals or motivations that
> it tries to achieve through these actions. Depending on the type

---

* The simulation of personality by software goes back to Joseph Weisenbaum's "Eliza." About a recent, much more sophisticated version of a MUD persona, called "Julia," Sherry Turkle says the following: "Julia is able to fool some of the people some of the time into thinking she is a human player. Mauldin [Julia's programmer] says that her sarcastic non sequiturs provide her with enough apparent personality to be given the benefit of the doubt in an environment where players 'make a first assumption that other players are people too.'" From Sherry Turkle, *Life on the Screen: Identity in the Age of the Internet* (New York: Simon & Schuster, 1995), 88.

of environment, an agent can take different forms. Autonomous robots are agents that inhabit the physical world; computer-animated characters inhabit simulated 3-D worlds; while software agents inhabit the world of computer networks.

According to the same posting, there are three main categories of agents:

"Software agents" provide active, personalized assistance to a person engaged in the use of a particular computer application. Software agents differ from current-day software in that they are: (1) proactive (taking the initiative to help the user by making suggestions and/or automating the more mundane tasks the user normally would have to perform); (2) adaptive (learning the user's preferences, habits, and interests as they change over time); and (3) personalized (customizing their assistance according to what they learned about the user).

An avatar, on the other hand, is like a digital mask that you wear to identify and position yourself, in full screen view, in the new 3-D virtual environments created on-line under such names as "Alphawords" and "Worlds Away." These environments are tours de force of graphic design made possible by the creation of a new Internet-based programming tool called VRML (Virtual Reality Markup Language). In some of them:

Participants select their avatar—human, animal or alien—and navigate it through virtual environments to meet and talk with other people on-line. Unlike chat forums, which are text-based, participants speak in real time using a microphone on their home computer. The avatars closest to each other on the screen will be heard the loudest—as in real life.[4]

These worlds are stable and reliable enough to support long-term communities. They are a step beyond text-only MUDs and MOOs (on-line, interactive role-playing environments), which have been building enduring communities and solid human relationships for some time, but without benefit of the representation of either place or person. The representation of person is the concern of the avatar.

In the world as we know it, personal identity, the you in "you," is very much dependent on the habit of reading and writing. What creates our separate and distinct identity in the world is the exercise of processing information in our heads, organizing it in a space where the images came from our memories, and the memories from our senses. We have sculpted our selves, our identity, by reading fixed words on a page. You might think: Why would the inherent mobility of words on a screen change to that? Aren't you still processing the information, translating an abstract series of symbols into images that are creating your imagination? Of course, you are. But the important distinction is that, on the screen, which is accessible to our input, what we experience is a dialogue, an exchange that goes back to an earlier time of preliterate orality when information was processed externally, through our interactions with the rest of the world. Meaning, in other words, arose out of action rather than through contemplation. It was with contemplation, with internal processing of information provided by the fixed words of the printed page, that the "self" arose.*

On the Net, identity becomes very flexible. You can present yourself in any way you like. As the dog in the cartoon typed to the other dog working at a terminal: "The nice thing about the Net is nobody knows you're a dog." The identities of people on the Net are instantly changeable and routinely altered. There are many stories of people switching gender, changing age, swapping nationality, changing even their very basic tastes. According to Sherry Turkle:

In cyberspace, hundreds of thousands, perhaps already millions, of users create online personae who live in a diverse group of

---

* The *Essays* of Montaigne were essays in development of identity.

virtual communities where the routine formation of multiple identities undermines any notion of a real and unitary self. Yet the notion of the real fights back. People who live parallel lives on the screen are nevertheless bound by the desires, pain, and mortality of their physical selves. Virtual communities offer a dramatic new context in which to think about human identity in the age of the Internet. They are spaces for learning about the lived meaning of a culture of simulation.[5]

The message of the medium of cyberspace is touch, body, identity. These are precisely the three areas of our being that pessimistic critics say we are losing to technology. But isn't it clear, too, that to put them in jeopardy is also to bring them out in the open? Until now the body, as Stelarc often says with a devilish chuckle, is that thing that we often only get to know when it stops functioning. By losing something of their physical presence on-line, people are made aware of the fact that they *have* a body and that they are lucky to have one. The same goes for identity. Even as you project yourself on-line through your avatar in the guise of your choice; even as you disguise your gender, race, nationality, age, and physical condition; even as you put this completely fabricated electronic mask forward, you remain physically attached to a being—right then and there— that you recognize as being uniquely yourself.

Here, in the words of one of the creators of a world made for avatars, is a description of how far the notion can be taken:

A few weeks ago the new TechnoSphere site from London opened on the World Wide Web. The site represents a unique exploration of the interactive potentials of electronic networks, of practical aspects of user interaction, and of the formation of virtual communities. It offers the visitors access to a three-dimensional virtual landscape which forms the natural habitat of TechnoSphere's artificial creatures. The users design these artificial life forms by choosing component body parts and by selecting from a range of behavioral characteristics.

After a creature has been released into the TechnoSphere, it begins to live there and to interact with the creatures that have been designed by other users. The whole system is self-organizing according to the laws that have been set by the team of developers. The creatures have to find food—they can be carnivores or herbivores—they join up with others in couples or groups, they procreate, eat each other—all depending on their given properties and needs. From time to time, the creature will send its parent/designer an e-mail message with a report about its current location, and about significant events in its evolution like having created a tenth generation, or about its death. The users can also request an image of the creature in its environment. Already a lively exchange is developing between the TechnoSphere team and users who request new possibilities for interacting with their creations.

The project raises important questions about the development of artificial life in electronic networks, and about the relation between art and technology. It tackles the widespread cultural unease about computer simulations of nature and makes a statement about possible future developments on the Internet.[6]

Interestingly, two of the individuals most closely associated with advanced simulation of human environments, Jaron Lanier, often credited with coining the phrase VR,* and Mark Pesce, first developer

---

* Writer Julian Dibbell posted what appears to be the definitive derivation of VR on the Internet newsgroup "CYHIST Community memory: Discussion list on the History of Cyberspace." It first appears in 1938 in an essay published that year by theorist/playwright Antonin Artaud, entitled "The Theatre of Alchemy." Dibbell reports that he conveyed this fact to Lanier in person, evoking the following reaction: "He was tickled. He insisted he hadn't been consciously aware of the reference at the time he (re)invented 'virtual reality,' but he did allow as how he'd read a lot of Artaud in college, so that who knows, you know? He added, too, that he liked the connection a lot, that he was always trying to convince his more anti-technological friends of the organic relationship between technology and the arts, and that this might help do the job." <<cyhist@jvvm.stjohns.edu>>

of VRML, have expressed deep reservations about the value of such simulations. Both have felt enough concern over the issue of this delegation of our selfhood to agents to make their views known on-line. Lanier posted a long message on the Net which included the following explanation for his aversion to agents:

Here is how people reduce themselves by acknowledging agents, step-by-step:

Step 1) Person gives computer program extra deference because it is supposed to be "smart" and "autonomous." [People have a tendency to yield authority to computers anyway, and it's a shame. In my experience and observations, computers, unlike other tools, seem to produce the best results when users have an antagonistic attitude towards them.]

Step 2) Projected autonomy is a self-fulfilling prophecy, as anyone who has ever had a teddy bear knows. The person starts to think of the computer as being like a person.

Step 3) As a consequence of unavoidable psychological algebra, the person starts to think of himself as being like the computer.

Step 4) Unlike a teddy bear, the computer is made of ideas. The person starts to limit himself to the categories and procedures represented in the computer, without realizing what has been lost. Music becomes MIDI, art becomes Postscript. I believe that this process is the precise origin of the nerdy quality that the outside world perceives in some computer culture.

Step 5) This process is greatly exacerbated if the software is conceived of as an agent and is therefore attempting to represent the person with a software model. The person's act of projecting autonomy onto the computer becomes an unconscious choice to limit behaviors to those that fit naturally into the grooves of

the software model. Even without agents, a person's creative output is compromised by identification with a computer. With
agents, however, the person himself is compromised.

Mark Pesce fears that "holosthetic media" (as he calls total surround simulations, whether vr- or vrml-based) are "the most potent
technology for mind control since the advent of human culture":

> The potentials for addiction and enslavement do not outweigh
> the potential for creative play and communication, but to ignore
> one and focus on the other is both shortsighted and foolhardy.
> The decisions made today by the architects and designers of
> holosthetic media will set the tone, define the mythos, for the
> coming community. We must do our best to construct a vivo-
> genic cyberspace, one that supports both individual and com-
> munity, where every person can extend their creative potential,
> free from pathogenic influence.7

My own view of this begins with the observation that one of the
dominant design themes in 3-d modeling and vr computer graphics
is tunnels. Throughout the multimedia environment there seems to
be an obsession with the seduction of going through a tunnel. It
could be attributed either to our memories of the passage through
the birth canal itself or an unconscious image of birth, but it seems
as though all these little creatures running through dark tunnels are
being born. Meanwhile, what is really being born is the cyborg—a
Transformer—a weird creature who is half human and half mechanical and whom we find coming out of the other end of the tunnel,
weightless and horizon-less, in a state of wonderment before the
world. Ourselves.
 Something approaching an inversion of the relationship between
man and machine is under way. It used to be so comfortable to say
technology is an extension of the body: it is less comfortable to say
the body has become an extension of technology. Nevertheless, that
is what is happening, because there is more and more of it (the body)

out there, so much in fact that the balance between what is "out there" and what is "in here" has changed completely. It is quite obvious that we are becoming the organic core or organic extension of our own brilliantly sophisticated machines. We must ask ourselves whether we want to go along with this.

The more extensions we have, the more we cede to them, the more we become like them. Jaron Lanier's diatribe is echoed in a stunning work of art by Jeffrey Shaw which did not achieve the recognition it deserved, perhaps because it was so critical of the very technology it was using. *The Golden Calf* is a pedestal with nothing on it, standing in the middle of the room. Around it, patrons will find small, flat panel screens with instructions to hold them towards the pedestal. If you hold the screen at a certain angle, you will see something on the pedestal. It is the 3-D image of a gold-plated calf. The high-ground, moral message of the piece is clear enough. But Shaw has added an extra twist, which he explained to me. He has set up the installation in such a way that nowhere does the full image of the calf appear sharply or fully. This forces those who approach the piece to adopt all sorts of contortions to try to see the virtual calf better, "as if they were in supplication," says Shaw with a wicked smile.

But there is another interpretation of this work. We want our machines to respond, which is part of the man/machine inversion. This response is a new mirror, one which we need more than others. It is the mirror of our feelings, the mirror of our interior. We are beginning to have an interior, an inside, again, which is why I call the culture of interactivity "depth culture." We are only beginning to find out that we are still human after the transition from an era in which we felt the notion of "human" was attached to the literate personality. We lost that humanity during two world wars and we are now trying to rediscover, or rather rebuild it. Sherry Turkle recounts this telling anecdote:

At the end of the 1992 Artificial Life Conference I sat next to eleven-year-old Holly as we watched a group of robots with distinctly different "personalities" compete in a special robot

Olympics. I told her I was studying robots and life, and Holly became thoughtful. Then she said unexpectedly, "It's like Pinocchio. First, Pinocchio was just a puppet. He was not alive at all. Then he was an alive puppet. Then he was an alive boy. A real boy. But he was alive even before he was a real boy. So I think the robots are like that. They are alive like Pinocchio [the puppet], but not like real boys."[8]

One of the early myths of industrialization, the story of Pinocchio tells us something about this process of humanization beyond the machine. Pinocchio was a puppet, that is, a creature made in the image of the mechanical age. But the main ambition of Pinocchio was to become a live boy. After going through the bowels of a whale—riding on another myth of transformation, that of Jonas—Pinocchio does indeed become a real boy.

We are all electronic Pinocchios with our hands on our keyboards, lying through our teeth as we try to pretend that, no, nothing has changed, we are still the same, it's the technology that has changed. . . . The wish to become human again, at the other end of the technological metamorphosis, is what drives the intense research into humanoids.

CHAPTER FOUR

PRESENCE,
REAL AND VIRTUAL

E VERY YEAR since 1994, the McLuhan Program has organized
with the help of another institution a series of video conferencing seminars on culture and technology. The first series was
conducted with the University of New Brunswick, then with York
University in Toronto, with the University of Orléans in France,
and, in the fall of 1995, with three universities simultaneously in the
Netherlands.* The idea behind The World Series on Culture and
Technology is to garner the thoughts of the best minds available
in the world today in various countries, in various cultures, in various languages. It is an extended worldwide benchmarking of the
state of reality. The World Series is also an experiment in distant education. We test different approaches to learning, including three in-
terlocking media environments: a global interactive classroom where

---

* In collaboration with the Netherlands Design Institute in Amsterdam and the
University of Toronto's McLuhan Program in Culture and Technology in
Canada, with the support of Origin and Telindus, among others, ACS-interactive organized The World Series in Culture and Technology during the fall of
1996. The central theme of this series of lectures, which were held simultaneously in four different locations, was the interaction between modern culture
and new media technologies. A video-conferencing link with Toronto (the
McLuhan Program) enabled the audience at three different Dutch universities
(Amsterdam, Delft, and Groningen) to "attend." Every week an artist was
invited to perform an experiment using the video-conferencing link.

attention is focused on a person on a TV monitor instead of a black-board; a Web site for the work in progress, bibliographies, resources, and, of course, on-line forums and lists of hyperlinks (the Web is not only a tool, it is one of the prime objects of study); finally, the series produces documentary material in video and in CD-ROM.

The interest at the McLuhan Program in video conferencing goes back to 1985, when I learned of an experiment in long-distance communication by artists Sherry Rabinovitz and Kit Galloway. It was called *Hole in Space: New York-Los Angeles, 1980* and it consisted of an unannounced, but very public video-conferencing link between New York and Los Angeles. A camera and monitor were set up in a storefront on a busy New York street, and a similar setup was established in Los Angeles. People walking by would look into the window and see other people in the monitors. Sometimes, the monitor people would be waving. At first, the passersby wouldn't realize these people were waving *at* them, but if they paid attention, they recognized there was communication going on. The next thing they discovered was that those people on the monitor were not some-where else in New York (or Los Angeles), but in Los Angeles (or New York). On the first day of the experiment, people just ran-domly got into contact with each other. By the second day, word had gotten around and families got together to wave hello from Los Angeles to New York and vice versa. On the third day the media were there. And, of course, with the media involved, the whole art event became pop culture fodder. The beauty of that simple experi-ment was a kind of artistic epiphany and I began to understand that distance video communication is a very significant development.*

---

* The McLuhan Program acquired its own video-conferencing equipment, a Picturetel 4000, connected by two digitally switched telephone lines in the fall of 1992, with help from BSO, Michael Paine, our benefactor from Boston and direct support in the form of a sizable rebate from Adcom Electronics in Toronto. We have never looked back. Eckart Wintzen is very fond of teasing me about my passion for video conferencing. He has taken me to task publicly in the Dutch World Series, but I am glad to report that both he and Origin have taken leadership in the use of video conferencing in the Netherlands.

PRESENCE AND TELEPRESENCE

What is so magical about video conferencing? In spite of the poor quality of the picture, the quirky jerkiness of the motion and the awkward kind of hieratic posturing people are obliged to adopt in front of the camera, the magic of seeing people instantly through a void that could take hours to cross in a 747 never fails to stir me. Then again, I must confess I still get a mild kick out of telephoning across the Atlantic. Maybe it's just an Atlantic sensibility that goes back to my early immigrant years. Regardless, it seems just plain wonderful to add a living image to a living voice and to be in the presence—or telepresence—of people who are so far away.

Which raises the question: What is presence? What, exactly, is "present" in a person you meet in the flesh, face-to-face (f2f in the lingo of the Net)? Clearly, there is a body there, and a body projects all kinds of information. Bodies talk to bodies at levels often ignored or set aside by minds when they are busy saying or thinking something else. After years of continuous fascination with the issue of presence, from the deeper spiritual sense of the total, absolute presence of being, and the stark "thereness" of the world, to the mundane issues of communications engineering, I have identified what I believe are four essential conditions for the sense of presence to be effective in telepresence:

1. A clear and shared evidence of the source of the presence. Nervous people often report experiencing ghostly, imminent "presences" somewhere in their immediate vicinity. The sense of presence may be as real to them as anything you or I know, but if the evidence of the source is not clear to anybody else, the experience is not shared, nor then the sense of presence. The evidence does not have to be visual—quite the opposite; touch and hearing are more reliable evidence of presence than the eye. However, it has to be shared.

2. Shared space. The fact that the shared space may be purely electronic or "virtual" rather than real takes nothing away

from the reality of the presence itself. This is critical to understanding the vast difference between virtual reality as a communication device and just plain old VR. If there is a real person (or object) behind the apparatus, behind the interaction, then there is a real presence; otherwise there isn't.

3. Shared time. On the phone, as during video conferencing, people who communicate obviously share the same moment in absolute time, if not necessarily the same "time" as established by their time zone. By contrast, while voice-mail does give one the illusion of presence, there is no shared time between the source and the receiver, hence there is no authentic telepresence.

4. A clear evidence of the "interval." The interval is the most sensory aspect of telepresence. It is a sensation of the other truly being there that comes through real communication. It is what makes live television reports different from video conferencing and it might almost be a tactile conclusion drawn instantly from visual and auditory cues. In a live television report, there is no interval because there is no shared communication: it is all one-way. The moment may be shared in "absolute" space (our previous, literate way of understanding space), but there is no two-way connection between locations.

So what is presence? Ask a lover. It is something quite physical. It involves more than the eye, the ear. It does not need to involve the hand, but it needs the skin or something like it. It is entirely interactive. It is a gentle form of pressure, or the sense of a person, an animal, or even, at a lesser degree, an object's aura. It feels almost like a very fine magnetic field. I remember a time when I distinctly felt the presence of a rather nice and intelligent-looking dog as if it were a big gust of warmth. As I moved in and out of the field of power of that dog, the difference was tangible. The presence of people is many times more complex, but nevertheless experienced all at once, without need to decode any of it. It can be impossible to describe in words.

Among persons face-to-face, all of this is easy to recognize. What happens when machines get involved as intermediaries? Let us ignore, for the moment, machines that do not fulfill the above four conditions. There are only three distant communication systems that meet the requirements of evidence of source, shared space, shared time, and the room or opportunity for interval: they are the telephone, video conferencing, and the nascent on-line virtual reality. And incipient both in technology and in the culture, there are two basic forms of telepresence, one using analogue communication technology to extend the face-to-face interaction, and the other using digital computer simulations to create shared environments where real people meet in the guise of avatars. Each has different business and social applications; both have inherent problems.

Analogue telepresence is now mediated by a growing array of technologies ranging from the humble telephone to telerobotics for remote surgery. While some of these technologies are accessible only to expert users and only at great cost, others are available off-the-shelf, such as, for example, the hackers' delight *CU-SeeMe,* appropriately named in baby talk because it is really still an infant technology. However, it is neither infantile nor superfluous to see one's interlocutor on a chat line or on a Web site, even if the image is black and white and postage-stamp size, refreshed only every five or ten seconds. The experience is all the more impressive if you are also using a phone connection which gives you at least real-time audio. It is certainly enough to reassure distant lovers who do not benefit from access to more sophisticated video conferencing. *CU-SeeMe* is also useful for sharing other visual data, such as charts, photographs, and designs, in a manner that is more direct and intuitive than faxing or e-mailing the evidence.

Off to a very slow start, but now picking up speed, cheap and efficient video-conferencing technologies are now in the process of educating educators and business executives to the opportunities of creating, offering, recording, and even reselling their own content. The effect of this is to further weaken broadcasting's exclusive gatekeeping prerogative on content and to help users to graduate from consuming to producing TV.

Two people talking to each other from Vancouver to Miami on a desktop video-conferencing system can establish such accurate eye contact and lip synchronization that it feels as if they were really face-to-face across a windowpane, even though both are aware that they are thousands of kilometers apart. But what we see via video conferencing is the result of a complex series of technical processes which come close to simulating the processes of our own nervous system. These prostheses are externalizations of neural processing, a technical continuation of our eyes and ears. The telephone provides for the ear and the voice, two baseline connectors capable of real eloquence despite the limited bandwidth. Video conferencing adds vision, a spatial sense, movement.

How do these synthetic "telepresent media" compare with the "real thing"? Well, they are fun, they are helpful, and they can be used to good effect in certain contexts. But where presence is concerned, they are guilty of continuing the disastrous split between body and mind that began with rationalism. What they are missing is *touch*. Not the kind of banal conception of touch as in people holding hands; after all, you don't need to hold hands to conduct a business meeting. But you need the sense of interval. The telepresent technologies still come up short in the interval. Strangely enough, phoning is more effective than video conferencing in terms of interval because it is so intimate. The real-timeliness is more intensely experienced. Video conferencing, on the other hand, adds a substantial sense of presence.*

Of course video conferencing, already perfectly adequate for business and academic purposes, will improve. But are telepresent technologies going to be confined to business and academe? Telepresence,

---

* After the end of an interview, professional sound technicians usually record a few minutes of silence. They call it "the room tone." It is used as reference for editing purposes, and also to add gaps or blanks to smooth out editing. It is qualified by a unique identity. There is a room-tone to video conferencing sessions, something that you can verify immediately by turning the "mute" button on: the electronic silence is dead, but the human silence of an attentive audience is full of life and energy.

surely, is going to create new forms of human interactions, new forms of presence, and who knows, perhaps new habits of gesture.

At the McLuhan Program, our study of this area began in earnest in 1986, when I took a delegation of twelve artist-engineers from Toronto to Salerno, Italy, and then to Paris for our first efforts at transatlantic art. The Salerno episode was a riotous debacle. We couldn't connect by phone from one house to the next, let alone across the Atlantic. In Paris, because we were at the Canadian Cultural Centre where the phone system is specially imported from Canada, we had next to perfect communication and we could test a few things.

We discovered, for a start, that for tactile extensions requiring ultrasensitive feedback, real time is essential. We learned this when Toronto artists Doug Back and Norman White inaugurated the Transatlantic Arm Wrestling Experiment between Paris and Toronto, June 4, 1986. The idea was to create a force-feedback system that would allow two persons to feel each other's physical presence by phone. In Toronto, at the now defunct ArtCulture Resource Centre on Queen Street, Doug Back would apply pressure on a mechanical contraption connected to a computer connected to a modem connected to a phone and the pressure would be sent as digital data to another modem connected to another computer connected to another mechanical contraption in Paris, where Norman White returned the pressure. Because of a 250-millisecond delay on the telephone line, it was impossible to get a true instant feedback. Those of us who tried it had to be very creative in our interpretation of the "interval" condition. Our whole being was required to fill a 250-millisecond hole in reality. Arm wrestling that way doesn't work. Still, the experience, at this early stage in telepresence experimentation, was exhilarating.

Despite being a rather modest imitation of what has been available to telerobotics in industry and military technologies for decades, this performance was breaking new psychological grounds precisely because it had no other purpose than to make the audience perceive itself in a completely new way, with an added dimension.

For many people who witnessed the event, it seemed as if, for the first time, they were beginning to understand that our human proportions have expanded from the immediate to global surroundings because we can now, with a simple electronic gesture, reach out and touch someone on the other side of the ocean.

During the same event, we also tried to transmit by musical sounds over the phone the complexity of bodily presence with David Rokeby's *Very Nervous System* (described in Chapter 2, "The Biology of Interactivity"). On the Canadian side, the installation was in Ottawa, at the National Museum of Science and Technology, where a dancer performed in front of David's camera and computer. The sounds created by the dancer's movements were digitized and sent via modem to Paris, where another dancer responded to those sounds. This was a way of making the telephone "tactile," we hoped. Like everything else we did in those pioneering days, it sort of worked. While the movement-generated sound was indeed picked up in Toronto and reproduced in Paris as continuous musical variations, what we missed was clear evidence of the source of the sound. Our ideas were always slightly ahead of our technologies.

Graham Smith, another of the artists on the tour who was pushing the limits of communication technology, is the person who first taught me the word *telepresence*.* His transatlantic performance which bore that name consisted of teleguiding three-wheeled robots by telephone signals to send and receive slow-scan TV images back and forth between Paris and Toronto. Besides having had to design and build the two robots from scratch, and to test untried connections between modem and direction controls, Smith had to contend with still-immature digital switching in the international telephone system. The slow-scan TV was atrociously slow at the Paris end, and the gray-scale images appearing on the Mac Plus sitting on the robot were all but unrecognizable. You had to have been there to know that, yes, that was indeed the general appearance of the ArtCulture Resource Centre in Toronto. Today, the remote-control device that

---

* The first of many companies created by Smith was called Telepresence.

comes with even moderately sophisticated video-conferencing equipment makes such video snooping easy.

Since then, Smith has been able to adapt his Telepresence machine to the "Supply Student" concept. This places in a classroom a video camera which can be controlled remotely by a student who is unable to attend school because of illness or other reasons. The practical—and poetic—value of the Supply Student is that it allows these children to keep in touch with social and academic life in school, to partake of lessons, games, and the general ambiance.

Graham Smith is one of the world's masters of video conferencing. I don't know of anyone else who has tried as many variations on this technology as he has. As director of our Virtual Reality Artist Access Program (VRAAP), Graham was the instigator of seemingly endless new ways of exploring video transmission and total surround video. At the McLuhan Program we also used video conferencing just to keep informed of what was going on elsewhere in the world, inviting artists, engineers, intellectuals, business people, and others to discuss what was current. Our regular collaborators in this venture have been the people and guests of the Electronic Café in Santa Monica, run by Kit Galloway and Sherrie Rabinowitz. Graham became so accustomed to communicating with Kit and Sherrie over the video-conferencing system, that he felt uncomfortable when he was just on the phone with them. "It feels like having my back turned to them," he said.

Another group of artist-engineers connected with the McLuhan Program is Toronto's Vivid Effects. With their interactive system *Mandala*, Vincent John Vincent, Francis Macdougall, and Steve Warrame have found a way to command events on a large screen without even having to get close to it.* In this system, your movements are recorded by an overhead camera and reported via a computer as a

* Vincent John Vincent, Francis MacDougall, Sherrie Cohen, and David Maubray have all contributed to the invention of *Mandala*, an interactive video system which enables the user to operate graphic and musical as well as robotic computer functions at a distance without touching the screen or any peripheral.

digital image appearing on screen. You can turn your image into a giant cursor and discover that you have just become one big mouse able to command and control whatever happens on the screen.

Graham, Vincent, and Steve used *Mandala* to do many delightfully silly things like playing Pong across the Atlantic to wrap up a conference organized in Sophia Antipolis by France Telecom. Every time Vincent would put a ball across his opponent's net, the two hundred Frenchmen could be heard applauding. It was fun, but it was also serious work because what we were really trying to figure out were some basic issues of telepresence.

Such as: where is the ball, really? What happens to me when I see this kind of experiment is a strange sensation of disorientation. I am connecting the ball with the "other side." I "see" it get hit by the other player's racket, and it comes back to "our" side. Somehow that doesn't make any sense at all. Truly, where is the ball, and where are *we* when we are together on that screen?*

It is worth exploring this process in some detail to bring out the complexities of another video-conferencing experiment, this one, a performance piece by Paul Sermon called *Telematic Dreaming*. In this truly dazzling and puzzling piece, Paul has installed beds in each of two galleries in Finland, 350 km apart, connected by video conferencing. The image of the occupant of each bed is projected onto the sheets of the bed in the other gallery. On the video-conferencing screens, the

---

* Technically, the ball is a simulation displayed on video by computer commands at one source and simultaneously displayed by video conferencing at the other location. The video images of the players on both sides are digitized in real time into the computer program by a special coder/decoder card called Live!tm. Chromakey, or blue-screen video-trickery, allows the separation of foreground from background. You keep the foreground images (the players) and put each one on one half of the screen. Then you substitute both backgrounds with the display of the computer program and you've got it. The image of the movements of both players can affect the course of the image of the ball because the transmitted video image of that player comes as source to the real-time video to digital decoder, just like the image coming from the on-site camera. But in the end, the ball is nowhere, just like a thought experienced only by the people who were there. And that, of course, is what interests the technopsychologist in me.

images of both beds are aligned so that both distant occupants are made to appear as if they were on the same bed. The entertaining side of what you see at either gallery is that one of the occupants appears in the flesh, while his or her bedmate appears flattened out in a 2-D image. Both occupants can see the effects of their paradoxical meeting on a large monitor placed next to each of the beds.

The people who meet that way can caress each other and see, in real time and total interactivity, the effects of each other's caresses. Are they touching? Or are they not touching? If you define "touch" according to cause, then they are not touching; only their images are touching. But, if, by "touch" you mean the effect or response, then it is quite evident that they are touching.

With *Telematic Dreaming,* Paul Sermon has created the first fundamental aesthetic paradox involving touch since the development of trompe l'oeil in the baroque era. By bringing together two people hundreds of kilometers apart on the same screen, and making them interact in real time, he is proposing the central paradox of telepresence: can you really touch someone by sight alone? This what Susan Kozel, a professional dancer who has tested the installation, has to say about it:

> Members of the public in the second gallery had the option of joining [Paul Sermon's] projected image on the bed, braving the social and personal connotations of being on a bed with another person, even if this other person was an electronic image. . . . The effect was astonishing: it was one of contact improvisation between an image and a person, between ghost and matter. . . . Virtual materiality is what it's about, an interactive, physical engagement with space, time, and meaning.

The point Kozel makes is at the core of the paradox of telepresence, both real and virtual:

> In his work Paul's body became virtual (i.e., a projected image), yet the rapport between image and person was very real and

evoked a social and sexual dynamic familiar to us all. Paul admits that his use of a bed in *Telematic Dreaming* was deliberate, he fully intended for the sexual and social implications to play a role.[1]

Here, the evidence of the interval, far from being choppy and evanescent as it is in standard video conferencing, is extremely strong, stronger in some respects than the intimacy of the voice in the privacy of the phone. Evidence of interval and evidence of source coincide. That's a lot of presence.

ON CYBERSEX

It takes an artist of the calibre of Paul Sermon to pull off such a stunt without generating jeers. I showed a video of *Telematic Dreaming* in Hamburg, at the 1993 Interface Conference, to introduce the notion of "electronic touch," only to find in the following morning's papers disparaging reports about a Canadian professor who was promoting "ersatz sex"! For better or for worse, the issue of sex in telepresence cannot be avoided, nor should it be. The sexual encounter is, at least in Western cultures, already such a rich mix of real and virtual, body and mind, flesh and fantasy that technology can only play right into it.

There is no doubt that with video conferencing, in particular when the partners can be made to share the same virtual space, the age-old sex trade will get a new boost. Safe sex to boot. One of our guests at our Virtual Reality Artists Access Program video-conferencing seminars was a very attractive and apparently successful phone sex operator who spoke to us from California. We showed her a tape of *Telematic Dreaming*. She was amused by our suggestion that she could set up shop with a video-conferencing unit like the one we were using to address her. I don't think that she wanted to let on how far she would consider getting into it, but she did give us a very proper yet unquestionably erotic simulation of a phone sex conversation, keeping her clothes on, of course. (By late 1996, sex by video conference had become a major industry on the Net.)

Unfortunately, most of what passes for cybersex is neither stimulating nor innovative. The on-line pornography that gets our regulators so worked up is as dismally boring as its glossy counterparts in paper magazines. There is a lot of it available, but all in all, according to a recent survey of a search engine's most frequent queries, it accounts for less than 20 percent of all data traffic on the Internet. And that's almost the same proportion of sexual traffic you will find in the average person's head. The really interesting sex on-line will have to address touch, not vision. And, yes, there is a memory of touch in even the most mechanical forms of interactivity, such as dressing or undressing "Virtual Valerie" or helping her to reach orgasm. While this activity is extremely limited, bordering on the moronic, it is undeniably combining the thrill of voyeurism with the surreptitious transgression of the other's privacy. But surely the simplistic transfer of our old contents to the new medium is not that medium's message. So what is?

Our visually biased culture has tended to think of sexual attraction as an issue of appearance, not one of presence. In the world of telepresence, looking good is not good enough, you have to "feel" good, too. Many interactive tactile experiments are being done. When they are merely interested in sex, they tend to be naive and predictable. But some of this work is authentic research.

For example, two artists, Stahl Stenslie and Kirk Woolford, worked together at the Cologne Academy of Media Arts on a system that created a mild sensation a few years ago. The system called *Cybersex* allows you to feel vibrations through electronic sleeves placed on various parts of your body. These vibrations, transmitted by telephone lines, are triggered by the movements of your partner at the other end. While Stenslie has continued to explore the marketability of the system, Woolford went in another direction. His question was that of feedback. What is the point, he thought, of touching anything if you have no idea of how it feels, if you have no feedback. Woolford's point addresses the very nature of touch.

Touch, to be effective, must always communicate in both directions simultaneously. Claude Cadoz, one of France's best researchers in virtual touch, has identified this condition as "transduction."* What Cadoz means by transduction is the two-way communication of touch from feedforward to feedback in real time. Until recently, he explained, people thought touch was one of the least articulate of the senses. Experimental work had shown that if you put two sharp points on a blindfolded person's arm, at first the sensation will be reported as two different points. However, if you move them closer together, the body very soon interprets them as a single point. However, says Cadoz, the really interesting data are in the relatively unexplored areas of many varieties of pressures, temperature, and textures that the human body is actually capable of distinguishing.

Cybersex is a field of such obvious potential for exploration and even more obvious potential for profit that we can count on continuous, rapid development in both serious and trivial applications.

DIGITAL TELEPRESENCE

Imagina, the Festival of New Images in Monte Carlo in 1993, featured a work called *Le rendez-vous de Cluny,* in which two people meet by teleconferencing in the same virtual reality environment. Using VR goggles and gloves, they enter into a digital reconstruction of the old Abbey of Cluny which was destroyed in the late nineteenth century. Two VR platforms, one in Monaco and the other in Paris, were connected to the same VR environment by a high-speed data line. Madame Vincent, in the form of a digital representation,

---

* Claude Cadoz is the director of ACROE, a research center in tactile simulations in Grenoble, France. Cadoz believes that we are only beginning to discover what it is to touch. For example, it is far more complex than the simple issue of making contact. It is only now that engineers like Cadoz are beginning to incorporate tactile sensation into technology that we can begin to appreciate that touch is also made of pressure, texture, interval, and sensitivity to minute variations of humidity and temperature.

but with her real voice, was guiding Father Di Falco from Monaco, also digitally imaged, on a tour of the digital Abbey. The three thousand patrons of the Imagina festival could watch on a big screen the two persons talking and walking into that imaginary space together.

One visitor is really in Monaco and the other is really in Paris, but together they are floating or levitating in, above, and around a construction in the nowhere land on the Net. This, of course, is quite different from sending an avatar. You are not merely seeing yourself in the picture, you are literally *in* the picture.* You can turn around and see the digital world around and below you; you can look at the person talking to you and see the expressions on the virtual face change according to what is said.

Télévirtualité, another project of the Institut National d'Audiovisuel in Paris, allows people to carry on real-time conferences on-line, using a lip-and-facial-expression graphic synchronized with their real speech and expression as registered by an on-site camera. The possibilities of extending one's living room are endless.

COMMUNITY, REAL AND VIRTUAL

Alpha Worlds are virtual cities on-line. Sherwood Towne, for example, is a virtual city accessible to anybody with a PC on-line.** It has a population of 75,000 "immigrants," and at this writing, it comprises a few hundred buildings. These constructions are three-dimensional and can be built and/or visited from anywhere in the world. Whatever you build in an Alpha World, you alone can destroy and reconstruct, and you cannot unbuild someone else's construction. This is important because it ensures permanence and

---

* As you do when you remember yourself in given circumstances, such as taking a bath: do you see yourself in the bathtub, or do you remember the feeling of the water around your waist ?
** This particular alpha world works on PC only, but a Macintosh version is planned (http://www.ccon.org/).

reliability to the objective status of the virtual environment. Of course, you can share a chat line conversation, either alphanumerically or by Real Audio, with one person or more and with or without the support of an avatar.

WorldsAway is a "cyberplace" Fujitsu and CompuServe launched in December 1995, where on-line users create their own animated representations or avatars and socialize with other users all over the world in a graphical landscape. Within WorldsAway, users can portray their real personalities or create unique on-line personas. They can also convey emotions through facial expressions and gestures, as well as "talk" to one another in real time through text, as in traditional chat services. Objects in the virtual world also support personal expression and enhance world experience—for example, you can give someone flowers, decorate a room with furniture, share books, and use other objects to enhance your avatar's abilities to express its (your) personality.

Alpha Worlds and WorldsAway are more than "graphic MUDs,"* they are another level of networking, within but also beyond the Web altogether. They are like concretizations or precipitates of immateriality. They create a sense of space, of continuous, unbroken space across the screens of the visitors and residents. They are pockets of objective imagination in the networked synergy of tens of thousands of people. They propose a new form of common space, one that people have never before had the opportunity to share, except perhaps during the far-off times of legend and magic hallucinations. Though still crude and limited by bandwidth capacity and processing power, they already show the promise of a lot more to come.

Carl Loeffler's *Virtual Polis,* is a virtual community environment which allows you to access your personally designed virtual apartment complete with a virtual wardrobe stored in virtual drawers and bought at a virtual shopping mall next to a virtual amusement park in your virtual neighborhood. At some point in the not-too-distant

---

* Graphic, multi-user domains, a feature of the Web.

future, you will be able to don these clothes to meet real partners, also dressed up virtually for business or seduction or any other purpose you care to get together for. In such environments, everything is indeed "virtual," except that the people who meet there are "real."

The question is no longer how much, but what kind of presence there is in digital telepresence. In analogue media like video conferencing, the answer depends on the number of sensory channels made available, the quality of the transmission, the value and pertinence of usage. In digital media like VR, you cannot tell what is behind the presence that you are confronted with. The effect is like magic. A commentator has posted articles on the Web about the "Superman Effect":

> The Superman Effect manifests itself in the extra powers given to us without the aid of machines. Although most of us in Alpha World design structures that look held together by gravity, the absence of gravity enables us to realize our long-held and unfulfilled dreams of flying without using wings, or floating in midair, or lifting (seemingly) heavy objects with ease. The ability to walk through walls, move objects from a distance (without telekinesis) and travel at warp speeds are powers that in the real world, we can only give to our fictional heroes. I see this combination of real-world familiarity and subtle superhuman powers as our first shaky steps towards a very different future."*

Are virtual cities just a toy, or can we expect new forms of socialization and community arising from this kind of experience? In both analogue and digital media, for the sense of presence to occur, real-time interaction is indispensable. But in digital media, virtual space may be extended to permit a sense of belonging to a virtual community, in other words a form of extended "presence." From that point of view, a virtual community works like a normal city, which is another form of human concentration. A real city brings together at

---

* From an on-line posting, author unknown.

close range a great number of active human bodies and minds. It multiplies the points of contact among people, that is, the opportunities for exchange of useful information. But you don't meet more than a fraction of the city's inhabitants at any one time. The remainder are carried in what the poet W. B. Yeats called "an emotion of multitude." A similar human and social energy is exuded by virtual cities.

By a predictable, but happy turn of events, real cities are transferring some of their status to the Net, first by creating flattering Web sites, and second, by creating a distinctive Net image or metaphor (*Digitaal Staadt, Telepolis, Virtual Polis, International City-Berlin,* etc.). *Digitaal Staadt,* for example, was one of the first to appear, the first certainly in the Netherlands. It began as a text-based Internet service in Dutch and in English, a navigation system to help people to find useful information about Amsterdam. Although you couldn't really meet people there, you could go to different places such as the Town Hall, the Kiosk, the Museum, the Coffee House, the Library, and so on, where you could find information and leave a message. Recently, it has added on-line discussion groups and chat, and a richer, graphical interface.[2]

However sophisticated and intriguing they may become, these new forms of telepresence will always have more to do with actual presence, than with virtual experience. Despite the fact that it is now possible to add virtual dimensions to our communication via on-line technologies, it is the reality and the targeted pertinence of on-line communication that is its principal value. Just as people can never be reduced to machines, human communications can never be reduced to the appropriate distribution of content, nor can the rich presence of people be excluded from the joyful task of making sense together, sharing information, advice, and skills.

PART 2

HYPERTEXTUALITY

CHAPTER FIVE

ALL ABOUT
HYPERTEXT

WRITING about Ted Nelson in *Wired* magazine, Gary Wolf observed that the prolific idea-monger had discovered the notion—and coined the name—of hypertext as a way to keep the productions of his scatterbrain mind under control, allowing each strand of an idea to carry on without suffering from interruptions by the other ideas:

> Xanadu, the ultimate hypertext information system, began as Ted Nelson's quest for personal liberation. The inventor's hummingbird mind and his inability to keep track of anything left him relatively helpless. He wanted to be a writer and a filmmaker, but he needed a way to avoid getting lost in the frantic multiplication of associations his brain produced. His great inspiration was to imagine a computer program that could keep track of all divergent paths of his thinking and writing. To this concept of branching, nonlinear writing, Nelson gave the name of hypertext.[1]

Hypertext was born out of a hyperactive mind. I think I know something about that problem. Clinically, it is a condition sometimes dubbed by French psychoanalysts *délire d'interprétation*. While the severe cases of this delirium tend towards hapless rumination over obsessive themes, the milder forms enjoy associations for their own sake and find a natural habitat in certain fertile minds. One idea—a word or a certain turn of phrase—triggers another; a memory calls forth a thought and vice versa, in swirls and swirls of intersecting associations and panoramic mental vistas. In effect, hypertext was a breakthrough borne out of the breakdown of the linear mind, a condition often linked to television and blamed for children's having trouble learning to read. In truth, it is the whole electronic culture that has gone nonlinear, and hypertext may be the beginning of an answer to the havoc this transition has wreaked on the previous literate culture.

Nelson, who may have been treated more harshly than he deserved in the *Wired* profile, is painted as a "Jack-of-all-ideas, master of none." But the fact is that he did master the principles of hypertext in his Xanadu project and, short of a few key applications he is said to be still working on, the World Wide Web is, for all intents and purposes, the realization of his dream.

Nelson's own succinct definition of hypertext appeared first in 1965: "Non-sequential writing with reader-controlled links."[2] The basic principle underlying hypertext is that any part of any text stored in digital form (text being made of strings of characters which are recognizable and addressable by a computer program) can be associated automatically, instantly, and permanently with any other text stored in the same way. Activating a hypertext link usually involves "clicking" on a piece of underlined text, which instructs the computer to implement an address hidden "behind" the link, which in turn takes you to the associated text, whether it is in the same document or in another database in some other computer accessible by network connections. As a way of dealing with the contents of one's personal memory and imaginings, hypertext has the advantage of being comprehensive. Fully implemented, hypertext is actually more reliable than a human memory because it allows comprehensive scanning of all potential connections of all data present in the "search space."

And the search space can be the whole world. The Web allows people on-line to link up automatically to all sorts of digital content wherever in the world it may be, in whatever database, by clicking either on a key-word or a "button."* On the Web, you can ask a question, and be transferred instantly anywhere in the world from Ottawa to New York to Tokyo to Johannesburg. Ray Hammond makes the point in perfect clarity when he asks readers of his book, *Digital Business,* to slip the complimentary Netscape Navigator disk into their PCs and to click on the underlined words they come across in the book as it appears in its on-line incarnation on the World Wide Web. This is Hammond's *mode d'emploi:*

> You will have noticed already that quite a few references in this book are underlined. This is not to emphasize the importance of such text, it indicates that in the on-line version of this book, these are "hyperlinks" on which you will be able to click and be transported around the Net directly to the company, person, or resource to which I refer for the very latest information.[3]

The principle of hypertextuality allows one to treat the Web as the extension of the contents of one's own mind. Hypertext turns everyone's memory into everybody else's, and makes of the Web the first worldwide memory.

Hypertext would not be familiar to more than a handful of scientists and academics today if the creation of Mosaic by Marc Andreessen had not turned it ipso facto into "hypermedia," in which not only text, but graphics, sound, and moving pictures may be linked. People born and bred on almost fifty years of TV need the sensory values that plain old text didn't have. (For the purposes of this book, hypertextuality is taken to include hypermedia, as long as whatever is identified by these often confusing terms is on-line.)

Hypertextuality spells the future of all the traditional industries of content or information, such as news and entertainment media, statistics, and research. It also holds the future for many objects, such as books, records, tapes, paintings, and sculpture, and the future of

---

* The Web's programming language is called HTML, which stands for Hypertext Markup Language.

their storage and distribution centers, including shops, malls, libraries, museums, and galleries. Hypertext will eventually affect architecture as well, because it is in itself an architecture making new demands on user access points, processing and distributing conditions, networking environments, and many other cyber- and real-space combinations.

Each time we invent a new medium, we seem to accelerate the rate and volume of information processing. Writing introduced a formidable acceleration of human processing abilities (Warp 1). With their alphabet, the Greeks moved from nowhere in information processing to an advanced state in less than three hundred years between the seventh and fourth centuries B.C. And with the printing press (Warp 2), the West was flooded with usable data, pushing mechanization further along the path embarked on by the Greeks and the Romans. With radio and TV (Warp 3), we had a force which increased the volume of information to the point of swamping the globe. Then, just when we were beginning to suspect that the reign of the private mind was over, computers once again accelerated individual minds at Warp 4 speed. We are now accelerating to Warp 5, where text meets hypertext, interactivity, and multimedia on-line. While the Internet allowed for the interconnection of contacts, the Web moves the whole process one giant step ahead and deeper by allowing for the interconnection of contents.

Hypertextuality creates the potential for new levels of acceleration in the circulation, elaboration, cross-checking, and simulation of ideas for commercial and scientific, as well as more playful, applications. Today, the Web is deemed to contain between thirty and fifty million pages which average about five hundred words or seven kilobytes a page. In May 1996 it was estimated that the Web contained "somewhere between 200 and 330 gigabytes of text" and that "these numbers [were] growing by 20 percent every month."[4] By the time this book is out and in your hands, the total content of the Web could equal the "roughly 29 terabytes in the current Library of Congress."[5] Having at your fingertips the equivalent in current information to the whole of the Library of Congress seems to be an impossible dream. Or is it a nightmare?

In one of his lesser-known plays, Molière has a character say mockingly, "A gentleman is a person who knows everything without ever having had to learn anything." By this definition, by virtue of having access to the memory of the world on the Web, we are all gentlemen! But exactly what is it that we have access to? The answer is "everything and nothing." In the big memory that constitutes the Web, there is everything under the sun and most of it is of no interest whatsoever to you, though of great interest to often ridiculously limited numbers of other people. That in itself is a new wrinkle in the economy: as with personal memory, there is a "direct address" quality to this new environment.

The trend towards direct or random access through digital technology is irrepressible, because we experience it all the time as one of the most precious of our mental faculties; that is, having instant access to whatever we need in our own mind exactly at the time we need it without having to go through a complicated routine to get there.

Nonlinear media or hypermedia share this quality and make their linear predecessors seem clumsy and slow. However access is not all; pertinence of access is. In the mass-customizing economy we are now fully entering, every contact, every address can potentially be made as precise as the human neural configurations that locate one thought in a trillion. The law of the Web is the inverse of the law of mass media: value is created in the relevance or pertinence of each connection, its appropriateness to the need being addressed, rather than in serving the lowest common denominator of a mass audience.

TIME AND HYPERTEXT

Real time is the speed with which, in our mind, we can summon an image or a thought. That is the speed at which consumers will want hypertext to operate. And that is what they will get from service providers of the future. The only thing standing in the way of instant distribution is the relatively low data-transfer speeds made available by the carriers. The telcos control the spigot. But that is also changing. The talk about cable modems with their essentially broadcast formats had hardly died down when "Web TV" arrived, a box that for a few hundred dollars will connect you to the Internet via your humble TV set. Sony, Philips, Mitsubishi, and others went a step further by integrating the whole package in one box, a television set with an extra channel for the Web. If that doesn't bring the Internet to the masses, nothing will. Let us observe, in passing, the irony of the Trojan Horse Internet breaching the walls where the vaunted Information Highway couldn't go. . . .

The latest trend throughout the economy is to do more and more of everything in real time, just in time: just-in-time production and delivery, the just-in-time association, just-in-time learning or just-in-time data processing. Indeed, thinking is a just-in-time technology. Just by thinking, you can change the content of your mind in real time with colors and motion and sound and texture and all the other simulations we process every second of our mental life in our private virtual reality. The flexibility of data processing we experience in our mind is the standard that network media engineering must seek to achieve.

It is the permanent availability of content that determines whether it can be delivered just in time or not. While the storage and delivery of traditional media content absorbs much of the time and energy of conventional publishers and broadcasters, the content of all digital, networked communications is potentially available anywhere, all the time, on demand. Being everywhere at once, the Net is the ultimate decentralizing force. It suppresses all distances and all delays other than those inherent in the transmission technology.

In principle, all media benefit from collective input, even radio and TV where a small group of people process information for the many. But radio and TV are called "time-based" because they follow a linear and irreversible orientation of time. To conduct e-mail and related Internet activities, one needs a different sense of time. The difference is that the time in use is not linear. It is not real time because inputs or messages are not guaranteed an immediate response. However, the exchanges are not really out of time like the content of books, for instance, because they are almost as contextualized as a conversation is. They are like a telephone conversation in slow motion (and, of course, in text). This is the "secondary real-timeliness" of the Web. One might call it "expanded" or "nonlinear real time." The time of the Net is expanded to include and accommodate the same level of context as an oral exchange, but over multiple entry points. This is critical to the improved processing of intelligence.

The real time of the use of any content, whether in face-to-face conversation or in complex media synergies, is predicated on the level of urgency defined by the context. In many cases, there is not a pressing need for immediacy. What I mean by "extended real time" is the duration of pertinence of an exchange-in-progress. Or, in the metaphor above, the time over which the "slow-motion telephone conversations" (in print) take place. While the concept is not useful in any face-to-face conversation, it becomes applicable in networked communications. There, the duration of the "real-timeliness" can outlast the moment locally, and transcend time zones across the world. A further comparison between on-line contact and a telephone conversation makes clear the virtues of extended real time. To engage in a telephone conversation, two people have to be available in given locations simultaneously. Their exchange is deemed, quite appropriately, to be happening in real time. However, posting a message (note that the word is not "sending" which implies travel, but "posting" which implies immediate presence) allows the parties to connect in the full context and urgency of the message without having to force themselves into the constraints of simultaneous real time. The telephone's pertinence of address and content remain, while the continuity of our lifetime, our most valuable resource, is left untouched until we decide to engage in the deferred communication. In the same sense, even our own private mind is an extended real-time technology: the information, in one form or another, is always there, always available, but many things are worked out only over a period of time during which, however, the fullness of thought and context remain.

The combination of instantaneous access to everything and synchronous distribution of everything everywhere makes all contents and all activities on the Web simultaneous. A useful observation by Paul Virilio, an astute French critic of today's technology, is that electronic communication brings out a new quality of time, which is depth. He compares depth of time to depth of field in cinema. In film, depth of field defines how far back behind the foreground the camera is able to keep objects clearly focused. The same idea can be applied to time on the Web. Indeed, as we probe the Web to retrieve information about this or that, we can decide how far back we want to go, how deep in time, just as we can decide how defined, how prepackaged or open-ended, that information should be. Depth of time may well become a feature of digital product distribution.

The shape of time, once purely and exclusively linear, now becomes spherical, like the operating milieu of bats. Bats are exceptionally well suited to act as metaphors of the new world we have entered. To dispel a myth, bats are not blind. In fact they see better than we do. However, they supplement their already acute perceptions with echo location techniques similar to radar or sonar. These can work in different ways, either specifically aimed at a target in a *Star Wars* laser-beam fashion, or in a simultaneous probe of the complete surround of the fast-flying mammal. This is the condition of man today, riding full speed on the crest of the electronic wave, surfing the fields of all expertise with the zapping precision of a video game. The bat's real reference is not a point of view, but a point of being. The Web brings up all information now.

SPACE AND HYPERTEXT

What is a library? It is a place in a unique space with smaller spaces, where you put books, which are spaces which have letters; neat little spaces on pages, also spaces. A book is a real object because it is actualized and made continuous in space. A text on-screen is truly *immaterial* because it is nowhere to be found before or after its appearance on that screen. The text on screen is merely *virtual* until it is actualized. Hence, it doesn't need to be anywhere, while fixed written forms are entirely predicated on classification in spatial terms. To find them you normally have to go to a library; that is, move in space, something which can be just as tiresome for some people as having to deal with ordinary "snail mail."

The space of hypertext is, of course, cyberspace. People plugged into the Net have different bearings than the horizon and the cardinal points. These are substituted by URLs (Universal Resource Locators). URLs are addresses, not places. They are referred to via hypertextual buttons which work like triggers, just as a need to recall something in your mind triggers a thought or an image. Instantaneous direct access removes time and space, duration and extension, from the imagination of cyberspace.

The use of the word "posting" to describe what people do when they put something on-line is paradoxical. A poster used to be something hyperlocalized. You would put it somewhere, say, on a telephone pole, and hope that someone would pass by and notice it. You would hope even more that the someone would actually read it. Posting on-line is instantly universal. Whatever you post will be accessed by others not through happenstance, as in real space, but by pertinence. People connect to your message because they need it, and only if they need it, unless they happen upon it during surfing sessions.

Publishing is an operation that requires large investments of matter, energy, and time, demanding in turn forms of rationalization that lead to mass production and established, proven patterns of distribution. Publishing is part and parcel of what I call the "broadcast" model of the economy. The standard relationship of publishing to the public is one of persuasion or coercion, not necessarily pertinence or relevance. This is amply proven by the cable industry, a typical "publisher" of audiovisual programs, which takes advantage, wherever it can, of its de facto monopolies to impose content that people only halfheartedly want because there really isn't much else available. Posting, in principle anyway, is an open, noncoercive mode of content delivery. It doesn't cost a lot so it does not require economies of scale.

Publishing, on the other hand, has to face all the resistance of materials, hardware, storage, transportation, damage, loss, obsolescence, cycling, and recycling, all of this misery for what remains, ultimately, a hit-and-miss operation. If stores run out of a book when it is in demand, chances are the demand may already be over when the second printing finally makes it to the market. Posting, though, is eternal as well as ubiquitous. While old posters on telephone poles may fray and fade, your message on-line stays there until you—or your sysop—remove it. The upside of posting for the publishing industry is that it will eventually reduce the volume of wasted production and bring back to books the value they enjoyed in the manuscript culture. Posting will eventually turn all books, not just the coffee table variety, into art objects. Their cultural content will be carried in their physical embodiment to a degree made much more obvious than is the case at present, because their literal content will be available in plain vanilla form as text on the Net.

What will posting do to objects and their sacred status in galleries and museums? Howard Besser fears that "people are likely to visit museums less frequently":

> As more and more people have access to digital representations of museum objects without entering the building itself, the authority of the museum (and its personnel) will rapidly erode. In libraries, we are already beginning to see that the people who have traditionally served as caretakers of on-site collections are instead becoming designers of access to collections that may reside either on or off site. [6]

The reconstruction of lost or damaged or inaccessible cultural objects in virtual form in high definition supported by presentations of pertinent learning is what will bring more people to the museum. The objects themselves, when available, will stand next to their replicas as witnesses to the substantive reality supporting the simulation—like the bullion that once supported the dollar, only in full view. Far from losing interest, people will develop a fetish for objects. They always have.

The ethereal aspect of cyberspace means that it doesn't leave traces. Let us suppose, for a moment, that all the utterly wrong predictions about the so-called paperless office had actually come true, and that, as in Ray Bradbury's *Fahrenheit 451,* or in Jean-Luc Godard's *Alphaville,* the world is entirely without books or paper of any kind. The first consequence of a world without physical books or other printed text would be that, while writing might still appear on our screens, it would exist only virtually.

And the distinction between the virtual presence of writing and its real presence on the page is a radical difference not to be taken lightly. Sven Birkets comments that the difference between the word in print and the word on-line is the difference between a noun and a verb. One is a static reference, a "product" as Birkets calls printed text; the other is a dynamic appearance, a "process." Indeed, by potentially becoming hypertext "buttons," words on a screen become like icons, actors in a dynamic play of meaning. Just as icons themselves have shifted from the status of mere illustrations to that of grammatical effectors, keywords in hypertext, like verbs, have power of action.[7]

NAVIGATION: THE GRAMMAR OF HYPERTEXT

Until recently, the most common complaint about the Internet and the Web, after the fact that they were too often painfully slow, was that they were impossible to find one's way around in, to navigate. Indeed, as more and more sites were opened, supporting the private and public agendas of more and more people and organizations with little concern for how whatever it was they were posting would connect, confusion threatened to make the whole Web enterprise irrelevant.

Having done my share of aimless surfing, I will never forget how I felt when I was told about Yahoo! and shown how it worked. It felt as if access to substance and meaning that had been forbidden until that moment had suddenly been authorized. Yahoo!, as a name, is a delightfully silly way to express that thrill of release from a major handicap. It is today's version of Eureka! The Web leaped back into relevance. I began to use this early "search engine" (though it was not yet called that) to find out about "Art on the Web" and I was flabbergasted by the number of sites already available. My next thrill came from trying "Virtual Tourist." The idea of clicking on the map of the world to gain access to a precise point in that world was nothing short of magic. Yahoo! was quickly followed by Lycos, Alta Vista, Webcrawler, OpenText, and a host of search engines usually working in collaborative modes, often referring to each other and recommending each other for more specialized access.* Search engines are a natural outcome of the urgent need to find one's way through the maze of randomly accessible data. They make palpable the World Wide Web's capacity to connect directly to a source, just as the mind does in calling up a memory.

The groupings and connections in hypertextual information are not organized according to a table of contents, as they are in a book. On-line, the organization of information is predicated on the index, which is a very different thing. The grammar of linking amounts to reducing immense complexity to utter, machine-ready simplicity. First base in this mass processing is what is called the "inverted index." As Steve Steinberg explains in *Wired:*

> An inverted index is simply a huge table, where rows represent documents and columns represent words. If document x contains word y, there will be a binary 1 in row x, column y of the table. To find all documents that contain a specific word, the computer simply scans for 1s in the appropriate column. With a little added work, it is possible to do more complex searches: Find all documents that contain the word "wired" and not the

---

* The way search engines work with each other is in fact a perfect example of the kind of collaborativeness fostered by networked industries, as opposed to the devil-take-the-hindmost competitiveness of traditional business.

word "amphetamines." The table helps speed up the process because only the appropriate columns, instead of the documents themselves, need to be examined.[8]

However, as Steinberg points out, "operating just on words is too low-level" to be consistently useful. To get to second base, a search engine must go beyond the merely mechanical listing of words and begin to emulate that exquisite capacity for placing in context that which we carry in our minds. This, as Steinberg discovered, is a two-step process.

The second base problem involves dealing with homonyms and synonyms. Homonyms are words that share the same spelling but have different meanings. Synonyms, on the other hand, present the inverse problem of two different words having similar or closely related meanings, for example, *husband, spouse, companion,* and *consort.* Synonyms present a less difficult challenge to automated sorting techniques than homonyms. To automatically differentiate the meanings of similar words, a computer needs instructions to recognize that word's meaning when it is associated with other specific words in its vicinity. The way this is done is to classify documents by statistical analysis of the clusters of "semantic fields" making up the contents. A semantic field is the cluster of words which are related to, or likely to be found in association with, a given keyword. For example, all the associated words in the various categories supported by the single word *line* are part of the semantic fields of each use of the word. Thus, the word *line* appearing next to "on-" in a document that also mentions *computer, hypertext,* and *data,* will be deemed by the search engine to belong to a text on networks and not on fishing, since there happens to be neither *rod* nor *hook* in that document.

The third base challenge is enormously more ambitious. It is to get the computer to understand the text (and, from that understanding, to be able to guess the context). This, in Steinberg's words, would be "a program that can not only analyze a sentence and figure out information such as what the important nouns are and how they are being modified, but actually understand the written word from the reader's point of view."9 This apparently impossible task is in fact being realized right now by Oracle's ConText research lab where lexicographers—experts in word shapes and meanings—are entering comprehensive semantic fields of different words down to a very fine tuning of real contexts. This Herculean task is reminiscent of Balzac's mission to replenish the French language in *La Comédie humaine,* by researching every region and every condition of life in France in order to identify professional or local jargon, so as to be able to use it in his novels. Steinberg continues:

> The result of all this effort is a nine-level hierarchy—with each level offering increased specificity—that currently identifies a quarter-million different concepts in English. The scheme also includes approximately 10 million cross-references between related concepts, such as Paris and France, roadways and death. ConText uses this data when it automatically analyzes a document and then decides which of the concepts best describe the document's topic. 10

Of course, a word, or a concept, or even a whole context, doesn't mean anything in and of itself. People, not words, make meaning, and as Steinberg also observes, ConText is quite incapable of dealing with metaphors, irony, double entendre, poetry in general and small talk in particular. This problem has plagued the dogged research into automated translation for decades. Still, the results of research on search engines will undoubtedly find a place in development of software agents and customized bogosity-filters, automated evaluation systems endowed with fast neural networks and generations of fuzzy functions.

For example, Patti Maes and her associates at MIT are developing search systems that are actually like viruses. Rather than destroying what they find, they compete or collaborate for that information with other search mechanisms to get the best out of specific assignments in given search spaces. What is even more astounding is the notion that these virus-like "agents" can be endowed with self-motivation. Maes explains that they are equipped so as to ensure that the maximum effort of intelligence and collaborativeness will be exerted: the motivation of an open, free-wheeling system should always come from within the system, and not from without.

"Bookmarks" and "hotlinks," that is, the easy point-and-click filing of useful or interesting Web sites, and the embedding of direct, instant connections to assumedly highly relevant contexts, are two more features of the Web that help enormously in navigation. Still, hotlinks are little more than currents in an ocean. Surfing is the Web's equivalent to the much-vaunted literary serendipity. Serendipity occurs when I go to the stacks in the library and, instead of flipping through the pages of the book I need, fall into ravished contemplation of something in the next book on the shelf, which has strictly nothing to do with the object of my visit. One wonderful thing about books, which indeed could otherwise be lost in hypertextuality, is that they are information free-for-alls. By comparison to the just-in-time, pointedly apropos information of hypertext, books begin to look more like newspapers. When you open your newspaper you seldom read only what concerns you. There is a randomness or a serendipity inherent in the printed page which will never be duplicated by another medium.

But surfing on the Web is nevertheless a very aleatory thing to do. You can flit from one button to the next like a butterfly, attracted by pleasing design or the prospect of interesting, though not immediately pertinent information. In its randomness, surfing carries within it the hypertextual version of the serendipity associated with reading a newspaper. There could well be a new industry in developing surf engines that create interesting connections for those whose surfing seems to adopt a certain pattern. A useful surf engine would require a good grasp of the user's mental routines, and might provide a new heuristic device specially suited to hypertext, like a throw of dice left not entirely to chance.

You can already get enormous help from a little digital critter called Personal Web Manager that gets to know your favorite topics

and routes and can give you a traffic report on access conditions
before you waste your time on laggardly connections. The results are
displayed in traffic-light red, yellow, or green.[11]

If ConText indeed manages to get to third base, the home run
will happen when I talk to my computer, and I ask it to search for
the key developments in search engines in 1996, especially around
the summer, and to bring out information about why they were so
critical. For the moment, we must content ourselves with learning to
surf adroitly.

HYPERTEXT AND MIND

Digital and networked-based technologies are working on our
minds much more comprehensively than books and TV have been
credited with doing. The instrumentalities that assist our thought
processes in our multimedia, teleputer, on-line environment can
shape that thought much more thoroughly than TV ever did. For
example, anyone who has practiced word processing on a screen will
be aware that it is a mode of writing that comes close to the condition of thinking.* Thanks to our habit of reading, much of human
thinking is based on organizing linguistic structures in our minds.

---

* Word processing actually brings people into a very new and unaccustomed
relationship with language. It is as if writing had been invented with the sole
purpose of giving birth to thinking of a particular kind—a thinking that is
largely constructive; that is, made of constructs, with words to label or support
them, interior voices to argue them, and a tendency to trust (or question) words
rather than feelings. It may be useful to recognize in such a context that the
newly fluid nature of hypertext writing is getting closer and closer to the nature
of that specific form of thinking which was itself one of the major effects of
alphabetic writing. The relationship between thinking, the way we know thinking, the way we practice thinking, and the practice of writing is central, determi-
nate; it is not an accident. I am not saying that humans cannot think without
learning to read and write, but I am saying that the kind of thinking that has
been developed in Western cultures is entirely predicated on the way we have
treated information by writing, and of course by reading.

ASCII files—whatever typographical garb and formatting they may be given—are a kind of instant, fluid writing. There is no substantial presence. It happens like thought. On-line, the immateriality of the text and all its sensory accoutrements, say in VRML or in Real Audio, is even more thought-like. At the same time, the private mind we are accustomed to is also changing. Our individual capacity to engage more than one stream of information at a time has been in training since the first split-screen techniques in commercial cinema (*The Thomas Crowne Affair*, 1968; *The Day of the Jackal*, 1973) through to picture-in-picture (PIP) television and multiple windowing on our PCs. Windowing can oblige the mind to configure itself as a hypertextual structure, handling several operations at once. Once familiar with this process, we can code and decode our everyday environment with the tools we've learned to use from the supporting media. Cinema taught us to split-edit ambient reality in split seconds and VR is showing people how to live in two or three environments simultaneously.

The relationship between language and thinking is transformed by the fact that the world of books is no longer yielding to television, but to the new screen presence of the written word. Pierre Lévy also sees in hypertext an extension of our reading habits:

> Hypertext, hypermedia or interactive multimedia continue the age-old process of virtualization of reading. If reading is a matter of selecting, schematizing, building a network of internal references to the text, of associating notions to other notions, of integrating words and the images they evoke in one's personal memory in perpetual reconstruction, then the hypertextual technologies constitute a kind of objectification, externalization and virtualization of the processes of reading.[12]

In principle, this should be good news for educators and literate persons. Like books, screen-based literacy appears to allow each reader a measure of individual control and mastery over language. But it could be an illusory power. The present danger of hypertextual data links and computer-assisted reading is that the decisions of the mind will not remain the exclusive preserve of the reader but will be shared by the system, the computer or the text. The more the information processing is interactive, that is, shared by the system, the less it leaves to the responsibility of the reader, and the more it can control the reader by the sheer power, speed, and complexity of its operations.

The judgment of Stephen Talbot on this issue is harsh:

> The computer took shape in the human mind before it was realized in the world. What we embed in the computer is the inert and empty shadow, or abstract reflection, of the past operation of our own intelligence.
>
> The computer gains a certain autonomy—runs by itself—on the strength of its embedded reflection of human intelligence. We are thus confronted from the world by the active powers of our own, most mechanistic mental functioning. Having reconceived my own interior as computation, and having then embedded a reflection of this interior in the computer, I compulsively seek fulfilment—the completion of myself—through the interface.[13]

Of course, Talbot is right on target for each point he makes and it is a rare quality of mind that we see at work in his thinking. However, he is simply revisiting the same biased concern that Amon Râ, the sun-god of the Egyptians, expressed to Thot about the invention of writing: "You fool! It is one thing to invent a thing; it's another to know the consequences. You think you have invented a remedy for the failures of memory, but what you have made is something that will make people lose it all. Having access to everything, they will think they know everything and they will become insufferable babblers."[14] Neither Râ nor Talbot seems to have recognized that the nature of memory and intelligence had just been fundamentally changed by the innovation that concerned them so. Indeed, Talbot equates the belief that there is some sort of extension of our minds out there with the loss of interiority:

The Net is the most pronounced manifestation yet of our tendency to reconceive the human interior in the manner of an exterior, and then to project it onto the external world. Look at almost any aspect of the human being, and you will find its abstracted, externalized ghost on the Net. The outer substitutes for the inner: text instead of the word; text processing instead of thinking; information instead of meaning; connectedness instead of community; algorithmic procedure instead of willed human behaviour; derived images instead of immediate experience. At the same time, by means of a ubiquitous metaphor of mentality, popular discourse levitates the Net somewhere between mind and abstraction. . . .

Of course McLuhan had predicted this inversion a long time ago, suggesting that the effects of electronic technologies would be to turn literate men and women inside out like a glove, exposing to the world the innards of their central nervous systems. But Talbot pushes the point further:

We can only project those inner contents of which we have more or less lost awareness. It is the progressive dimming of our interior spaces that enables us to imagine them out there, objectified in some sort of global, electronic, "central nervous system."[15]

Yes, we have embedded the outlines of what we know about intelligence in our computers. It is only natural that we would build into those machines the things that we know best, and the things that we know best are our most recently outmoded, and equally artificial, methods for survival. All we have really done is to dump the contents and the processes of the literate mind into this super-literate accelerator we call the computer. Are we really losing that interiority? I think not. I see more real presence in the generation of my own children who are growing up with the Net than in many of my colleagues who have grown up on books and TV. The interesting question is not what we have lost, but what we have gained in the transition.

Michel Bernard is a lot closer to the mark when he proposes the idea that hypertext is the "third dimension of language"[16] and reveals a qualitative progression from the inarticulate utterance which he compares to a point, to hypertext which he sees as a volume in space. Oral speech he presents as a line and written speech as a surface. If Bernard is correct, then the kind of mental concentration, the kind of acceleration, and the kind of social consequences to be expected from this new modality of language should also be of a qualitative order. An emergent order, to be precise.

CHAPTER SIX

THE FUTURE OF NEWS

T HOMAS DE QUINCEY, adventuresome opium eater but no etymologist, wrote: "Mails from the North—the East—the West—the South—whence [. . .] comes the magical word NEWS."[1] Ezra Pound offered the self-serving suggestion that "poetry is news that stays news." Digital oracle Nicholas Negroponte insists, "If your early morning flight is delayed, that fact should appear as the lead headline in your personalized newspaper."[2]

McLuhan, who knew the future of everything, said somewhat dismissively, "The future of news is old hat." Nevertheless, news is having to respond to digital networks and hypertext just as it did to the telegraph and television, and we would be well advised to monitor the outcome if we value our democratic institutions. The basic question remains: What's news?

My own definition is that news is human utterances that can be supported by any number of channels but have four things in common:

- nowness
- newness
- pertinence
- publicness

The condition of nowness—or currency—requires that whatever is news is either happening now or is, for one reason or another, made more relevant now. Nowness is something we assume we all share in, because in real time we all move at the same time, in the same direction, and at the same speed. Newness—or novelty—means that whatever it is, the information is fresh and/or has not occurred to you before, at least not in that form. Pertinence—or relevance—is the quality of being of interest or concern. Then again, news that may be of extreme relevance to us cannot be called news because it is "private." In publicness, we find both the sense of community (beyond the gossip group) and a common or shared destiny.

Not all these qualities are supported equally well by all media. News as a consumer good has been shaped by the media that support it. Whether you agree or not with the idea that the medium is the message, there is no denying that the medium does modify the selection, the content, the display, and the distribution of news. The balance of ratios between nowness, newness, pertinence, and publicness changes from medium to medium.

Print reduces the news to silent words and invites the reader to rebuild the scene mentally, select the text, provide the context, and make the connections. Print news is simultaneously public and pertinent to a high degree, but nowness suffers: all printed news is deferred news. The delays accompanying print processes are measured in terms of days, at best.

Radio is instant and continuous. Radio delivers on-the-spot reporting and a connection to news that is otherwise impossible, short of actually being there. Radio has a powerful voice that can exhort to war or to consumerism. But unlike the newspaper, radio is not interactive, and it presents its information in linear, one-at-a-time fashion, which affects the ratio of publicness to pertinence. Much of what is news on radio affects the individual listener only peripherally, and the only options open to that listener are to wait out the irrelevancies in the hope of finding pertinence further down the newscast, or to switch off the broadcast, or change to another station. The same applies to television, which delivers the news "in the flesh," so to speak. However, while radio is a companion that permits you to do other things while you are listening, television is a dominatrix demanding your full attention.

For a while, computers didn't provide news at all. Now, via the networks, they can and they do. News via computer networks maximizes nowness, newness, and pertinence, but it doesn't do a whole lot for publicness. The relationship of public and private is in fact inverted. Publicly available news is tailored to private interests when made to blend with the user's specific profile; private news posted on the Net becomes public domain. Public domain information, digitized and delivered on-line, becomes private property if it is processed through proprietary standards. Normally, rumors affect the stock markets more than the real news which arrives just a touch later. Even that is about to change. We can anticipate real-time, fully-informed investing, because now the news is simultaneously available with the rumor.

The new medium brings important new benchmarks to news gathering, formatting, and delivery, namely continuity, versatility, and ubiquitous access. Continuity, or in the current jargon, "streaming," relates to the real-time flow of data available on-line; it equates to the stream of the present. Versatility describes that quality of the digital format that allows the transferring of the data to any medium, any support.* Ubiquitous access arises out of the trend to mobile communications, which is destined to achieve maximum dispersion and decentralization of human receivers. Ubiquitous access and its partner ubiquitous sourcing allow for maximum decontextualization

---

* According to Nicholas Johnson: "Digitization means, among many other things, that any content (such as video drama, text or still pictures) can be stored on any media (tape, computer disk, CD) or transmitted through any medium (wire, ether, infrared, optic fibre). A computer hobbyist can send computer files through the telephone system or, with an amateur radio station, through the air. Stock market prices can come to a home screen from a computer database, or through the air on the 'sub-carrier' of an FM radio station. A voice 'telephone' call can go through a twisted pair of copper wires, a 'cable television' coaxial cable, an optic fibre—or the ether ('cellular phone'). A remote-control device for a television set can transmit instructions through a wire, or an infrared beam. A CD-ROM can contain music, or a 30-volume encyclopedia." From a transcript of "Television in the Electronic Supermarket: The Confusion of Interests," a paper delivered at the Cologne Conference (on television and its market), June 7, 1994.

and recontextualization of news, in other words, optimal customization to achieve maximum nowness, newness, and pertinence.

As we begin to partake in what technology consultant George Gilder calls a "global ganglion of computers and cables, the new worldwide web of glass and light,"[3] how will other media fare?

For example, how does the impending revolution in news delivery affect the newspaper industry? Says Warren Caragata: "Not far down the virtual road, publishers fear that papers will lose their franchise as one of the community's main sources of news."[4] Many newspapers have responded to the challenge by going on-line. This allows them to offer customized services and charge for them. The *Washington Post*, the *Wall Street Journal*, the *New York Times,* and the *Los Angeles Times* have all secured gateways to the Internet. News, tailored to your specific needs, is becoming ubiquitously available, in a range from real-time satellite data to context-relevant, layered, fully documented, and archived information concerning the tiniest item in a want ad. The (Toronto) *Globe and Mail,* Canada's national newspaper in the English language, has been one of the quickest to take advantage of the new opportunities. It took its first, tentative steps into on-line services as long ago as 1977.

In its 150th year, having survived the busiest period in the history of the world's technological transformations, the *Globe and Mail* stands at the hinge of two eras, that of paper and that of electrons, and it belongs to both. As the general manager of Globe Information Services, Michael Ryan says, "If you think you're just a publisher, you will die; the answer is to create a universal database with any number of output formats." The *Globe* has understood the meaning of "mass customizing."

In mid-1996, two media-specific news services appeared on the Web and began vying for market share. One is Timecast, a Real-Audio service that offers semipersonalized, radio-like news. You can register your "Daily Briefing Preferences" for an automated preselection of the news. It is extremely easy to use: just check the boxes next to the sources of your choice and start it running with the click of a button. If you are not interested in the item you are currently listening to, you can instantly switch to another. You can also revert to the standard programming of any one of the radio stations listed among the available choices, thus bypassing your briefing preferences and getting back to regular radio fare. The customizing allowed by Timecast is limited, but the degree of pertinence of the news delivered in this way from the familiar, conventional medium of radio is much enhanced. It has the hypertext-based merit of respecting the rule of real-time continuity. And, of course, that exclusive advantage of radio over all other news media is retained— i.e., the fact that you can keep on doing other things and still get your news. It is like having your time and spending it.

The other news source is PointCast, a service that offers subscribers a wide selection of text and news graphics in selectable categories. The PointCast Network (PCN) broadcasts news and information directly to the user's computer screen. Information can be "pointcasted," or customized, according to interest. Pointcasting combines the best aspects of traditional broadcasting—in which top stories are identified, researched, and delivered to audiences by news professionals—with the ability for each user to receive personalized, up-to-the minute headline information.

PointCast grants the Web surfer a much greater level of personalization than Timecast. Here is a sample of the contents PointCast lists in its Fact Sheet, posted on PCN's Web site in July, 1996: Reuters national, international, business, and political news headlines. To view the full text of any story, users click on a headline. Business news includes access to charts with six weeks of stock prices, volume data, and a scrolling stock ticker provided by Standard and Poor's Comstock, along with news from PR Newswire and Business Wire. Users can select the companies they want to track. Current temperature and precipitation readings from AccuWeather for user-selected cities scroll across the screen. Satellite images, radar maps, and national weather maps are also available. Sports are covered by a sport score ticker and schedules for baseball, football, basketball, golf, and tennis. There are also categories for news specific to various industries, special interest magazines, lifestyle, horoscopes, winning lottery numbers, selections from *Time Daily, People Daily,* and *Money Daily,* the *Boston Globe,* the *Los Angeles Times,* and for Canada, the *Globe and Mail.*

It seems clear that this is television's future. The same streaming technology used for Net audio presentation is also available now for continuous streams of video images. Where once there was a need for tedious, time-consuming downloading of bit-hungry video, it now plays as you go. Interactivity is provided within the video by "temporal annotation generators," or TAGs. TAGs, the creation of a Canadian software company called Digital Renaissance, allows viewers to click on objects within a video stream to get more information from the vast resources of the Web. From a commercial point of view, TAGs can be embedded in CD-ROMs so that catalogue companies can change pricing or availability of products listed on a CD without having to make and distribute a new disk.

Accessible by wireline and wirelessly, with satellite and cellular audio and video, all news will soon be as easy to receive—and send—as radio news is today. Knight-Ridder, the U.S. publishing consortium, is working on plans for an all-electronic, continuously up-dated, personalized newspaper that will be accessible through a flat-panel, legal-pad-size computer screen wherever you are, whenever you want it.

Magazines are also getting into the on-line act. Most magazines are community building and support devices, but magazines in print can accommodate only a minimal number of edited responses from their readers. An on-line magazine such as *HotWired,* the digital companion to *Wired,* permits the posting of unlimited numbers of reactions and comments on-line. There is also an innovation that the magazine *Interactive Age* calls "real-time letters": a magazine will select some articles to post on the Net or distribute via e-mail in advance of publication. Letters are solicited on these articles and published in the magazine, along with the article, in the same issue. Needless to say, in the magazine's on-line version there is unlimited space to accommodate any and all responses; the editing job becomes one of sifting through them to highlight the best.

Let's face it, though: reading off a computer screen is no fun. McLuhan said that you plunge into your morning newspaper the way you plunge into a bath. Streaming electrons on a computer screen won't wash. The letters are not stable and the light coming at you through the screen is aggressive. Scrolling the data demands more physical effort and postural adjustments than holding a book or unfolding a paper. James Fallows' opinion on the matter reflects accurately my own and those of many people I have asked:

> Reading from even the nicest computer screen is so unpleasant—and the expectation is so strong that the computer will always be doing something more active than just displaying text—that computers will remain better suited to jumping from topic to topic than to the sustained intellectual, artistic, or emotional experience that print can provide. People can read books by the hour; it's hard to imagine anyone spending even ten minutes straight reading a single document on a computer screen. [5]

The only kind of reading I can stand to do on a screen is material I am personally involved with—either incoming e-mail letters, or my own work-in-progress. An understanding of this shortcoming of computer screens is critical to the displaying of news items on a Web site such as PointCast. Quite apart from the quality and precision of the news the site delivers, it must package the text in concise, at-a-glance formats which invite your reading to be ideogrammatic and nonlinear.

Trust and reliability are twin issues of real concern for news on the Net. In the print world it is not uncommon for four editors to handle a story; on the Net there is no stopping solitary semiliterates from learning enough HTML to create a site. The problem of accuracy, however, goes well beyond the issue of orthography. It includes the verification of facts, and that, on the Net, must be the job of a trusted editor. The job of the newspaper on-line is the same as that of the published book: to make authority.

Another problem with Net news is, of course, that not everybody is on-line. Not yet. The present estimate of Canadian households with computers equipped with modems and using them to get on-line is just over 30 percent. This is a very high proportion, considering that it represents by priority the socioeconomically advantaged members of the working population and it is still on an upswing curve. The major roadblock to even more rapid growth is the sustained high prices of the ever-more-powerful computers needed to handle the ever-more-complex software used for Net applications such as browsers.

What will happen to the numbers of people on-line when Web-enabled television sets and set-top Internet adaptors are widely available, making this investment either unnecessary or much reduced? WebTV, for example, is a set-top box that sells for a few hundred dollars and which provides high-speed Web access via cable modem but also allows the use of a regular TV set as a monitor thanks to software that markedly improves screen resolution for text. Sony provides a similar product adapted to telephone lines. This is the invasion of TV by the Internet. It means that the market for Net users is going to expand by orders of magnitude. The critical mass to trigger this explosion is already there.

Have printed newspapers, then, become irrelevant to social needs? Not if we look back over the last eighty years. In spite of ever-more-fierce competition from radio, television with its "people-metering," in Canada, the ratio of newspaper readership to the general population has hardly budged from 20 percent over the decades from 1910 to the present. The odds are that personalized electronic news services will no more eliminate paper than the much-anticipated paperless office did. Once again, the medium is the message, namely paper itself. Why? Paper remains the best, the fastest, and the most democratic interactive medium around. Recent polls conducted by Environics Research indicated that during the last national elections in Canada, people routinely went back to the newspapers for detailed information and opinion that they could not get on TV. To put the matter succinctly, television may give you the experience, but the newspaper gives you the meaning.

Nevertheless, professional jeremiads have been lining up to prophesy the end of paper as a medium. According to Russell Neuman, a communications professor at Fletcher University in Medford, Massachussetts: "The current generation of professional journalists and publishers who have ink in their veins will have to die off before the next generation realizes that the newspaper industry is no longer a newspaper industry."

The fact of the matter is that we all have "ink in our veins" and that it will keep flowing there as long as we prize our psychological autonomy. The condition of our mental freedom is to have language still in front of our eyes. Anything else is an invasion. When you are given a newspaper to read, you do the scanning; you take control. On-line, and especially with the help of agent-controlled, personalized news services, the scanning is done by the program, and you become a mere extension of the display.

The printed paper is the best "random-access memory" available. I may think that I only open the *Globe* or the *Times* for the arts, the sports, or the business section, but I wouldn't want to be stuck with a screen that only reflected my previously known personal news needs. No flickering screen will ever quench the insatiable thirst of my peripheral vision, glancing sideways at a headline that catches my eye.

The greatest advantage of the traditional newspaper is that it provides an all-at-once, random-access view of reality for the day. The job of the newspaper is to sort out the items which are relevant to public interest, over and above those which address purely individual needs. A major newspaper each day performs the task of boiling down four hundred or more hours of reading material to an average of three to five hours' worth. On the average, readers only find time to read about fifteen minutes of that. The rest is that part of the public life that your eye catches only subliminally.

In the immediate future, business, professional, and academic news will in all likelihood trend towards the customized end of the news delivery environment. But national or local news delivery is better suited to the paper format, or to the radio and TV broadcast. Indeed, the most significant difference between personalized media and the conventional models will be the difference between private and public application. This is not to suggest that public news cannot be found on-line, which is clearly not the case, but to point to the difference between the physically based community and the just-in-time, on-line community. Personalized—or even community-oriented—news arriving on-line is closer to the chatter of a gossip group than to the formal quality of objectivity associated with material objects like newspapers. By the same token, extremely personalized news can isolate individuals from a community, much in the way that extreme specialization tends to isolate academics from their colleagues. If the newspaper and news broadcasts were to disappear for good, that public part of life which defines the day-to-day meaning of a community, or even of a country, might well disappear with them.

CHAPTER SEVEN

THE FUTURE
OF THE BOOK

J UST AS THE DEMISE of the newspaper is regularly predicted
by prognosticators of our digital future, so is the book almost
daily declared obsolescent, if not obsolete. Bruce Powe has said:
"Yet we are the children of electricity, and post-literacy is our frontier."[1] My colleague Robert Cook believes:

> The book has already been eclipsed as a storage format. It is
> expensive to produce, to store and to circulate. It is hanging on
> because of user interface. Does anyone really prefer reading text
> on screen? The end of the book may not be nigh, but it is imag-
> inable.[2]

Their pessimism, if that is what it is, may not be justified.

What is a book? In French, I would say, *"Un livre est un lieu de
repos pour des mots écrits."* A resting place for words. It sounds trite,
but in fact the printed page is the only place where words do have
a rest. Everywhere else, they are moving: when you speak, when you
see them on a screen, when you see them on the Net, words are moving. But a book is a restful place. The printed word is, and always
was, still. There is an old adage: *verba volant, scripta manent*—
spoken words fly, but written words stay. On-line, that is not true
anymore. *Scripta* are *volenting*, in fact, much faster now than the
verba.

The effect of this acceleration of words is that we live much faster today than we used to. Not only because we do more things or because we have more access to distant places or because we have more information coming our way, but because the segmentation of textual information has changed. When Henry Fielding published *Tom Jones* in 1749, his public was reading by candlelight (not bad in terms of luminance, by the way!). That could give an average book an active life of a month or more, at the rate of consumption of a few pages each evening. And the book had little or no competition in its field. Now, suddenly, as in the movie of *Tom Jones,* you have a whole book compressed to two hours. Furthermore, any single shot in *Tom Jones* that is sustained for more than five or six seconds seems endless, almost a bore. Movies have taught us to process and deal with information at breakneck speed, so that, today, we have to look at the screen as a measure of our time. We know, for example, that if an advertiser puts together a commercial with fifty edits in a single segment of thirty seconds, that spot will not shatter the mind of the viewer. On the contrary, the speed factor will work to very good effect on the viewer's body, as well as his or her mind. Thus the speed at which we process information today has increased because the units of information processing have shrunk.

Today, words and images packed with distilled meaning zip about everywhere as slogans, headlines, jacket covers, logos, and so on. Hypertextuality turns the content of books into sound bites. The magical power of words in a hyperlinked computer program, or the fluidity of writings on our electronic walls, turn information processing into a quasi-mythical job (*muthos* was the ancient Greek word for *word*). We seem to be returning to the habits of earlier times when laconic people packed meaning into mottoes, sayings, and proverbs, crunching information maximally in minimalist vehicles.

THE DESTINY OF BOOKS:
"IT'S THE REAL THING"

Today, only 35 percent of publishing involves books. The rest of the worldwide flow of restless words and images ends up in less formal vehicles for print, or on video, in CDs, and, of course, in electronic databases of one kind or another. Beyond the confines of the library, public or otherwise, the proportion of information on paper is rapidly losing ground to the amount of information on-line or in other digital forms. According to *The Economist,* industry analysts estimate that "by 2000, electronic products could account for up to 40 percent of the turnover of the publishing industry as a whole."[3] This amounts to a kind of mass disembodiment of information processing.

With the speed and flexibility of electronically processed information and the sheer volume and complexity of the available data, the role of hard copy will change. Paradoxically, the role of print will evolve from its traditional use as a vehicle for "hard" information (factual, theoretical, regulatory, didactic, etc.) to giving precedence to the very thing that print has traditionally tended to spurn—imprecise, fuzzy, judgmental information: in a word, opinion. Factual information will have to be automated and hypertextualized to speed access, while opinion will require hard copy because advice is not trustworthy if the original text may be tampered with.

Another way of looking at this is to suggest that we are evolving different speeds for different types of information. Information travels at different velocities in different vehicles. Some data need higher speeds than others; for example, much stock market information is worth a lot of money in the first twenty minutes of its appearance, and then nothing at all after that. Literature, on the other hand, while potentially benefiting from hypertextual links based on thematic or content analysis, will not tolerate much tampering with the original text. Literature, like most printed information, travels at a slower, more meditative speed. The printed word is a time-stopper.

The criteria for printing anything will center on whether or not the content needs to be fixed. The fact of the matter is that, even in our digital era, there remain plenty of words that benefit from being fixed and well warrant the effort. Some information that needs to be slowed down:

- Medical, scientific and legal facts, and processes that serve as solid ground to knowledge.
- Opinion, criticism, literature, and other content issuing from people whose opinion has acquired value.
- Manuals and textbooks which are addressed to educational and professional communities for the transmission of step-by-step, linear information unlikely to change much over the longer term.

If the word "publisher" is still spelled b-o-o-k-s, it is with good reason. The reverently bound copy of well-typeset text on quality paper still carries the image of reliable, if somewhat austere information. There is currently a real danger of inflation of the value of often unreliable data posted on-line as opposed to being published in the traditional sense. Indeed, one of the main problems of today's scientific or professional on-line publication is a lack of enough time and adequate staff for thorough editorial review, with the result that much on-line scientific material is losing credibility. While many scholarly journals are now simultaneously published in hard copy and on-line, a growing number are put on-line only, to accelerate delivery, reduce costs, and allow "instant" reviews and commentary. Moreover, the appearance of authors/publishers who put themselves on-line so as not to have to endure the often capricious scrutiny of an academic publisher's editorial board is a challenge to the whole publishing industry.

The real issue is authority. The book is destined to take on more and more of the burden of credibility lost in the fluidity of electronic data. The professional publisher may not survive on books alone, but to survive at all, he or she will have to acquire the image of authority. That way, publishers may continue to attract authors who might otherwise be tempted to sell their works privately on-line, rather than share the profits (after much inflated production costs) with the professional publishing business.

Today, opinion has returned to rule the roost in public affairs, whether in the media with celebrity opinion-leaders, in courts of law with expert witnesses, or, more formidably, at the stock exchange. We are witnessing the return of *doxa*.* Thinking about the rise and fall of market value McLuhan quipped, "In the electronic age rumors are 'the real thing.'" Fiction, opinion, criticism, commentary, empirical observations, expert testimony, statistics, heuristics—anything involving the explicit or implicit expression of judgment will require fixed forms appropriate to the new authority it conveys.

The irony is that most of the efforts of the great publishers from the sixteenth century onward, like those of the great encyclopedists, have been devoted to arresting or fixing "the world on paper" (to use an expression coined by my colleague David Olson), with a special emphasis on facts, on historically and scientifically verifiable statements. But when all information is available all the time, everywhere, it is the process of selection and analysis that gives it value through relevance. If I were an ancient Greek sophist, I would be able now to give many valid responses to Plato's criticism of *doxa*. Plato railed against those whose advocacy was based on opinion, rather than on truth; on provable—or disprovable, if you accept Karl Popper's definition of a scientific truth—facts. ("Well, I know all the facts, Doctor, now what's your opinion?")

But rather than picking a bone with Plato, who has already muzzled his critics by pointing out that the author of written words is not there to defend them, I would like to address an argument of another one of my colleagues at the University of Toronto, historian Robert Bothwell, who writes:

---

* According to Plato, the mind has two faculties: knowledge of the real world and belief in appearances, or *doxa*. *Doxa* denotes what "seems" to exist or to be true or right. It falls somewhere between belief and opinion.

I think there are too many books being published that nobody wants to read. What we have in North America is a vast production of theses and an academic promotion system that demands publication. So we're communicating information that nobody really needs and we're doing it because there is an expectation, largely on the part of university employers, that their staff have to produce these things. But in practice if you look at what is produced, there is no sale, there is no readership. These books are being produced for what I call "ritual purposes." I am opposed to that and I think one way to start pruning the system is to end book subsidies.[5]

While I often feel that the grist of the mill of university scholarship grinds impossibly fine, I cannot agree with Prof. Bothwell. Far from being a mere ritual, the scholarly publication and all its attendant modalities of checks and balances is what it takes for a society to equip itself with information that is as reliable as it is humanly possible to make it. I remember being utterly shocked by a statement made by Jacques Derrida at a conference on the nuclear threat in 1984: he said that the scandal of the bomb was not that it could destroy all life, but that it could destroy all texts, all the archives of the world. While I still think Derrida's statement, like the bomb, is overkill, in the light of what Prof. Bothwell has suggested I am beginning to understand what he means.

Few people may ever be exposed to any given item of scholarly minutiae, but its fixed presence in a library somewhere will serve as a constant reference as against all the combinations and permutations that the text could or will be subjected to by hypertextual manipulations in electronic databases. The relationship of printed matter to electronic distribution devices should be one that serves to support the authority of information, just as gold bullion serves to support the value of money. There is a cost attached to this, but, in the context of current military budgets, it's not a whole lot and it, too, could provide a line of defense against some future "enemy" intent on erasing digital archives.

I do not for a moment want to imply that electronic data can never be trustworthy. Rather, it has different uses and presents different opportunities for the publisher. Here, too, an interesting reversal may occur. In the past, publishers looked for permanence, for the definitive edition, the most complete description, the lasting classic. Today, they have to be "just in time," attentive to the latest developments. They have to remain flexible, and tolerant of conflicting approaches and interpretations. Two qualities make on-line information closer to oral communication than to text on paper: on-line information is as close to real time as writing can ever get, and it is interactive. This means that what appears on screen, remaining fluid and adaptable like the spoken word, is more closely bound to the *context* of the information delivered, than to the *text* of that information. In other words, while text-based information bolsters credibility, context-driven information nurtures pertinence. Pertinence in publishing is a function of knowing your customer's needs even as they change. Today, publisher Wolters Kluwer's slogan "Partner in information and education" calls to mind that in the new electronic environment, the professional customer has become a full-time partner of the professional publisher. (The same could be said of many other areas of industry and commerce.)

This is the secret of so-called mass customization. The more specialized the customer, the more customized the product must be. The more, too, it must be subjected to a constant dialogue between the publisher and the client. The idea, at a certain point, is not to think in terms of product at all, but in terms of service. Being a "professional" more and more means having access at the right time— just in time—to the right strata and the right blends of reliable and contextualized information. Economies of scale require, and actually demonstrate, that what is less specialized, and therefore less time-sensitive, is also less expensive and more appropriate to long-term publication, while highly customized information is much more expensive, and, paradoxically, less durable and less widely distributed.

A side issue, although not an unimportant one, is that of intelligent retrieval software that is now being developed to cut down on human time consumed in basic data collection and sorting. Publishers are known to scoff at the likelihood that these digital agents will one day be sufficiently functional to compete successfully with human librarians, journalists, and researchers. The fact is, however, that sooner or later intelligent software will begin to nibble at the edges of the domain of the publisher. Many private professional users, rather than rely on the authority of a publisher, may one day soon prefer to resort to computer-assisted scanning of the available information on-line. The degree to which this happens will depend, of course, on how much potentially pertinent information will be available on-line in the future, having escaped the grab of prescient publishers.

In an astute response to the decentralizing impact of hypertextual access, and as part of the general trend to "just-in-time business," digitally savvy Xerox is introducing a new concept, and a new supporting technology it calls "printing on demand." Because hard copy will remain easier to handle for many purposes other than electronic data, most documents will continue to benefit from being printed at one time or another. The major problems associated with printing are delays in production and delivery, and waste of materials. Xerox's idea is to set up sophisticated printer/binder and packaging units at various strategic points, just as many cities are now well-equipped with photocopying centers, usually at walking distance in busy areas. The copy would be downloaded into the unit from an on-line source and a finished, bound, and packaged book, brochure, pamphlet, or "special edition" would come out at the other end. When will Xerox add a shredder, recycler, and a paper-waste maker to their wonderprinter?

In brief, then, how should professional publishers respond to the pressures of hypertextuality? They have to become as scientifically and instructionally reliable as universities, but better able to cope with immediate and urgent information demands. Why a university? Because the on-line learning process accessible to their customers will be constant, with benefits as real and tangible as a diploma. In this environment, the professional publishers' level of specialization and their collaboration with libraries and customers will be what ensures that the information they supply is professionally updated and market-worthy. Their close collaboration with their customers will constitute an international, multidisciplinary think tank of which buyers of information services will be proud to be members.

Four recommendations summarize the issues of speed, authority, pertinence, and content for publishers:

- Connect, get wired, get bought by or buy yourself a cable operation. Alternately, secure speedy delivery by multiplying your contacts with printing-on-demand units.
- Protect your reputation of authority in your chosen fields; one of the university-like functions of the future publisher may be to establish guidelines and review processes for whatever comes their way on-line, so as to sell or resell such information as value-added with authority and pertinence.
- Consider the professional client as being the defining parameter of the content of any publishing service.
- Generate as much client-produced content as is market-worthy (i.e. more than might ordinarily be published in book form); it will create a sense of the connected intelligence associated with the publisher's operations.

Just like Coca-Cola, the publisher, pointing to any of its books, should always be in a position to proudly affirm: "It's the real thing."

THE DESTINY OF LIBRARIES IN THE PUBLIC DOMAIN

The greatest challenge to public libraries—indeed, to the very notion of public domain in the sense of the *res publica* of the Romans—is the networked electronic data environment that is growing up around them. Because of networks, the very nature of public information, not to mention information storage and distribution, is changing.

In keeping with that country's tradition of excellence in everything to do with the printed word, some of the most vigorous and creative thinking about libraries is conducted in Holland. G. M. van Trier is among those who have understood the nature of the technological future for libraries. He recommends: "Research should be encouraged into issues of information retrieval techniques for large full-text databases and multimedia information, focusing on the application of advanced computer and information science techniques such as artificial intelligence, linguistic technology, and neural networks." His research recommendations read like a wish list for a company like Philips to grant:

> The use of electronic information should be stimulated through research aimed at:
> - the development of a full-page size, high quality, flat panel display;
> - the development of reading software, creating an electronic display browsing capability, improved search and retrieval, and spin-off to private files;
> - enhanced convenience, especially regarding system operations: data input, operating systems, and file management.[6]

A great deal of the future of the communications industry is implicit in these requests. Because they make communication devices light and portable, flat-panel displays like those incorporated into current laptop computer designs, are now the spearhead of domestic product research in Japan. Reading software, from optical character recognition (OCR) for scanning and digitizing of text for use in computers, to digital agents for automated filtering and sorting of information, is the cutting edge of software research today. Customizable reading software will be the publishing phenomenon of the future. We can already foresee that the combination of scanners, parsing software, neural networks, and object-oriented technologies will bring us something like "computer-assisted reading," wherein texts will be scanned and partly judged in a man-machine dialogue at very high speeds.* And van Trier adds: "The government should create the conditions for the development and use of a differentiated telecommunication infrastructure for the benefit of information services. Broadband communication for the transport of images and multimedia databases is especially important."

The potential for cable delivery of library holdings has caught the attention of others, as well:

> Not too far down the line, local library resources will be fully incorporated into your cable service. You'll have access to all the automated indexes, full text, and multimedia that the library has collected. Conceivably, you could see something on a TV show that baffles you and just zap over to the library channel to look it up.[7]

So predicts James Larue, outspoken director of the Philip S. Miller Library, Castle Rock, Colorado. The future of libraries is circumscribed neither by time nor place. Access to information online—provided that there is sufficient bandwidth capacity—is instant. And it is the mountain that goes to Mohammed. This is the defining distinction between the old concept of *dissemination* and the new one of *delivery,* according to the director of the San Francisco Public Library, Kenneth Dowlin: "Basically, dissemination has meant: come to the library and get the information. I am talking about delivery of information to your desktop or your home—instantaneous delivery." Pursuing this train of thought, Dowlin urges librarians to change their approach from that of banking to that of connectedness: "Essentially, this is moving from

---

* With the help of the appropriate software, a reader can conceivably scan vast amounts of data, cull the relevant items, sort them in automated judgment categories, distribute the results instantly in pertinent locations, all as part of the process of consulting the original books and databases.

the just-in-case collection syndrome to just-in-time information delivery."[8]

The fact that references to banking pop up regularly in library discussions is no accident: the history of the two institutions are closely related. In banking, as with the library, content (in this case, money) arrives, is logged and deposited and then redistributed. The rate of circulation of the content is what determines the institution's productivity. Today, electronic phone transfers are making banks go through the same digital hoops as libraries, striving for connectedness.

Indeed, the existence of a global network suggests the notion of a global library. While communication on the Net has mostly developed through private and individual initiatives, a new concept of the public realm could well develop out of it. Alluding to the "big picture" of libraries' operational and institutional frameworks, Colin Steele, the university librarian of the Australian National University, suggests that one of the technology-driven changes affecting his profession is the shift of emphasis from "local storage to global access."[9] In fact, with improvements in the functionality of the Web, and with multiplication of library access points via that route, the inverse relationship, i.e., "local access to global storage," may turn out to be a more accurate depiction of the future.

Once the public libraries of the world become interconnected in what visionaries such as Steele and others are calling the "one library concept,"[10] the notion of a "global public domain" to which all the public libraries contribute their resources can be entertained. However, to make this fundamental shift possible, the contents of the archives have to dematerialize. This means enormous expenditures of energy and money to convert our hard-copy universe to software. It also means, at a deeper level, a profound change in personal and social psychology.

In a networked world our autonomy as individual people needs to be defended on two levels. In order to ensure a reasonable amount of individual autonomy, we have to resist the temptation to automate everything, including our mental responses, by excessive interactivity and hypertextuality. At the public level, it is the responsibility of governments everywhere—and soon the condition of their survival—to protect the public domain from takeover and control by private industry.

The urgent question is: How can we protect the public realm from privatization by huge "consciousness industries" (to borrow Hans Magnus Ensenzberger's brilliant phrase)? Under the pretense of improving competition, telecommunication and cable industries, often controlling large publishing interests and media, are pushing for acquisition and mergers. As this is written, the most recent in a continuing series of strategic mergers and takeovers by corporations wishing to secure market dominance is Disney's acquisition of the American television network ABC. The earlier acquisitions of CBS by Sony and NBC by General Electric and, in Canada, the acquisition of the publishing consortium Maclean Hunter by the giant cable operator Rogers Communications are leading to vertically integrated monopolies and oligopolies that deserve more than the polite expressions of deferential concern they've elicited from government.

Microsoft's Bill Gates has been courting museums and galleries of the world to secure exclusive rights to distribute the digitized images of their collections. In their material reality, these public art treasures will remain accessible to their usual publics, but their digitized versions, soon to be more in demand than the real thing, will only be accessible for a fee, paid, of course, to Microsoft and its distribution licensees. The paradoxical outcome of this can only be that the existing communities of users of public domain material will become smaller and smaller as against a growing proportion of users paying for the same services in their virtual form. The saga of the cable industry tells pretty much the same story: "How we got the public to pay for what they used to get for free, i.e., broadcast television." And the cable story tells us as well that the issue is not only that we may have to start paying for what was once free, but that the integrity of what we are provided with in return for our money is threatened by the priority of profit over service and the slatternly trend to "infotainment."

U.S. Senator Bob Kerrey saw the danger and urged Congress to consider a bill for state-based electronic libraries:

While we were asleep, the late twentieth century public library has been eclipsed by video stores, cable televisions, and the ever-expanding world of entertainment. . . . For the sake of our culture, our democracy, and our economy, we urgently need to turn this around. . . . I believe the State Electronic Libraries could be the resource needed by communities grappling with this challenge.[11]

But far from shoring up the public media, whether in printed or audiovisual form, governments are drawing back. According to John Blegen, there is evidence of an historic pattern of much reduced funding for public libraries in the U.S.:

To read the annual reports of the major public libraries during the 1920s, 1930s, and 1940s is to see the functions of a vital information resource, much supported by public use and accustomed to the importance of its role. Budget problems are there, to be sure, and staffing is never sufficient. But there is a confidence that begins to weaken in the 1950s, and to disappear in the 1960s. By the 1970s, the large urban public libraries that lead the public library profession are without any question the suburban systems.[12]

On the other hand, the idea of using libraries as public access points to the Net is catching on, at least in Canada, where the School Net Program will see all of the country's 16,500 schools and 3,400 libraries on-line by 1998. However, the vision is still not always very clear. The imagery of transportation, the dominant technology of a previous age, peppers government reports and ministerial speeches. It began with Vice President Al Gore and his unfortunate "Information Highway" metaphor; in Canada one of the recommendations of the 1995 Access Subcommittee of the

Information Highway Advisory Committee to the federal government reads:

> To make sure that all Canadians have the opportunity to exploit the economic, social, and cultural benefits of the Information Highway, there will be a need for low or no-cost access centers in every community. Affordable community access could be made available in a variety of locations such as schools, libraries, shopping malls, airports, or other transportation terminals.

To bundle transportation terminals along with schools and libraries as potential access points seems to imply that, in these circles at least, "access" is defined as "outlet." This view does not propose a radical departure from industrial age, broadcast distribution psychology, which is primarily the mind-set of business. The pipeline remains the principal image of the day.

Why should we care? If, while governments battle deficits and sagging economies, industry is ready to pick up the tab and install the most important public infrastructure ever, shouldn't we be thankful it is happening at all? Or should we, as taxpayers, clamor for public electronic highways, public access to vital information? A growing number of people are asking for governments to establish something like a charter of information rights. Mark Surman, creator of the concept of the "electronic commons," a public arena of social and political discourse, warns:

> We must constantly remind ourselves what this whole grassroots media thing is about—human beings and community. . . . If access to the new systems does not include literacy and the demystification of technology, we will have created a system that makes class barriers and cultural exclusions bigger rather than smaller. If we leave people in the South to sit on the periphery of the Net, getting sick as they build computers for the rich, the electronic commons is a failure. As we build a movement for a new electronic commons, we need to remember the primacy of

all these things, to remember why we care about information democracy in the first place.[13]

The future of democracy—assuming that democracy is still a valid concept for technologically assisted human behavior—lies in maintaining the difference between public and private, not eliminating it. Because of their twin commitments to the written word and to public service, public libraries are among the primary arenas where this critical contest of humanity will be played out. The public library may be the place where democracy takes refuge against the complete electrification and digitization of our connected mind.

Why, in the era of hypertextuality, do we still need books? Because hypertext is not a book. The book is fixed, and that fixity is crucial. Why? Because today the challenge is not to accelerate information, but to slow it down. Information is already going fast enough by itself. Because our culture is absolutely hell-bent on accelerating to the nanosecond every aspect of human activities and how we relate to them, what we need is to decelerate and make sense of our relationship to information, to deal with it in a rhythmical way. And the book is a consummate decelerator.

The nanosecond generation takes its shoe and hits the screen because it isn't booting fast enough. Each new generation of computers has to be faster and pack more processing power than its predecessor of three or four months earlier. Time is on fast-forward and out of control. To control time, you have to play golf, or read books.

Thought is stopped in a book; thinking is laid bare as if on a dissection plate, revealing its inner structure. The structure of thinking is nowhere in evidence on the Net. As in all computerized media, the structures of thinking are imposed in the guise of programming, but you don't see them.

Books will remain necessary for two main reasons:

- They are decelerators of information (and subsequently accelerators of thought). The inversion of the previously existing relationship is worth considering here: in a predominantly oral culture, books played the role of accelerators of collective intelligence; more people could benefit from the contributions of thinkers and discoverers. Each major book read and discussed by key people and shared by larger groups made an impact on the collective lore. Culture was thus accelerated continuously to this day. However, in an electronic environment, the role of books is to decelerate information, so as to give people the time to think about it and turn it into serviceable knowledge.

- They are distillers of information and resist manipulation by the new "hypertextual/interactive" reader. The fundamental polarity at issue, one often ignored by educators and publishers, is that of the complementary objective/subjective realities of the book and the reader. Reading and writing give the literate person individual control over language. In turn, this special control over language gives that person a separate identity. This kind of separation between the individual and the social group is quite impossible in an exclusively oral society. The fundamental condition of mental—and political—freedom is that the "objective" world outside be stabilized, while the subjective mind is free to roam within it, picking and choosing according to one's needs and personal plans. This power of control is greater if the text is fixed and the mind of the reader takes all the decisions regarding the elaboration of meaning.

Unlike either networked interactive or oral communications, books hold up a fixed mirror to individual development. Thus, the printed book is indeed a necessary condition of the existence of private identity. Education and government need to inform themselves about the relationship between literacy and the privacy of mind. Every medium is what you could call an epistemological option.

Epistemology is the science of how we know things. It is the study of how we relate, globally as complete human beings, to the environment and to other human beings. It is the study of how we structure our own thinking, our own bodies, our own feelings, our own sensations in relation to information "out there." Books and writing represent one of the few fundamental epistemological options offered by the history of our civilization. Hence, the idea that books could disappear forever without leaving a trace is out of the question; it is just impossible. Educators should understand that books are not going to be replaced by television or multimedia or computerized information or virtual reality or any interactive system, including the Net. We should all realize that they *must* not be, that it is critical to maintain the presence of books not just as technologies of information processing, but as technologies of being.

CHAPTER EIGHT

MUSEUMS, REAL AND VIRTUAL, AND THE TYRANNY OF "POINT OF VIEW"

M USEUMS AND GALLERIES are statements about the cultures they represent. The Musée du Louvre, the first museum to go on-line in Europe, was also the first large public museum in the West, an unlikely child of the French Revolution. It opened its doors on August 10, 1793. Not only was this public collection mostly composed of objects which had belonged to the French monarchy, but the building itself was part of the king's city palace, where much of the affairs of state had been run. It made sense to show "the people" the objects which had delineated the differences between them and the previous ruling class. It was a secular temple, a mausoleum for past artifacts, but, as an expression of the psychological revolution underlying the political one, it was a concrete representation of the contemporary mind.

Now that our revolutions have become more technological than political, what should our museums say about us, and how should they say it? As retrieval systems for the significant concerns of a living culture, museums are fairly coherent representations of value hierarchies, and in their changing nature we can find clear reflections of the shape of our own evolving psychology.

The cognitive processes of nineteenth-century man are well represented by the stately architecture and the orderly interior compartmentalization of museums since the opening of the Louvre. Toronto's Royal Ontario Museum, London's British Museum, Brussels' Musée du Cinquantenaire, to give only a few examples, are all well-dressed gentlemen with huge quantities of objects stuffed inside them, all properly labeled, in what is essentially an anal-retentive archival classification system. Information appears in the guise of objects, rather than as relationships or constructs: a sort of obsessive literalism is at work.

But the most striking characteristic of these institutions was their unconscious commitment to the Victorian ideal of mental privacy. Though meant for the general public, they were closed in on themselves, like the human mind; a world within a world, a quiet place of meditation where history, learning, and culture would connect with personal dreams. Their walls were heavy and deep, their ceilings high, and many rooms had no windows. Like the mind of Western humanism, they seemed to be built for eternity. Visitors would find themselves sharing a collective model of their own private minds.

Today, however, museums are built of glass and steel, as we move from the Holy Roman Empire to the empires of the multinationals. As art historian Helen Searing points out:

> From the temple you have the museum becoming more like a loft building, or an office building with large open spaces which then can be supposedly rearranged with ease. I think the extreme of this point of view is found in the Ideal Museum project of Mies van der Rohe, a project of 1942 for a museum in a small city, which simply has a floor, a roof, columns, and glass walls— where paintings float, as it were, in space, where the sculpture is placed throughout this flowing universal space . . . a museum truly without walls.[1]

Changes in architecture reflect changes in psychology. One of the effects of electronic media has been to open up people's mental space for all to see, as multiplying communications systems cross all boundaries, personal and collective. Consequently, as Marjorie Halpin, curator of the University of British Columbia's Museum of Anthropology, observes:

> Museums have been in an identity crisis that began in the 1960s. And what we do at all of our professional meetings and in our literature is ask the question: What is our purpose? What is our goal? What are we doing here as professionals? We're still doing it the way we did basically in the nineteenth century. So what are we about?[2]

Halpin's concern is echoed by art critic Thierry de Duve who, reflecting on the status of Paris's Centre Georges Pompidou ("Beaubourg") at a retrospective of the previous decade in art, proposed that "every museum curator knows that the two principal functions of museums, conservation and exhibition, are contradictory; hence the two ideal forms which haunt the imagination of the museum architect: the coffin and the showcase."[3]

De Duve goes on to explain that the Beaubourg architecture resolves this dilemma by inverting the proposition of cultural dissemination. Indeed, by treating the plumbing, heating ducts, and the structural features of the building as ornaments, Beaubourg presents the image of a momentous reversal: instead of bringing people to culture as so many prime cuts from the contemporary carcass, this museum treats culture as a kind of bouillon made up of all the bacteria and germinations of our daily lives. "Do not expect the museum of tomorrow," warns de Duve, "to create a protective barrier between the inside and the outside, between the sacred space of art and the profane space of life; rather be ready for it to treat all the cultural signs, be they art or not, as instant art, for the time of their appearance, at the time of your appearance . . ."

Beaubourg, as it were, wears its technological heart on its sleeve, showing outside what is ordinarily inside—and showing inside, ordinary life, i.e., the outside world. This could be seen as a direct consequence of technology itself: when electricity invades buildings and our lives, older mechanical forms are taken over and pushed out, so to speak. With electricity, it is the hidden, the personal, the intimate that is drawn outside of structures and institutions. Beaubourg is like a lady appearing in public in her underwear.

By comparison to Beaubourg, Toronto's very dignified Royal Ontario Museum could be suspected, in its recent and decidedly restrained renovations, of "trying to keep up appearances." The ROM has become deservedly the benchmark for excellence in a country which is beginning to acquire a reputation for the high standards and the innovative spirit it brings to protecting its heritage. But the ROM has its problems, not the least of which is the question of what to do about our condition of galloping "reality" and the masses of artifacts and information this frantic accumulation of experience churns out. Objects in a multiplicity of categories have been pouring into the consumer's cultural environment ever since industry discovered mass production. How can museums handle so much information in so little space? Some answers have begun to appear.

Indeed, another Canadian institution, the Ontario Science Centre,* is nowadays doing its best to rapidly and continuously renew its exhibits, treating culture as a passing parade, a monthly magazine of artifacts. This is a dramatic change from the earlier inclination to wrap up the new, and make it old immediately: "Freeze the bloody thing before it gets out of hand." Just as Beaubourg picks up the feel of the Zeitgeist, standing at the interface between cognition and recognition, the OSC and other science and technology museums around the world are more and more committed to the exploration of the present. They go beyond the coffin and the showcase controversy to become cultural accelerators.

The modern confusion over interpretation, including the problem of deciding whether a museum is a coffin or a showcase, starts with a basic misconception about who we are today as people. Like

---

* The Ontario Science Centre has often served as an example for European imitation; its influence can be seen for example in the Paris Museum of Science and Technology, LaVillette.

the Beaubourg museum, we too have changed inside out: we have been unfolding outwards like a rubber glove does as it's removed. As McLuhan pointed out, with electronic technologies, our central nervous system is pushed outside our own bodies: we ask electricity to do, externally, everything that we used to do within our bodies, including thinking, counting, imagining, dreaming, and so many other intimate processes. Who knows, one day we may ask it to do our loving for us. On the other hand, with telephones, radio, and television, and first videotex technologies such as Minitel in France, now the Internet and the Web, all of which reach into our homes, the world is invading our interiors. The world is pouring into our souls via electronic media, and we in turn are looming high and wide across the globe by dint of the same technologies. Can we seriously ask the new museum, that image of our developing psychology, to reflect, enhance, and clarify that condition?

The problem is that, although our way of handling information both collectively and personally has changed, our image of ourselves has not. We remain helplessly stuck in the Renaissance outlook on reality, which is: "I stand here, and I embrace all that my eye can see; I judge and select, I order, I classify, I use it when I need it, I store it when I don't; I am reluctant to throw it away because it surely has a reason to exist and it might be useful someday." This attitude, which is unquestionably commendable, has been translated into a vast reality tidying-up operation which has spanned four centuries, and which became science, law, history . . . and museums.

The "point of view" was a cognitive technique used to classify and set out in hierarchies of objective categories all personal information, which would then furnish our mental theaters. The point of view is also a technique to which many curators of museums are deeply committed because it reinforces their idea of the museum as a box, of artifacts as inert matter and of the public as innocent gawkers whose education must proceed in show-and-tell fashion. It is probable, however, that as a psychological referent, the point of view is obsolete. We may have to begin exploring different ways to sort out our relationships to reality.

With a point of view, you can only be at one place at a time, just as you can occupy only one position at a time in a theater, in front of a painting or a photograph, or in the local landscape. With the new media, you are everywhere at once, a mode of reality which is continuously supported by radio, television, and computer networks: they bring the Earth and the moon to your living room. That this condition ought to find a reflection in the museum of today seems to have been understood by the developers of Cologne's Media Park, and the more modest Peterborough (Ontario) Artspace, each of which incorporates in its own way the notion that a museum should be technically as well as metaphorically a kind of cultural accelerator taking information in and sending it out again into the community.

In fact, my quarrel with the Renaissance point of view amounts to an objection to the way it puts blinkers upon an otherwise fascinating possibility: we can replace the notion of the museum as a repository, whether coffin or showcase,* with that of the museum as a central node, a grand central station of intense interactions coming and going rather than simply going in and staying there. All museums, whether of art or natural history or science and technology, ought to be cultural amplifiers which give a spin to the visiting public, sending it out again energized with a new understanding of the present. Museums of the past and of the present differ only in their labels: the ideal function is the same—to make all times now.

Paul Virilio points out, correctly in my view, that the most important current issue in technological matters is not the management of space, but the management of time.[4] We are the nanosecond generation. If we seem less attentive than ever, it is not because of a shortage of time, but because we are processing information faster than ever, and our attention span is that much reduced. If the average gallery patron's pause before an object is limited to a duration of eight seconds, it is partly because that is all the time it takes to discover what there is to know about most of today's artwork (unless you are a

---

* The new entrance to the Louvre, a large glass pyramid, seems to turn the contradiction between coffin and showcase into a monumental pun.

specialist), and partly because we are taught by TV advertising and by the increasing speed of home computer activities to capture information in quick glances, leaving it up to our internal cognitive processes to synthesize whatever it is that we might have missed.*

Thus, in today's man-made environment, there are very few things that merit looking at for any length of time, except computer and video screens, which, like autonomous mirrors, reflect in instant feedback loops the powers of our own intervention. Interactivity appears to be a necessity in the retooling of museums and galleries because today's patrons are more and more accustomed to participating, as opposed to judging from a safe distance.

Museums must also deal with the fact that even simple objectivity is threatened: the status of objects as objects is no longer secure. When matter was everything, as in the eighteenth-century view of things, objects were revered. But mass production, planned obsolescence and the multiplication of reproduction techniques (as Walter Benjamin has explained in his oft-quoted book, *The Work of Art in the Age of Its Mechanical Reproduction),* have devalued the status of objects. We have been moving in the direction of what Jean-François Lyotard has cleverly dubbed the "immaterials."5 In high technology research and marketing, the movement from matter to non-matter follows the chain of priorities that places design above substance. Well-made fakes are about to be on a par with the real thing. The trend in all technologies to achieve perfect simulation may have been nothing but an unconscious, quasi-Hegelian attack on matter to better control it by transmuting it into program, i.e., non-matter. But how do we then know what's the real thing?

Virtual galleries with digital displays might, on the other hand, cause us to reevaluate the worth of unique objects. When everything is available in digital form, it is the real object which becomes the

---

* Television expert Herbert Krugman has suggested that children exposed to television before they have learned to read might have learned to see with quick, recursive glances, in a way which does not conform to the sustained attention required of the written page.

rarity. Assuming that the future economy of abundance does not reverse all the values of scarcity, uniqueness might well be "in" again, in the not-too-distant future.

It takes a visionary to know even slightly ahead of time the changes that perceptual faculties are about to experience. Artists were the first to discover the formal, "natural" rules of perspective as it would be accepted during the aftermath of the Renaissance. Just as television was a technical realization of the Pointillists' understanding of light as emanating from an object rather than being reflected from it, today we are invited by holograms to remember the lessons of Cubism, to explore simultaneously the inside, outside, back, front, top, and bottom of any object. Holograms are currently being investigated as an appropriate method for conservation. They are faithful to the original, next to indestructible, and they don't take up any space.

One more thing soon to be available to us, and to curators, is the precise and intimate sensation of touch and sound at great distances. In the classical museum, we were not allowed to touch the objects. Their visual presence, authenticated by the label, was supposed to be truth enough. Kids wanted to touch anyway, because that's how they get to know things. There were all kinds of good reasons not to allow touching, not the least of which was the (Platonic) notion that true intimacy was deemed to be obtained not by direct contact, but by holding the memory of the object in the privacy of one's mind. In the modern museum, actual touching may become impossible because most objects will be presented as images, holograms, screen ghosts from video disks or Web sites. The desire to touch, however, will remain a gnawing void in our psyche. How can we verify anything without knowing that, if we really had to, we could put our hands to it? Because, in its essence, electricity is really a tactile medium, we can confidently anticipate technologies which will deal imaginatively with touch.

Finally, there is the question of reach. Why go to the museum when you can bring it home? Or why stay within the mental, emotional, and cultural confines of your own neighborhood when you can have access to the best information from the four corners of the globe? The computer terminal at the end of a telephone line has become the output appliance for the senses of hearing, sight, and touch. We might reasonably expect at some point to be able to collect images and objects on-line in real time, by scanning the object exposed in a museum or a gallery.

Among the first institutions to establish sites on the Web were museums and galleries, with scanned images and navigable itineraries. Perhaps Nicolas Pioch's private posting of treasures of the Louvre in early 1993 can claim to have awakened people to the possibilities of the Web. Today, a simple tour of art-based Web sites via the Yahoo search engine opens up access to so many sites that it's already too late to hope to visit them all. Sites and home pages devoted to art galleries and museums, public or private, famous or unknown, number in the thousands.*

It is as a distributor of simulations and the purveyor of information that I see the role of museums in an age of networked information. Some of them, such as the Art Gallery of Ontario, are already equipped with storage facilities for videos, image databanks, and videotex networks. Others are considering equipping themselves with simulation rooms for displays such as those devised by MIT's Spatial Data Management system, or any number of virtual reality programs depicting in high-definition simulations of ancient cities, such as Karnak, Çatal Huyuk, and Pompeii, not to mention St. Peter's Basilica in Rome, the Abbey of Clunya, and the Tomb of Nefertari.

---

* For individual artists, creating a home page has the advantage of providing a venue for showing their work at virtually no cost. As a means of distribution to art patrons and collectors, the Web is unparalleled: it guarantees targeted, instant, and even participatory distribution. Thanks to the global nature of the postings and the sites, the potential buying public is hugely and instantly enlarged. While much of the conventional artwork seen on the Web is little better than sidewalk painting or graffiti, it is also possible to access and preview art collections and antiques auctions. On-line bidding and payment by credit card makes the whole process easier and accelerates the circulation of the art market.

Baudrillard observed that, in the baroque age so absorbed in exploring all our senses in the light of new learning, stucco was the simulator of all textures, all materials, all substances.[6] In the same way, it is becoming apparent that digitization is the simulator of all previous technologies. However, regarding this practice of simulation, to which many a museum curator will have to resort, there is an objection, made by gloomy moralists, which ought to be acknowledged. This is the idea that technology today increasingly replaces experiences, substituting ersatz for the real thing. Television thus is seen to replace private imagination, video games to replace dexterity skills, computers to replace thinking, and so on. The possibility of simulating any environment has even led some to suspect that the entire Apollo space program with its lunar landing was in fact scripted and shot in an isolated desert studio.

I would like to suggest a brighter possibility: every time a technology simulates a human activity, it is not to replace it, but to enhance it and to bring attention to new potentials and new areas of interest. Our musical instruments now produce more complex sounds than ever before. To what extent can we say that they are merely simulacra, or devalued technomirages? To anybody who would argue that the intense psychological reactions engendered by the novelists of the nineteenth century, or the filmmakers of the twentieth, were in some way synthetic, I would respond that the emotions were both new and authentic, and thus enriched people's lives.

Acknowledging that patrons are more interested in special events and social occasions than in the art displayed at the museum, the Art Gallery of Ontario's marketing director, Liz Addison, suggests that "it's part of a trend towards participation. A lot of museums are trying to get the visitor to have an interactive experience. People are not content to have a contemplative experience. They want to have action."[7] Under the conditions created by the emerging psychology, chances are that the satisfactions derived from the conventional highbrow cultural values will not continue to support museums' attractive needs. It is difficult to be simply a consumer today. Most people—except for couch potatoes—want to be part of the action.

They have recently become doers and producers, rather than consumers. The computer has presaged an end to the promotion by television of mass consumerism. People turn to their video recorders, their computers, and their modems with their own programming in mind. They are rapidly recovering the autonomy they lost by being exposed to TV without remission.

Just as microscopy has helped us to experience directly, by extending our vision, realms of unsuspected beauty and complexity, the results of artists' explorations in the digital world are inviting us to perceive levels of sensitivity and integration that we would otherwise never have known. The role of the museum thus may be first and foremost to help artists to make new experiences available to ever larger audiences, even if it be under the guise of simulations.

One of the great trends which distinguishes Victor Hugo's nineteenth-century ideal of "art as chosen reality" from McLuhan's twentieth-century ideal of "culture as our business" is the shift from selecting the best examples of reality (for storage in museums) to simply quoting reality as it happens. This "quoting of reality" may be precisely what is required from museum Web sites today. Just as news media—radio, television, cable news, etc.—highlight the personages and events of experience, the museum's role is perhaps to probe and cite the *context* of experience, just as postmodern architecture reveals hidden context by advertising historical allusions on the exterior walls of structures.

There is simply no way to interpret today's multisensory, technologically extended reality through the traditional box-bound museum. When your whole nervous system is outside your body, tied to everybody else's nervous system, it is ludicrous to hope to perceive the complexity of the environment's interrelations by cutting a pie-shaped piece out of it, labeling it and putting it on display in a glass case.

Of course labels have long been among the principal means whereby a museum curator would help fix the public's point of view; nothing helps to resolve the anguish of ambiguity in front of an abstract painting like a label describing it. As Tom Wolfe observed in

The Painted Word, you can take any logical abuse from a painting as long as it is properly labeled. The meticulous researchers timing the dwindling duration of a patron's stay in front of gallery paintings have determined that, on the average of eight seconds, five seconds are devoted to leaning forward and reading the label. Trying to avoid the tyranny of the text, Marjorie Halpin experimented with an exhibit where she and her colleagues at the UBC Museum of Anthropology presented objects without any labels. She recalls with excitement that people would find their own rules of unity and form in their absence: "If there's a unity, where does it come from? Well, I think it has something to do with our bodies, with our receptors, with the way sensory information comes in . . . what I'm clear on is that there's a unity."[8]

Halpin's experiment may itself have found inspiration in McLuhan's suggestion to museum curators in New York:

> The senses that are relevant to most of the artifacts in the museum are those of what we would now call an extremely backward country, in which they used, not their eyes in our way, but their whole sensorium. They would practically live in a world of ESP. When your whole sensorium is in action you don't really use anything except ESP. The whole skin of man, when it is acting as a perceptive agent, is intuitive. It doesn't need any special message. It gets the message very quickly from just the slightest change in the environmental pressure.[9]

Another issue facing museums and galleries is that of classification. In established urban environments, museums specialize in a given line of artifacts, or in a given period. This may run contrary to need to have access to many different sources of information at once. Libraries have moved quickly to adopt electronic techniques of information retrieval and have established international networks among themselves. Museums are also, tentatively, taking part in such networks, but they may be required to do so systematically in the future. Networking will inevitably tend to overshadow specialization.

We rack our brains to make museums more attractive, more relevant, more showy . . . but is that the way to go about it? We should attend to the public's intuition that a museum is not exclusively about past memory, but also about present cognition. People go there not so much to see what was, but to seek answers as to what is happening now. Says Halpin: "Museum exhibits are normally about answers, and the answers are always about differences. But it's much more exciting to pose questions."[10]

PART 3

CONNECTIVITY

CHAPTER NINE

WEBNESS

I N THE DAYS before electricity, technology was tame and obedi-
ent, and life was evenly paced. There was a real world out there
called "objective," there was a real person right here called "subjective," and there were a lot of printed words to bring order to their
relationships. Things were clear, at least in the industrial countries
founded on alphabetic literacy, because a strong polarization distin-
guished individual humans from the world beyond them. One pole,
the human self, was constantly evolving and adapting within the
confines of a private conscious realm, while the other, the "worldwide world," remained stable—and conveniently dumb. There was
no mind in it. Or at least it appeared so. This was the blessed time of
noninteractive media: time and space were fixed, and private minds
and bodies were free to roam without losing their bearings or blur-
ring their boundaries, or sharing with machines the responsibility
for making up their minds.

Today, thanks to technological change, we are faced with the
potential for a major psychological watershed. The social and psychological conditions of humanity have always been closely related
to technology and this is true more than ever today because of the
electronically driven, exponential increase in the numbers, power,
and reach of technologies invading both the social landscape and the
intimacy of the physical and psychological being. Because major
new technologies have demonstrated their power to seed chaos in
the existing social and psychological order, the challenge is to make

sense of the changes and discern the new conditions for stability and social order. Among the principal features of today's technological wave to consider are:

1. In the realm of hypertextuality:

-   over the past 150 years, since the development of the tele-graph, the world has seen the proliferation and accelerating growth of a global infrastructure of layered, interconnected and integrated networks; the present condition is a still pre-carious but gradually more unified environment of increas-ingly complex and precise communications;
-   over the past fifty years, since the creation of the first digital computers, the digitization of as much material as possible has promoted both the homogenization* and standardization of inputs and that has in turn permitted infinite customiza-tion of outputs. With networks, access to digital processes has the potential to be ubiquitous—but there are new kinds of barriers rising in intranets, firewalls, and other virtual enclaves that threaten to hamper or prevent open access;
-   over the past five years, since the invention of virtual reality, the virtualization and convergence of the sensory values, tex-tures, structures, and properties of hardware are turning tra-ditional hardware contents not merely into software but more radically into "mindware."

2. In the realm of interactivity:

-   the recent development of improved interfaces, by allowing more intuitive and user-friendly interactions between the user and the computer, are introducing a shift from internal to external processing of information. This may be changing the

---

* The paradox of digitization is that by reducing all inputs to a lowest common denominator, 0/1, it allows for maximal differentiation and targeting of outputs; so what is meant here by "homogenization" is directly opposite to what people used to mean by that word when it was applied to the effects of television.

primary orientation of the private mind from within the body to without;

- rapid progress in intelligent software is opening avenues for the migration of psychological processes such as memory and intelligence from the inside of individual minds to the outside world of connected-knowledge media;
- the increasing effectiveness of sensory interaction in multimedia, hypermedia, and virtual reality, i.e., in direct-connect mind-machine interactions, is approximating that of our own mental processes, presaging a shift in emphasis from static memory-based media to the media of processing—dynamic and self-adjusting, intelligence-based media.

3. In the realm of connectedness:

- the increase in human interactions—personal, social, and institutional—through integrated networks is concentrating and multiplying human mental energy;
- the gradual self-organization and increasing autonomy of agent-supported databases is providing tools for emergent problem-solving skills;
- consequently, the degree of collaboration among individual people's minds is about to become vastly increased, tutored and focused by mediating software and hardware.

All of these changes are happening simultaneously and are interdependent. My hope in bringing them together under the banner of "connectedness" is to place the entire transformation in its proper perspective: not only is connectedness a principle that governs them all, but it appears to be an inherent goal of what is a largely self-organizing process. How else to explain the complementarity of trends in innovation, research and development, manufacturing, marketing and media, organized labor, and government behavior?

The evidence suggests to me that a diffuse and shared self-consciousness of the whole is arising in bits and pieces here and there, with people, like many of those who appear in this book, pushing hard the limits of their own minds, or like Bill Clinton suddenly deciding a month before his reelection that it might be a good idea to earmark half a billion dollars to improve the infrastructure of the Internet.* At this diffuse but effective level of semiconscious organization, what you know, what you don't know, what you don't know that you know, and what you don't know that you don't know, all seem capable of invoking a Lorenzian "butterfly effect" of the mind. In the predominantly software environment that technology is building for us, every thought connects, immediately, in some way.

What is "connectedness"? It is the tendency for separate and previously unrelated entities to be joined by a link or a relationship. Connectedness may be a property of electricity, an analogue to conduc- tivity. The electronic industry as a whole could be thought of as a technological simile for our organic, internal communication system. The continuity between the two domains, the technological and the biological, is established by the fact that there is electricity both within and outside the body, just as there is language both within and outside the body. It is worth noting that the telegraph, which was the very first electronic metaphor of our central nervous system, was from the start a carrier or a processor of language. The telegraph was the first outward projection of our central nervous system, but more importantly, the telegraph was the system which for the first time translated the alphabet into electricity. Thus, in the telegraph, there is a simultaneous and combined externalization of language and electricity. The telegraph took the first, albeit modest, step towards the present ubiquitous externalization of information-

---

* This is the toughest consequence to evaluate and predict because our literate grounding has tended to make us associate any thinking process with an originating point in an individual self; it is very difficult to imagine self-less, distributed, connective, emergent information-processing going on, as in the metaphors of beehive or anthill. The French philosopher Michel Foucault attributed to language itself, *"le discours,"* the power to self-organize into institutions and rule people's lives without them knowing about it (unless, of course, they were clever French philosophers).

processing from the intimate recesses of thought to public, computer-assisted and multi-user connections.

There is an uncanny continuity in the wiring of the planet since the discovery and first applications of electricity. The telegraph, the telephone, the Internet, the World Wide Web have followed upon each other as if they were stages in a single technological development. Each new stage brings new features which integrate with the previous realm and vastly increase the communication potential of the multilayered system. The telephone added real-time bidirectionality and voice to the telegraph, the Internet added multipath communications to the telephone, the Web added multimedia image, sound and color to the Internet, and so on. All of this could be interpreted as mere directionless progress, the blind elaboration of a technology according to its inherent possibilities or, on the contrary, it could be seen as a groping towards a purpose. What we are dealing with here is a hugely intelligent but mostly decentralized system that appears to be organizing itself, without a whole lot of people knowing or even having to know what's going on.

Technological networks have demonstrated a tendency to grow in bursts like the biological ones in our nervous system do soon after birth. Just imagine the Atlantic, bridged first with the telegraph's thin lines, then with a burst, by telephone cables and eventually with mega-capacity fiber lines snaking along the ocean floor. At the same time, radio signals had begun skipping from continent to continent, carrying information in war and peace. The next big burst was the era of television feeding back live images to millions in huge networks of information-processing systems. At the same time, the integrating machine, the computer, had been growing up in awkward isolation. Computers went from single-purpose, data-crunching mainframes (industry-controlled)—big, lumbering half-wit machines—to the personal computer (user-controlled), training you and me to connect our biological systems to the technological Web in ever-more intimate association. The last big burst, the one we are living through now, is the infiltration by computers of the worldwide telephone system. With this development, the process of self-organization has steadily accelerated through data-processing and e-mail and local area networks, to the Internet, and soon after that, to the linked retrieval system called the World Wide Web.

The interesting difference between the Internet and the Web in terms of the growth patterns of a connected environment is that the Internet is a web of addresses, nodes, places, but the Web is a network of contents. In the same way, the mind needs the connection of various lower-level functions in order to have the ultimate capability of connecting contents themselves. The linking of content is a second level of articulation of the network environment. Thus, the Web is an order of complexity beyond the Internet, a fact its commercial competitors, the BBSs (Bulletin Board Services) like America Online and broadcast networks like CBS and CNN, are beginning to appreciate.

There are still deeper parallels between the burgeoning of networked communications and the growth of organic human intelligence, especially at the childhood developmental stages. The Internet is growing connections exponentially like a brain in full learning status. As in the neurosystem of a growing organism, there seems a kind of demand-pull on the Net for more development, more production of contacts, more connections, and, eventually, more ideas. Indeed, the most baffling aspect of Internet history is the formidable demand. Everywhere in the world, even in developing countries, there is a clamoring for access that is undiminished by the very real technical, financial, and cognitive hurdles that must be overcome.* Millions of people spend hours on-line using their brains at top speed, suffering the agony of waiting for the data to download without worrying about who is going to pay them for all that overtime.

---

* People do not always really want telematic technology this badly. The case of Minitel is eloquent in that, while it did become a resounding success in the end, it had to be force fed to the French population for several years before it took off. The reason for the Web's more immediate success is twofold: one, that it was enhanced by the colors of Mosaic; the other, that its universality makes it closer to a total rather than a partial milieu.

The phenomenon is completely counterintuitive. In the past history of radio, television, computers, or even simple literacy, there is no precedent for such a rush to acquire what is still a fundamentally immature technology. Television, to give the most banal example, took more than thirty years between the time the technology was mature enough to be mass produced and the time its penetration reached critical mass in the world's households (1928-1958).

While it is still too early to know what is really happening, the recent proposal for the "embedded Internet" is one that points to an almost teleological thrust in the technology. In the words of David Kline: "The next big thing to hit the Net will be wiring together millions of tiny computers embedded into everything we use. This is no future vision—the products are hitting the market now." The mere idea, let alone the actually nascent industry of the embedded Internet is the *summum* of connectedness:

> Only the Internet can serve as the infrastructure for a truly connected world. As a medium, it is much cheaper than the phone network. It provides standardized interoperability between all types of disparate devices, networks, and systems. The Net is also a better platform than the phone system for adding intelligence and agent technology. And the Net's distributed architecture makes it more efficient at rerouting communications around damage and bottlenecks. But perhaps more importantly, the Net's packet-switched approach to handling communications is simply better suited to handling the billions—or even trillions—of relatively short data transmissions likely in a future connected world than is the phone network, where each connection essentially requires a dedicated link for the entire duration of the transmission.[1]

Embedded Internet's appearance on the scene is as if technology were discovering a way to emulate the physical, biological body within the social, technological realm: every part connecting to every other for an integrated functioning of the whole. If there is merit in this notion, we can count on industry to carry it to completion, and sooner rather than later.

One of the main effects of digitization is to make "liquid" everything that is solid. Anything that can be digitized can be translated into anything else that can be digitized. Just as the alphabet once virtualized sensory data to be reconstituted in the reader's mind into sensory images, our sensory modalities are now translated into digital data, virtualized and extended on-line. This very flexibility makes matter, once perceived as consisting of mutually heterogeneous and impenetrable substances, seem now as fluid as thought itself. By reducing all matter and all shapes to 0/1, the lowest common denominator of everything, digitization is a new meeting point between the material and the conceptual. As fewer and fewer material conditions present resistance to the storage and delivery of information, the fluidity of digital data brings it as close to the condition of thought as anything we experience in our own minds. Digitization turns hardware into software, and, by extension, into something close to a mental image, i.e., "mindware."*

EVOLVING CONSCIOUSNESS

Electronic technology is changing the fundamental orientation of the consciousness of the literate mind. The consciousness of the reader is in its essence the world inside the mind; the body looking inward. The thinking process is carried on by an internal eye looking at an internal field or stage where the information is processed. Have you ever observed how you position yourself in your mind when you read? Are you in the midst of the action, as in a dream, or in front of it, as you would be in a cinema or before of a television set? Do you "see" the scene at eye level, or from above? Do you "hear" voices, "smell" the scent of coffee; can you "taste"

---

* What I call "mindware" is software based on knowledge media, that is, software closely connected to processing by people, not merely machines.

Proust's celebrated *madeleine*? Whatever your answer, you will have
to concede that the experience of reading, even when you actually
feel something, is entirely internal. In fact, most people would agree
that it is more like an interior stage than a flat screen, hence the
close association that has existed between alphabetic literacy and
theater. The Greek invention of the theatrical institution was but
an external, standardizing means to facilitate the integration of
sensory inputs coming from within the self during the reading
process.

But we do not process information in our minds alone anymore.
With interactive and screen-based electronic technologies, the orientation is reversed: it's the body looking out. With television, for
instance, the screen is on the outside and replete with sensory information. The eye of the TV watcher is not turned inward, but outward. The place where the information is processed is out there, on
the screen. All meanings are controlled by the outside source and the
critical role of the viewer is merely to integrate the meaning as sensory inputs, much in the way the physical body makes sense of a situation in context. Even with computers, in spite of, or perhaps
because of, the interactive nature of the process, there is an intermediate stage of information-processing between what is behind the
screen and the mind. There is consequently a considerable inversion
of our psychology as it is moving from within, outward.

Virtual reality can be considered mindware in this context. VR is
constructed to represent the world more or less as we see it, but the
VR decor is in fact an externalized mental decor. The human mind is
itself a virtual environment, designed to process information in simulations and pre-enactment. The mind and its experiences are externalized by VR machines which extend our sensory inputs (touch,
vision, and hearing) to reconstitute an artificial consciousness which
is truly outside our own mind and outside our own body. VR provides a world of extended mind for education, for work, for play,
for love, and for health. Professionals will increasingly use VR to
make decisions, the way they play out scenarios in the privacy of
their own mind; architects and medical professionals already use VR

for test-driving the environments they create and for rehearsing delicate surgery.

VR is your imagination "out there" in front of you. You can "walk" in it. And so can other people. Once you are in it, you cease to be in front of the object of consciousness—you are *in* it, immersed, as you are in sound. As in *Tron*, the prophetic movie about a programmer cruising into his own program, with VR we not only talk back to our screens, we enter them. And with networks, we are now able to link these imaginations, one to another.

CONNECTED IMAGINATION

Let us compare two mental operations, one private, the other connected. When you think privately, when you picture something in your mind, you focus your attention inwardly and what you "see" is a more or less unified and flexible image. There is no particular "place" for the object of your attention, but you know that it is "there" somehow. It seems to be suspended at some central point, slightly forward, and slightly below eye level in your mind/brain. This suspended image is the result of the collaboration of millions of brain cells interconnected by contact points called synapses. In your mind, therefore, the collaboration of millions of activities can produce a single dynamic image. In the same way, the object of attention of hundreds or thousands of people in a network is a unified and flexible live construct.

Alone in front of a screen, especially in a text-based environment, you may not always be aware of the extent of the memory and activity behind it in the netherworld of the Internet. However, if there is a common image that every participant shares, for example, a groupware screen for collaborative work at a distance, or the 3-D stage of an Alpha World, then the paradoxical communality surrounding the object of attention surfaces quite readily. Each participant's screen becomes both a portal and a tool for connected thinking. What is accessed on the Net is the content of other people's imagination and memory. The screen of each individual user becomes the place where one's own imagination and memory meet the imagination and memory of many other people.

The art of the Web is the art of connected thought. For some people, it is nothing but a kind of shared hallucination. But for many others, it is a real live experience. In Andrey Tarkovsky's magnificent sci-fi film, *Solaris,* a team of astronauts falls under the influence of an unknown planet which projects thoughts in the shapes of objects and people that the protagonists believe to be real. The "projections" of people's thoughts on the Net are equally substantial and much more real than those of the movie. To gain some measure of the psychological and epistemological complexity of Alpha Worlds,* for example, it is only necessary to imagine their opposite: suppose that, in your own mind, there were fixed forms of thoughts that were put there by other people, with your consent. Whenever your circumstances would bring up these thoughts, they would appear fully formed, unchangeable and perhaps foreign. You could alter them peripherally but not fundamentally. They would be internal objective/subjective thoughts. Similarly, Alpha Worlds are objective/subjective realities, but instead of being internal, they are external.

Personally held beliefs are thoughts which are at the same time your own and shared with other people. They are things that you have learned from others and that you hold true. But, however deeply fundamentalist your approach to such learning may be, in the privacy of your mind, you still have total control over the shape of the imaging you choose to give to your beliefs. This kind of control is not available to you in the external realities of 3-D networked communications. But you do have an access to those external realities which is personal. Alpha Worlds are not beliefs, they are connected realities.

---

* These are virtual communities created collaboratively in the Web, featuring virtual environments such as buildings and open spaces in which visitors or "dwellers" can interact.

EMERGENT PROPERTIES:
NEW COGNITIVE
BEHAVIORS

Among the most valuable insights in her remarkable study *Life on the Screen* is Sherrie Turkle's identification of the "quality of emergence."* Emergence of a new order of integration from the simple or complex interactions of individual units is indeed a kind of "quality." Intelligence, typically, is an effect of emergence, and the expectation created by the Web could be that new kinds of intelligence are beginning to emerge. Connected intelligence is something that is most easily demonstrated by pointing to the Net. The Web, with its formidable linking ability, is a forum for real-time interactivity between tens, hundreds, or thousands of people looking for something. The pressure of human minds focusing on the same issues and the self-organizing abilities of the network create a potential for a great unity of purpose. All these organic minds can be assisted by digital media which vastly increase their power of synthesis and classification. The significance of the Web is not that it is yet another distribution system, but that it is a *distributed* system. The fun and the substance of the Web is in its ability to connect living minds at work in all manner of purposeful configuration. The minds on the Net are connected and they behave like liquid crystal in stable but fluid formations.

The so-called virtual community is more than just a large number of people involved more or less directly, more or less constantly,

---

* Turkle refers, for example, to the fascinating "connectivist" theory of the mind and the ego proposed by psychoanalyst David Olds: "For Olds, connectionism challenges ego psychology by providing a way to see ego not as a central authority but as an emergent system. Through a connectionist lens, says Olds, the ego can be recast as a distributed system. Consciousness can be seen as a technical device by which the brain represents its own workings to itself. Olds likens it to the 'monitor on a computer system,' underscoring its passive quality"; *Life on the Screen*, op. cit., 140.

in a common activity. It is also a real-time,* immediate, and contingent presence, like a mind at work. On-line communications have created a new category of mind—a connected mind, to which one "plugs in" or from which one pulls out, without affecting the integrity of the structure. The worldwide connections of "mind-at-work" are in their own right active, learning, self-organizing, and thereby growing in size and precision. So, let us concede that these new categories of mind, states that have both the permanence and the flexibility of liquid crystals, are a reality. They are here now, and growing. Many people believe that the whole postindustrial culture is being absorbed by the phenomenon of networks, a supposition made all the more plausible when we see that business and government are now looking at all of this with voracious eyes. There is an urgent need for artists to explore this new psychological condition, so that they can begin to prepare the antidotes to potential traumas, and reveal the extent of the new possibilities that we are offered.

WEBNESS

"Webness" is a term created by the jurors of the Art on the Web category for the 1995 Ars Electronica Prize, to make artists and their critics understand a feature which is quite specific to the properties

---

* What is "real time"? Technically, it is a term to designate the instantaneous and continuous response of a machine to a command. Metaphorically, the notion is an oddity: just as we never before had to distinguish between real and virtual space, we haven't had to think in terms of more than one "time" (unless of course we were post-Einsteinian physicists). The reason this question deserves attention is that, for the practice of connected intelligence, just as for estimating operative durations of the Internet, you have to allow for a kind of "extended" or "virtual" time. On the Net, there are strictly speaking no time zones, although there are specific times of day for rush hours and traffic jams. The real time of connected intelligence on the Net is the time it takes the communication to connect, mature, and produce a result. There is no precise limit to that kind of time. It is a sort of continuum; it has unity and purpose.

of the World Wide Web. What, the jurors want to know, is specifi-cally "Web-like" in a Web application; what character distinguishes it from other sustained colloquy on networks? The distinguishing difference is that it derives its power and qualities from optimal exploitation of network connectedness. The property of webness lies in the interconnecting of human intelligences by purposefully conceived connected interfaces, for purposes of innovation and discovery. While the Internet by itself has a little bit of webness, the World Wide Web is much more "webby" because it adds hypertex-tual links to networked communication. Something like connected thinking in slow motion is going on out there. Webness is also an aesthetic criterion in that there is beauty in patterns and qualities of interconnections.

For example, Firefly is a rather brilliant and innovative marketing tool. It provides you with a personal digital agent to seek and recom-mend entertainment items such as music or movies according to your taste. To train your agent in recognizing what you like, you must first indicate your preferences by entering on the site a precise evaluation of a sample of musical items. As it is described on the Firefly home page:

Firefly brings personalization and community to the Internet. Your agent belongs to you and whenever you use it, it intelli-gently navigates through the entire Firefly community space to discover the information and people who would be of most interest to you. In fact every member of the Firefly community has his or her own personal agent, so interacting with Firefly is like automating the word-of-mouth process. When you tell your agent what interests you, it goes out and locates those tastes, opinions, preferences, and idiosyncrasies most similar to you so it can suggest new music and movies that you might like or even people who you might like to meet. The more you train your agent, the more useful and accurate it gets. The more other people train their agents, the smarter the Firefly community becomes.[2]

The Ars Electronica jurors recommended Firefly—or rather its prototype which went under the name of RINGO ++—for a top prize, not so much because of what is described above, but for another feature which seems to have been left out of the latest version. That feature, the truly connected one, is that after having made an evaluation of his or her tastes in a sampling of twenty musical items, by clicking on a button the user could call up a map of the "taste community" that showed the statistical range of people from those who were closest to those who were the furthest away in musical taste from the user. Firefly is a kind of "connected taste bud," the first in a generation of connected sensory scanners which, if combined and cross-checked, could profile communities much more precisely and usefully than the best psychographic analyses in existence today.

While many Web sites process information, i.e., the content of human taste, thought, and imagination, other sites also process intelligence itself, in a kind of epistemological factory. This other aspect of webness is best illustrated by Idea Futures.[3] This site allows you to invest digital dollars in an idea or a hypothesis that you either post there yourself, or that you can select from an index of previously posted suggestions. As you might in a worldwide Monopoly game, you receive fifty digital dollars every week to invest. You can also connect with the idea's originator(s) and contribute to the content. Day after day, you can see the value and the complexity of your chosen idea grow before your eyes. Group mindware like Idea Futures weaves a seamless tapestry of intelligences.

DISTRIBUTED INTELLIGENCE

There is a growing body of theory and evidence that there is no need for intelligence to be centralized or even localized in any particular way to function coherently. According to Kevin Kelly:

Parallel distributed computing [the linking of several or many computer processors] excels in perception, visualization and

simulation. Parallelism handles complexity better than traditional supercomputers made of one huge, incredibly fast serial
computer. But in a parallel supercomputer with a sparse, distributed memory, the distinction between memory and processing
fades. Memory becomes a reenactment of perception, indistinguishable from the original act of knowing. Both are a pattern
that emerges from a jumble of interconnected parts.[4]

While Marvin Minsky evokes the notion of a "society of mind"*
and Kevin Kelly brings out the metaphor of the "hive mind,"[5] experimental work in digital agency demonstrates that given certain controlled conditions the association of many individual, single-
purpose agents can collaborate in unified and purposeful activities
by rapid trial and error and instant reconfiguring. For example, MIT's
Patti Maes is working on developing societies of agents that reduce
work and information overload, a "multi-agent system that discov-
ers, monitors, and filters information resources." Maes explains:

> Instead of constructing a large complex agent that will have to
> solve the whole problem, we are creating a society of smaller and
> simpler specialized agents, that try to solve the problem collec-
> tively. We introduce an artificial ecosystem of evolving informa-
> tion filtering and discovery agents that cooperate and compete
> in a market-like environment.

"Kasbah," for example, is an "agent marketplace for buying and
selling goods":

> The goal of the Kasbah system is to help realize a fundamental
> transformation in the way people transact goods—from requir-

---

* "This theory (society of mind) explores how phenomena of mind emerge from
the interaction of many disparate agencies, each mindless by itself"; from
a review of current research at the MIT Media Lab, posted on the Net at
<http://www.media.mit.edu>.

ing constant monitoring and effort—to a system where a soft-ware agent does most of the work on the user's behalf. A user wanting to buy or sell a good creates an agent, gives it some strategic direction, and sends it off to the agent marketplace. The Kasbah agents proactively seek out potential buyers or sellers and negotiate with them on their creator's behalf. The agent's goal is to make the "best deal" possible, subject to a set of user-specified constraints, such as a desired price, a highest (or lowest) acceptable price, and a date to sell (or buy) by.[6]

Strange new breeds of consciousness have begun to flourish outside our heads on the Net: real-time, self-adjusting databases; distributed parallel processing of converging data structures; intermediate, anonymous, synchronous, and asynchronous mind collectives on MUDs and MOOs; intelligent avatars meeting real humans on 2-D and 3-D Webs; enduring, cross-referenced, indexed, and automatically updated conferences and discussion groups on usenets and newsnets; self-adjusting expert systems with neural networks.

CONNECTING CONSCIOUSNESS

The development of intermediate stages of conscious processing is happening not only in terms of our personal relationship to computers, but also in the dynamics of computers within the electronically networked environment. Indeed, this artificial consciousness can be shared, and this sharing possibility allows virtual reality access to the principal characteristic of conventional, objective reality. VR pioneer Jaron Lanier rightly observed that in his invention RB-2 (Reality Built for Two), for the first time in human history, a world had been created where people could experience a form of subjectivity as if it were objective, without it being a dream. Five years before people even conceived of 3-D "worlds" on-line, Lanier predicted that VR would someday join the telephone and become what it was always meant to be, a communication system. The Internet delivers the promises of virtual reality, which is to make real-time, instant imagination "objective."

There are a number of developments in telecommunications and VR that point to a new tendency: reality is reconstructing itself virtually, no longer simply with the naive simulations of media park environments, but with real data. When the virtual serves to augment rather than to replace the actual, it becomes a form of "augmented reality" (AR), especially when it is endowed with real-time telepresence. Video conferencing is a sort of entry-level augmented reality. It does more than add visual cues to the voice on the phone; it extends space. The sense of the reality of the space at the other end of the video-conference signal is very strong, almost as concrete as in face-to-face presence. AR generates an active link between perception, technology, and world. As a significant and reliable extension of our sensory access to the world, AR may very well be the true destiny of VR.

Perhaps the most representative of these developments is T-Vision, Art + Com's magnificent geographical information system interface.* It allows users to travel digitally from outer space all the way down to the street level of a city, say Berlin, and connect seamlessly with data arriving in real time from satellites, or from film archives, or even from live video cameras. T-Vision is the projection of planet Earth on a screen in 3-D.

As you "fly" over Tokyo or Berlin, you can call up real-time satellite data about the city's weather conditions, or connect with one of its TV or radio stations for the latest news, or go to its stock exchange board, and so on. What you see, if you choose to "land," is an analogue image, in 3-D, of the streets of the city. If you want to enter one of its virtually constructed buildings, you can fly into it. You can even enter a virtual office, sit at a virtual computer, and perform real

---

* Although it is not quite out on the Net at this writing, T-Vision is one of the prime candidates for today's best interpretations of webness. It was granted the prize for the art form with the most significant potential impact on society at the 1995 Interactive Media Festival in Los Angeles.

data processing, if you so desire, taking advantage of the specific performance capabilities of the real computer represented by that simulation in that virtual office. If, perchance, you would like to see what is happening at that very moment in the real street outside the virtual office, just check the output of one of the video cameras looking out the virtual windows onto the actual street.

It is but a modest step beyond this to imagine that we might one day transport ourselves anywhere on the globe and land there in a "live" environment. In the same way, we would be able to travel in time via recorded or simulated data. T-Vision accomplishes the exact opposite of what *Star Trek*'s "beam me up, Scotty" transporter technology purports to do: instead of dematerializing the traveller, it dematerializes the whole world. The effect, however, is the same: you get to where you want to go. In that regard, T-Vision as a concept is closer to television, its namesake, than to the computer because TV brings you the world, while computer networks bring you *to* the world.

The T-Vision interface puts the world in the palm of your hand, so to speak. In doing so it may be indicating the point at which the new, digital media and the Net are merging because it is the interface par excellence for internalizing in each one of us our new body image, that of the globe itself. Of course, with the imminent rapid growth of high-bandwidth network pathways, students, engineers, entrepreneurs and professionals of every stripe could soon have access to a kind of instantly available Macro-Web of the real world. This would facilitate finding and processing of records, checking inventories, giving demonstrations, consulting and diagnosis, as well as multiplying the points-of-sale for business. But the destiny of T-Vision, though it will certainly need the support of business to be fully developed, is not to sell more stuff. (That it will do this goes without saying.) The deeper message is that instead of sending people off down yet another escape/fantasy byway like television, T-Vision, while being the *summum* of simulation, in fact brings the user back to the real. It establishes the potential for a direct person-to-planet continuity. In that regard, the T-Vision interface is without question one of the most important on-line creations, short of the invention of the Web itself.

PLANETIZATION

The development of networks and connectedness have given birth to a powerful new technological metaphor, which affects everyday space-time perception. The principal technologies of communication have until now tended to affect people's perception of their environment in terms of size, layout, texture, and, of course, limits. If literacy and print, by externalizing and focusing attention on local languages in visual form, created a consciousness of "the Nation" and the need to specify and control its "natural" boundaries, electronic media have tended to blow these boundaries away and thus expand the size of the mental representation of pertinent space. Television, for example, began the "planetization" of consciousness by giving its audience live access to various parts of the world. Satellite images, by highlighting the contours of continents, redefined geography for the average TV watcher checking out tomorrow's weather. What network connectedness is adding to these unconscious media influences is the opportunity for spectators to become participants.

The entire world can be perceived as an input-output environment. We are continuously projecting ourselves via all our senses, and with the electronic extensions of our hands, eyes, ears, and voice, we have acquired the ability to project ourselves far beyond the limits of our bodies and to receive the projections of others as if we could "wear" them. Our new skin is very sensitive; it is made of the millions of interactions of computers and electronic webs all over the planet. This is a tactile world. Indeed, the world is not "out there" anymore, it is right here, under the skin of each of us. Now that we are extended beyond the boundaries of our biological being, it follows that eventually our psychological makeup will be modified accordingly.

CHAPTER TEN

THE CONNECTED
ECONOMY

THE TELECOM GIANT AT&T reports that its network set an all-time record during 1995, by handling a phenomenal 61.6 billion calls, an increase of 10.8 percent from the previous year. On an average business day, the network handles more than 200 million voice, data, and video calls. The network is 100 percent digital for all switched traffic and includes more than 2.75 billion circuit miles of transmission lines. Other telcos such as the new titan British Telecom, now augmented by MCI, have similar resources in place. If this is the planetary medium, what is the message? More particularly, what is the economic message?

Unsuspecting people think that the economy is a concrete, tangible reality describable in facts and figures. Of course, it isn't. Grammatically speaking, the economy is just a "collective," a general term used rather loosely to include all the events, activities, and behaviors related to the way people earn a living and spend their earnings. It's a figure of speech and, more often than not, there may be little if anything of substance to justify the ways we speak about it. Nevertheless, "the economy" has become, over the last few decades, a powerful concept that has a constant feedback effect on the behaviors it is supposed to merely describe. It sticks in people's minds in a generally vague and abstract way, but wisps of hearsay about its machinations often motivate their career and employment choices and their most valuable investments.

Globalized and networked, endlessly commented upon by the media, the economy has now become a conscious reality unifying the purposes of business, government, and society at large. In effect, the economy is pure mindware, a mainly—though by no means exclusively—self-organizing entity that often materializes out of rumors.

In different parts of the world and at different times, the state of the economic mind fluctuates between open and closed, bull and bear attitudes. As can be observed any day at any stock exchange, the economy is highly susceptible to moods and feelings. As Robert McIlwraith, a professor of psychology at the University of Manitoba and a Senior McLuhan Fellow, suggests, "Increasingly, economic data are psychological data." We are now, he says, entering the era of the "feelings economy":

Today, feedback about consumers' behaviors, audiences' reactions, and voters' opinions is nearly instantaneous, and the outgoing messages themselves are just as quickly modified by those responses, the two in constant dynamic interplay or dialogue. Among the advances in feedback technology, I include: constant public opinion polling (including "push" polls, which help to shape attitudes or raise the visibility of issues, rather than simply recording existing attitudes); feedback on consumer choice via electronic cash register and inventory control technology; electronic mail; fax and the Internet. All of these contribute to making the public reaction to any new development almost instantaneously available to the marketer, the corporate decision-maker, the financial manager, and the government policy-maker.

McIlwraith concludes:

Feelings used to be an epiphenomenon or a reaction to things that happened in the areas of finance, industry, trade, and government. Now, feelings are the primary commodity of this speed economy. Feelings are the main data and the main products of the electronic economy. Major economic events don't need to happen, except in the "virtual future" which is constantly modifying the present. The instant, electronic economy is, to a large extent, functionally detached from and independent of tangible goods and services. Financiers, businesses, and governments contend with each other to produce a certain psychological result, a product, in the consumer: optimism, economic anxiety, hedonistic euphoria, caution, which feelings will enrich one or another sector financially. There's big money to be made (or lost) if you invest in the right (or wrong) feelings.[1]

There is an "economic unconscious" in most of us, which drives our decisions much more than rational examinations of our financial assets and situation. Even impoverished people budget what little they have in response to hearsay. For those who have money, investment seems to work by averaging hearsay with advice and hunch. There need not be a connection between the real and the invested value. The recent fortunes of such stocks as those of Netscape last year and more recently of Yahoo!, which jumped to 154 percent of its initial value in the first day of issue, bear witness to this emotional dimension of investment, and hence of the economy generally. The trust that people put in promising, but immature, technology can never be underestimated. That trust endures in spite of endless, highly publicized disappointments, perhaps because so many of the technological advances we've experienced in our lifetimes have arrived suddenly and exceeded expectations.

Noah Kennedy has observed that "the modern world has reached the point where industrialization is being directed squarely at the human intellect."[2] One of the striking features of networked communications is that while they may appear on the surface to be so much hardware and software, in reality, they are supported by a great deal of biological activity, namely, the people sitting at the computer terminals. It is really *people* who connect through networks, not just their machines. But they connect with the immaterial products of their minds. Business consequently has become accustomed to consider such imponderables as "intellectual capital" and "knowledge-based industries" as important assets.

Since the beginning of the Industrial Revolution, more and more consciousness has percolated through the activities that give rise to the economy. For example, during the heyday of television, the main driving force of the economy was not goods and services themselves, but, via advertising and packaging, information about those products and services. The primary effect of this early form of dematerialization of industry was to accelerate the production, delivery, and turnover of goods. The secondary effect was to accelerate the circulation of money. The tertiary effect was to include, accelerate, and render more complex the role of consciousness in the economy. Today, as the ratio of services over manufacturing in the economy increases continuously and as more and more material goods are digitized, the total ratio of "mindware" over hardware is also increasing rapidly. It is the increasing ratio of conscious to unconscious drives in the production, packaging, and delivery of goods and services that shapes much of the thinking about the "New Economy."

The law of network connectedness is that a simple linear curve of connections leads to an exponential multiplication of interconnections. In turn, this multiplication of interconnections gives rise to emergent markets made of new configurations within the network. One of the effects of instant communications networks on new forms of business developments has been spotted by economist W. Brian Arthur under the name of "increasing returns" which "are mechanisms of positive feedback that operate—within markets, businesses, and industries—to reinforce that which gains success or aggravate that which suffers loss." Arthur sees this new trend as something inherent in knowledge-based industries which, unlike the goods-based industries of the industrial era, are capable of indefinite expansion.

As the economy shifts steadily away from the brute force of things into the powers of mind, from resource-based bulk-processing into knowledge-based design and reproduction, so it is shifting from a base of diminishing returns to one of increasing returns. A new economics—one very different from that in the textbooks—now applies, and nowhere is this more true than in high technology. Success will strongly favor those who understand this new way of thinking.[3]

The phenomenon of increasing returns depends on two things: one, the unlimited expandability of software; the other, the instant feedback of current information. The idea could become one of the first principles of a new economy based not on scarcity but on plenty. As Arthur explains:

Increasing returns generate not equilibrium but instability: If a product or a company or a technology—one of many competing in a market—gets ahead by chance or clever strategy, increasing returns can magnify this advantage, and the product or company or technology can go on to lock in the market. More than causing products to become standards, increasing returns cause businesses to work differently, and they stand many of our notions of how business operates on their head.[4]

Kevin Kelly also includes "increasing returns" among the twelve main features of the New Economy and explains it this way:

Them that has, gets. Them that gives away and shares, gets. Being early counts. A network's value grows faster than the number of members added to it. A 10 percent increase in customers for a company in a non-networked economy may increase its revenue 10 percent. But adding 10 percent more customers to a networked company, such as a telephone company, could increase revenues by 20 percent because of the exponentially greater numbers of conversations between each member, both new and old.[5]

The basic theory is that while the old economy was constructed on material objects and the ultimate scarcity of resources, the new one is being built around the unlimited abundance associated with the production and distribution of ideas or mindware. The control strategies implied are very different: to manage growth in an environment of scarcity is to allocate limited resources among competing demands. To manage mindware growth is to multiply connections, checks and balances, applications, trial and error, in order to optimize uptake. Another "New Economist," Paul Romer, draws similar conclusions from the shift to software industries and the inexhaustibility of ideas. Inspired by Robert Solow's observation that 80 percent of economic growth comes from technological change, Romer proposes that "new ideas, embedded in technological change, drive economic growth and allow us to escape the gaunt future economists have so often imagined."

Today, an important business strategy in software development is to make it available for free so as to develop a client base, and then to cash in with ancillary services. The basic problem, as seen by both Romer and Arthur, is the risk involved in the front-end investment. In the economy of software, the price of market entry is very high. For Arthur, the whole exercise is one big gambling act. If you are clever and lucky, your idea catches on, finds associates, and snowballs to a critical mass of users before the competition has found the time or resources to undercut you. Even if your software isn't the best available, it can become the industry standard, as so many Microsoft products have. You have then hit the jackpot. However, you have at the same time become an ipso facto monopoly, so that when you think of, for example, buying out Quicken to secure control of all financial transactional software, antitrust regulation raises its democratic head. When the risk is so high, where is the incentive to invest?

The solution proposed by Romer might be called time-release monopolies. He suggests that regulatory authorities provide for "monopolistic competition," by which he means that in a given industry, say telecommunications, a company is licensed for a limited period of monopolistic privilege in the market until its product has been fully developed and partly distributed, at which point the protection is lifted and the competition is allowed to enter.* While a danger of this strategy is that it can allow industry complacency to set in, one way to moderate the risk might be to subject the monopoly holder to regular "creativity assessment" checkups, as a condition of license.

Money, of course, pioneered the trend from hardware to software. It is now shifting from discrete and batch-mode to continuous modalities. In fact, the intelligence of money parallels that of networks. Automatic banking machines created a unity of purpose and a seamless functionality worldwide long before anybody had heard about the Internet. Visa, Mastercard, and American Express went a step further in connecting banks both to people and to services and goods providers: their cards "hypertextualize" transactions, just as the Web connects not just databases but also the contents of databases. The next step is to emulate the "embedded Internet," that is, to go fully digital. Money is indeed migrating to the networks, as evidenced by almost monthly announcements of new on-line banking and payment services—CyberCash, Netbill, DigiCash, Millicent, First Virtual, etc.

Electricity and digitization allow any sequential process to be measured, scanned, priced, tracked, and debited or credited continuously. The ideal currency of the digital economy is the bit itself. In McLuhan's jest, "Currency is current," there are two—maybe more—layers of puns: one is that, what is actual and newsworthy is valuable and can be exchanged for currency; but the more profound pun is that electrical current is the latest form of money. Where cash was discrete, credit cards, debit cards, and "smart cards" are leading to continuous streaming of transactions. Where money was static and purely representational, on-line accounts will be dynamic and directly active. This could eventually change the status of money

---

* This is what de facto has occurred with Bell Canada, protected by regulation from competition by the cable industry for the delivery of telephone services, and with most of the European telcos, protected from each other until 1998 (or 2003 in the case of Portugal).

from a tool to represent value to one which actually *is* value, i.e., energy. You will plug into your digibank much the way we plug into the electricity network. Like the lives of a digital character in a video game, the infusions that you accumulate in your smart card, or your digital "mint," represent direct payment. You transfer power and energy from server to server.

Pierre Lévy, Nicholas Negroponte, John Perry Barlow, Don Tapscott, and scores of other observers note that the character of the digital economy is that its products can be given out without either losing their quality of originality or leaving the possession of the original owner, which is another key aspect of an economy of plenty. There can't be a conventional economy at all if expensive information, digitized and on-line, becomes both available for free, and open to perfect reproduction. Digitization, convergence, and public networked communications bring enormous copyright management problems to information-providers from the tiniest independent software creator to the biggest publishing corporation. Anybody and everybody can get the data on the fly and redistribute it either free of charge, or for a profit that is shared neither by the publisher nor the author. This is a very complex question and solutions will require collaboration and understanding on the part of governments, publishers, authors, communication industries, and banks.

One part of the answer to the copyright question may be offered by the digital technologies that caused the "problem" in the first place. In principle, all information can be labeled digitally and thus made traceable wherever it appears and is incorporated into a product, hard or soft, on- or off-line. This is done with encryption, a coding instruction system that writes a constant signature on the digital data stream.*

---

* To encrypt or label digital data, all that is necessary is to add a coded pattern in the combinations of 0/1 pulses that constitute the sequence of bits. This pattern is invisible, but ever present and impossible to remove without destroying the object data.

Encryption has three very important features that could pave the way for the introduction of a new payment system:

1. The encryption codes allow automatic monitoring, accounting, and copyright payment distribution.
2. The code is always present, even in the smallest segments of the stolen material, and thus will make fraudulent use traceable and actionable.
3. The digital data stream will never have to be stored in any one particular place. Libraries, for example, would simply be instructed to redirect on-line queries to the appropriate publisher's database, and they could even be allowed to collect a minor toll fee for the service of redirection, if their server was queried and prepared for precisely that configuration of data searches. This could generate a form of collaboration between authors, publishers, and libraries which would solve some, if not all, of the vexing problems of copyright infringements in the networked environment.

The inventor of hypertext, Ted Nelson, concedes that the Web is a rough approximation of what he had in mind—with one critical difference: the Web does not allow for automated copyright management. Nelson's Xanadu, the Web's prefiguration, goes a big step farther than simply organizing a way for people to receive their royalties. His notion of "transcopyright" is that any material used by an independent information-provider can be debited at the user and credited to the source through automated billing systems. In turn, the new content or framework given to the borrowed material is to be considered, in essence, to be new material. Any further use of the new combination of old content and new framework would bring revenue to the new user. This model of transcopyright would serve as an inducement to a collaborative rather than an exclusively competitive model of the economy.

Like the market, the corporate culture will change profoundly in the New Economy. Joel de Rosnay coined the term "coopetition" to express this new combination of competition and collaboration. While the existing one-way market psychology will continue, partly by the force of inertia, partly because there is still a real need for it in slower cultures, the leaders of the new industry will be those who have understood that the mood and the mode have changed. Something like a mutation is happening to the edges of innovation and communication. The electronic tribe is younger, less politicized, more interested in collaboration than competition, less hung up on short-term profits, and more aware of the needs of the whole ecosystem. They don't like war; they neither profit from nor by it. They can handle any culture in any number of combinations. They are connectors and networkers.

Knowledge-based businesses, from content-providers to software developers and media, need to consider decentralizing their operations if only to keep their best people interested enough to remain with them. Intelligence is not a hierarchical process, but a connected one. Nothing paralyses the individual mind more than a single obsessive concern, i.e., a top-down mind-set. Brian Arthur points out that the basic people-management strategy for ensuring increasing returns is different from more traditional approaches in process industries. For example:

> Competition is different in knowledge-based industries because the economics are different. If knowledge-based companies are competing in winner-take-most markets, then managing becomes redefined as a series of quests for the next technological winner—the next cash cow. The goal becomes the search for the Next Big Thing. In this milieu, management becomes not production oriented but mission oriented. Hierarchies flatten not because democracy is suddenly bestowed on the work force or because computers can cut out much of middle management. They flatten because, to be effective, the deliverers of the next-thing-for-the-company need to be organized like commando units in small teams that report directly to the CEO or to the board.[6]

In fact, the new trend is not merely to create small, efficient teams intramurally, but to go out and seek ideas from nonresident "wild men" and women, that is, nonexperts and consultants with far-out ideas. In an environment in which information is available all around you, it isn't what you know that is worthwhile, but what you don't know. The wilder the merrier. Properly framed, ignorance is truly bliss.

In one of his lesser known books, *Take Today: The Executive as Drop-Out,* McLuhan identified three main characteristics of the economy unfolding in the early seventies as:

- a general shift from hardware to software
- a radical decentralization trend affecting most economic and social activities
- a general shift from jobs to roles

The most original observation here is the one that concerns jobs, which are now becoming a dwindling resource for keeping people busy (i.e., for employment), and are being replaced by an attitude characterized by a general readiness to drop out and face any new situation as it turns up. Convergence of media is also leading to convergence of skills and abilities. McLuhan also predicted that women would be better prepared than men to face the requirements of a just-in-time economy, due to their wider-ranging skills and more generalized abilities.

In the late sixties and early seventies, many executives dropped out to "get a life." They wanted more out of their existence than the humdrum of the rat race. Today, I know many cases of people who, far from waiting for the ship to start sinking, jump overboard on the rising curve of their capabilities to start a consulting relationship with the very company they have just left. Even top executives frequently leave prominent or protected positions at the pinnacle of their careers to strike out on their own. The economist David Foot, a colleague at the University of Toronto who recently published a best-seller on current demographics, has created a chart which compares different "Career Paths and Associated Characteristics."*

Career Path	Job Mobility	Occupations	Organization	Reward
Steady State	none	one	rectangular	tenure
Linear	upward	two	tall pyramid	power
Spiral	lateral	five +	flat pyramid	skills
Transitory	lateral	many	just-in-time	interest

The number of jobs available in the first two categories ("Steady State" and "Linear") are dwindling as the enduring deficit-fighting economy is motivating closure of government services and the merging of companies and industries. As jobs become scarcer, professionals de-specialize to take on different roles, readying themselves for any circumstance. They have learned that beyond a certain time in one's life, too much expertise can be a liability. People dropping out, both those who have jumped and those who have been pushed, have to consider retuning themselves and creating their own job opportunities. It is from the last two categories that the new consultants are spawned, with highly developed skills and their own networks of business and government contacts. The connected economy provides them with more tools for survival than ever before.

The new connected economy unfolding is not one of clearly defined consumers and producers; it is an economy of networks. And the jobs of the future will involve creative and applied thinking on the part of everybody, not just the experts. These jobs will involve shaping, processing, editing, distributing, and treating information as a source of income and deep growth. They will involve connecting people at the right time in the right configuration for the right purpose. The connected responds best to autonomy and self-organizing principles. The Internet is not a mass medium: it is not a one-way medium. It is not even a two-way medium. It's a "my-way" medium.

---

* Reproduced, with permission, from a conference slide shown by David Foot at the CIBC Learning Centre, July 23, 1996.

When everything and everybody is on-line, everybody has something to say about what's worthy to be read, seen, watched, and done on-line. That means that the user, not the producer of information, is in the driver's seat.

The incipient trend is already plainly visible, away from the conventional broadcast model of production, distribution, and delivery towards a more flexible, personalized, and empowered network model. In the mass media market model borrowed from the old military-industrial complex, big corporations would identify or generate average tastes in goods and services, promote them by advertising, and deliver them in uniformly packaged products and deals. Today, thanks to the versatility of computerized data-retrieval and specification-design, it is possible to "mass customize" products. But the action is already moving elsewhere in small, fast, easy-to-assemble and disassemble units of production and consumption. Yesterday's customer was a docile consumer: today she has become an aggressive just-in-time producer, thanks to ever greater access to means of production. Karl Marx said that everything would be all right when the means of production were finally in the hands of the workers. What is in the hands of workers today? Desktop management, tools of information production, and network management or distribution.

Paradoxically, while so much of the overstimulated media coverage of the vaunted Information Highway is about the carriers and the infrastructure, ultimately the sectors of the economy which stand to gain the most are not the carriers, but the content suppliers, publishers, and users—that is, you and me, provided that we are given the means to put ourselves on-line (and "on-the-line"). It is user demand that will finally prevail in the rewiring of nations, not the industry's internal priorities. And it is the user who will provide most of the content that will eventually be bought and sold in the economy of mind. McLuhan suggested that if the medium were indeed the message, then the user ought to be the real content of his or her engagement with the medium. This is never more true than with connected media. It is quite obvious that anyone who speaks on the telephone provides the content of that medium. However, carriers who now vie to become content-providers don't quite see it that way, because they hope to make money from offering the content as well as carrying the data. The mistake being made by both big business and government regulators is in continuing to treat the general public and the potential networker as a consumer, rather than a producer. They continue to think in terms of numbers instead of configurations, to worry about controls instead of searching for new forms of collaboration with that public they often take for granted.

What is needed, and as soon as possible if we are to develop an authentic and durable connected economy, is access to "bandwidth on demand," controllable not only by the producer but also by the user of information. The quickest way to educate and retrain a whole population of workers is to give them access to network bandwidth, the way they have access to TV and to the telephone. They will produce their own content and find their own networks, and soon enough be able to live off these new relationships. Depending upon how radical the effects of computer education will have been on the present and the next generation, people with more brain and less brawn (*dixit* Don Tapscott) will grab control of their own economy.

It has often been observed that on-line, David and Goliath, you and MGM, are on a par. It's a great thought, and a great hope for a radical restructuring of the economy, but it is certainly not a given. Critics have been prompt to remind us that we have heard all of this before; we were to be liberated in turn by the invention of the telephone, of radio, of television, and most recently by cable. As Allucquère Rosanne Stone puts it so wittily: "Cyberspace can be viewed as a toolkit for reconfiguring consciousness in order to permit things to go on much in the same way." The example of the cable industry is a particularly apt one in that few communication industries have been better and quicker at breaking promises and making money doing so. As late as 1973 a cable industry spokesman claimed that "cable can become a medium for local action instead of a distributor of prepackaged mass-consumption programs to a passive audience."7 Of course, it didn't work out that way.

Democratically equitable and economically valuable access to the worldwide networks will eventually depend on how well big business and government collaborate to manage its distribution. This is assuming that governments stay in the driver's seat long enough to have a say in the matter! The present reality is that national sovereignty is threatened by global corporations as the multinationals of yesterday are replaced by global corporations. The very idea of nation fades away. Then again, the nation-state was itself a product of a defining technology, the printing press. With the ascendance of electricity, there is a consequent overriding of the print-inspired hierarchical management of precise geographical boundaries. The consequence of huge mergers such as that of British Telecom and MCI could be that the role of the corporate global state is no longer so much to establish and maintain national sovereignty, as to provide the unified infrastructure necessary for a renewed localism. The era of the single global village—the time of television's visual representations of a single, unified, real geographical space—is over. The concept best adapted to the networked condition is "global villages"—that is, real space locally, but virtual interactions globally.

The thinking of government in the advanced industrial states remains by and large stuck in the worn-out groove of apportioning scarce resources, whether in terms of bandwidth allocation or licensing of content delivery. This defensive posture is inherently weak. The assertive approach would be to do everything possible to optimize the connectedness of the nation. That translates, first of all, into encouraging and supporting—financially, if need be—cable, telco, and even hydro joint ventures; second, combining these initiatives with educational programs that put the power of creation and idea development in the hands of the people, rather than exclusively under the control of established developers and information providers; third, maximizing access to copyright-free public domain material. The people of democratic nations pay for cultural content through the tax dollars that go to educational and cultural, as well as national media institutions. Assuming that a suitable way can be found to compensate the original creators of content, the availability of such content to the people at large for reuse in new contexts should be unfettered. If every time I had a new thought in my mind, I had to rebuild and pay for all the bits and pieces of thinking I had done and stored before, I would probably never have another new thought at all.

In short, if governments the world over understand where their future lies, they will come to the inevitable conclusion that they should assume the leadership in promoting connectedness rather than leaving it to international corporations, as they tend to do today.

CHAPTER ELEVEN

PLANETIZATION

T HERE IS A LOT of loose talk in business, government, and education circles about "globalization." McLuhan is quoted knowingly and incessantly about the "global village." Hardly anyone, on the other hand, talks about "planetization." Though the word smacks of New Age babble, I find it useful in differentiating the inner from the outer point of view of the Earth. Globalization is the process of technological and economic expansion from here to there. Planetization, on the other hand, is the view from above, from the satellite. When people look at satellite images of the Earth on the weather report on TV, what they are watching is planet Earth. Thus planetization is an issue of human consciousness, namely the conscious integration of the Earth's dimensional reality, while globalization is an issue of geopolitics. Ecology, and the ecological sensibility which is now much in evidence among the newer generations in the advanced postindustrial countries, belongs to the "planet" side of the equation, since the fundamental reality of any ecological consideration, is, of course, the planet itself.

NETWORKS AND DEVELOPMENT

While it is clear that the Internet is growing faster than any technology in history, according to Dan Schiller, there are three sobering statistics to consider:

1. At the end of 1995, the total number of computers in the world was still under 200 million, against a global population of six billion which puts at 3 percent the maximum access to networks by individuals.
2. At the same time, over 75 percent of the world's main telephone lines served less than 15 percent of the world population.
3. A typical wired family in the U.S. (more than 40 percent of the total) earned over $75,000.

And, as if such obstacles to universal access to a unified networked environment were not enough, Schiller points out that there are four times as many closed networks, i.e., intranets, usually reserved to people with means, than there are open access networks within the Internet. His prognosis is not encouraging because he predicts that excessive privatization and crude commercial interests will tend to further limit network development to larger concentrated markets rather than expanding access across the board.

The University of Montreal's Michael Carter is no less pessimistic in his assessment of what's in store for the developing world in an era of networked communication:

The question of national sovereignty is related to the ability of a nation state to cope with transnational mega-mergers which have less and less national loyalty. If the global market paradigm holds, even in developed countries there will be some second-tier and second-rate players and in the rest of the planet a vast, information-dependent Third World.*

By and large, Carter is right about the fact that, in the present transitional state from the Industrial Age to the new era of information processing, the governments of the world have tended to delegate their responsibilities to big business. That is an unsettling development. Among the G-7 nations, for example, Italy and France

---

* From an on-line discussion about cultural and technological hegemony.

stand out for having decided to protect cultural interests locally, while every other country seems willing to delegate that responsibility to the market. But in a world of networks, which is where we assuredly are headed, whether or not the implementation of new technologies in the less developed countries is a happy experience is dependent on the degree to which people in authority understand the potentials and the pitfalls. The outcome cannot simply be abandoned to the machinations of corporations and the market.

The patterns of implementation of network communication differ from country to country. In the developed world the approach has tended to be "put in a backbone," analogous to the central spine of a nervous system. This is normally done by the telephone system. The backbone, however, is not typically the way less developed countries go about it, because they seldom have the required infrastructure in place. Furthermore, they seldom have the required cash or the ability to attract adequate outside investment.

One alternative is being pioneered in South America under the auspices of the Organization of American States. U.S.A. International Development, the World Health Organization, and several other United Nations agencies are putting together, with regional collaboration, the rudiments of networks and the rudiments of connections. Anywhere that it's difficult to make the connections because wires are lacking, a start is being made on packet-radio switching to close the gaps.

While institutional initiatives like this one are to be welcomed, the fact is that in network development, the hard work of individuals can make an enormous difference. Committed people are the hormones of this global nervous system. This is what I call the homeopathic value of communications: where there is a will, there is a way. Even in remote areas, people connect among themselves and then move ahead to create local networks.* For example, Africa

---

* These embryonic networks often run on pre-Internet software known as FIDO-net. FIDO-net is authentic grassroots technology which allows people to establish networks by connecting from one computer to another through existing telephone lines and in some cases using packet-radio links.

Online is the realization of the dream of a single Kenyan visionary. Its server has to deal with store-and-transfer problems and all kinds of obstacles at the technical level, but it's there. And a lone professor from the University of Rhodes in South Africa is largely responsible for wiring the whole of the south of that continent.

Bill Buxton, once my colleague at the University of Toronto, and now a consultant with Alias Research, is one of the most interesting thinkers on development issues and new technologies. However, we rarely agree on how to interpret trends. He says: "Fifty percent of the world's population doesn't have access to a telephone and here you are talking about the Information Highway in Africa! Who are you kidding?" He argues that there are three fundamental access issues in any country, developed or less-developed, when it comes to the communication infrastructure.

The first issue is technical, relative to the existing infrastructure in developing countries. This is a well-known problem in Africa, where telephone lines are what they are. Furthermore, the technical support for that infrastructure is often lacking or inadequate. The hardware needed for terminals, the required software, and software management and maintenance are also unevenly distributed. Where equipment is in place, it is often obsolete. There is no denying these very real difficulties, and so it is all the more heartening to discover that there is in fact anything on-line at all in Rwanda or Somalia. There is evidence that, at least in some African countries, the situation is improving.

With the rapid development of wireless technologies and the continuous drop in the price of mobile telephony, technical or infrastructure issues of access may not remain intractable problems. Wireless satellite communication is still in its infancy; eventually the technology will be ubiquitous and cheap. The technology has already made significant inroads in China and India. Among the uses of low-bandwidth data communications via satellite or cellular technologies, data transmission (i.e., the Internet and other networks) is beginning to move ahead of voice communication in line of priority. People now want a phone not just to talk, but also with which to do their work. The infrastructure obstacles facing the Third World may have a wireless solution.

As for the distribution of hardware, the solution is already evident in mass production of increasingly powerful and sophisticated computer chips. When we talk about media, communication, computers, and the technoculture that is just over the horizon, we should never forget that over the last twenty years motor cars have gone up in price and only marginally improved in utility, while during the same period, computers have plummeted in price and soared in service. It should also be borne in mind that rapid improvements in computer hardware and software render the previous generation obsolescent, and not obsolete. Used appropriately, older equipment can be of great value. One can even imagine a computer industry geared specifically to the needs of developing regions, producing robust, inexpensive equipment, perhaps from recycled components, for network access.

Buxton's second issue is financial. This is in fact a sticky problem, though not just in the developing world. Europeans, and not just the less developed countries, have traditionally used their telcos as cash cows. They constantly fiddle with rates and surcharges and oblige users to pay through the nose for what North Americans get very cheaply. As an example, university Internet access in North America is virtually free, while in France users are billed by the minute.

This is an exceedingly shortsighted strategy on both sides of the development gap and one that can cripple an economy vis-à-vis its worldwide competition. The only sane policy is to maximize use (and revenues) by making access universal and inexpensive. In practical terms, this is about a three- to four-year cycle of legislation, regulation, and implementation.

A related question is being asked in both developed and developing countries: where will the jobs of tomorrow come from? It's clear that government won't supply them, and business won't either—certainly not traditional business in any case. However there are employment opportunities in the information sectors of the economy and these are increasing in both number and scope as the Web continues to develop. So the issue of access is an absolutely critical one in terms of the new production environment. I would venture to predict that governments in Europe, certainly, will recognize the folly of imposing artificial financial barriers to access sooner rather than later. When, in 1998, the European Community opens its gates to true competition in telecommunications, at least for long-distance operations, there should be a rapid drop of rates in Europe, which will probably signal a decline elsewhere as well.

According to Buxton, the definitive access issue is neither technical nor financial, but cognitive. How well prepared is any given culture to absorb and deal with the new technologies? The first consideration here has to be the average local level of education. The problem is that with the less costly, text-intensive versions of networked communications, more or less fluent literacy is required of users. To the extent that network access is in demand in Africa, it is a demand which tends to be urban, professional, university, and business-based.

Let us assume, on the other hand, that the basic conditions of financial, technical, and cognitive preparedness for network communications are somehow met for the nations of Africa. What benefits might be expected to follow? Would the effort prove worthwhile?

At the moment, *80 percent* of what is known about Africa is in European and U.S. databases, not accessible to Africans because so few of them have access to the Web.

This is an enormous resource denied to people locally: it includes statistics about jobs and disease patterns, geographical information, environmental data, history, culture—basically, the memory of the continent. Perhaps even more distressing is the issue of "Lost Science in the Third World," as described in *Scientific American:*

> Many researchers in the developing world feel trapped in a vicious circle of neglect and some say prejudice by publishing barriers they claim doom good science to oblivion.[1]

Not only are Africans denied access to information, they are denied access to today's foremost means of information distribution.

The other side of the same coin is that African countries have better access to U.S. and European news than to news about their own neighbors. This is because the information moving between two neighboring countries in Africa travels on foot or by radio and television with all of their inherent delays and censorship opportunities, and it travels on-line instantly to the U.S. and Europe.

The less developed countries have other unique problems. Government policies may be unfriendly to Net access not just because of the cash-cow issue, but because of the need for governments to tightly control information in undemocratic societies. Even among the long-established democracies, including both France and the U.S., governments are loath to permit private citizens access to sophisticated encryption software: in France it is controlled under military secrecy legislation.

In 1996, China gave us an intriguing new example of government control. The leadership there dreamed up the nation-based Intranet. The ostensible motivation is to protect the people of China from too much foreign cultural influence. At the same time, Beijing does not want to miss out on the economic opportunities of networked communications. So the idea is to erect an electronic Great Wall to keep the enemy out. The so-called firewall technique is one used by many corporations to protect their internal networks from outsiders while still allowing employees to access the wider Internet. A firewall would allow authorities in Beijing to control access by Chinese citizens to the Internet, and access by outsiders to the Chinese Intranet. In theory. It is difficult, however, to see how Chinese citizens can be prevented from using long-distance telephone links to connect with Internet service providers outside their country.

Like the Great Wall, China's Intranet firewall plans are probably impractical in terms of the perceived threat of invasion. At a symbolic level, however, it may be quite effective. It is one more reflection of a fundamental concern of Chinese rulers from the early emperors through to Mao Tse-tung and Deng Xiaoping, which is the national unity of China. This ideal cuts across many languages and writing systems in China, but it means walling-in everything.

Political resistance to improving network infrastructure in developing nations is sometimes rationalized in terms of perceived dangers of *technological* imperialism or colonialism. This is a serious issue: after all, Western technology has already invaded a good half of the planet with the alphabet; now, with electricity, it is taking the whole thing. Is technological colonialism political colonialism in sheep's clothing, another threat along the lines of that presented by the insidious worldwide reach of the American television industry? Psychologically and technically we have done too much colonization from the West.

Neither should we underestimate the effects of the intensification of real-time, interactive distant communications in oral cultures already so sensitive to the amplification of orality. Radio has been used as an instrument of propaganda to disastrous effect in both the developed and the less developed world, and continues to be a very dangerous technology.* One can only hope that the Internet will prove to be more benign in this respect. My feeling is that it will be, because it is participatory, because it empowers the individual rather than putting people under the control of a central disseminating source as radio does. The Internet is not an authoritarian instrument in any sense. Although it is mediated by writing, anything that happens on the Internet is instant, so it resembles oral communication. Communication is archived and instantly retrievable. I think to that extent the Internet is a safe technology but I don't want to bet on it right now. Perhaps, by multiplying thus the possibility of private communication, the Net will help to tone down some of the power of tribal rhetoric typical of one-way-only radio transmission. This is a frail hope, I must confess, to offer a continent profoundly wounded by technology.

American television and the English language are two examples of world-conquering cultural technologies. A cultural technology is one that is so pervasive as to fundamentally influence the structure and behavior of communities. The old cultural technology of

* See Rwanda and Burundi for a lesson in the power of radio to foment hatred.

Europe and North America is still around and doing fine in the form of the self-consciousness created by the phonetic alphabet. It is true, however, that this literate mentality is being seriously challenged by the new electronic technologies, and that we are as yet only dimly aware of the consequences. (Most of us for that matter don't yet realize the extent to which we have been affected psychologically by learning to read and write.)

Every shift of media generates a new configuration of linguistic processing: the new configuration proposes a new mirror, and a new image of community to the users of the medium. The image is territorial and the size of the "land base" depends on the reach of the medium. The shift from oral to literate media, for example, introduced the need for well-defined national boundaries. Fierce colonial wars were waged against regional, nonconforming languages. National cultures were homogenized through the schools (among other means) but within those newly unified codes, individual personalities were permitted to develop and democracy eventually emerged in most Western nations.

With the shift from printed to electronic media, personal identities have been shaken and physical frontiers have been shredded. The impact on local language has varied; in some cases friction has arisen between linguistic groups. For example, the impact of television on French Canada helped to accelerate the *révolution tranquille*, the quiet but relentless development of Quebec's sense of separate identity, which has led to a quest for a "distinct society" status within the Canadian Constitution and growing agitation for outright sovereignty.

For a short while, electricity returned the Western cultures to oral conditions. Radio and television brought back the preliterate priority of context over text. They created instant mass audiences: Hitler's voice on radio helped to put Germany (and much of the rest of the industrial world) in uniform; television created a worldwide consumer society with its ideological center in the U.S.A. In the former Soviet Union, the power of electricity was muted by a totalitarian bureaucracy, with the consequence that local cultures were denied the right to evolve freely; today some of them resort to unspeakable violence to catch up.

The Internet is, without question, a cultural technology. In fact, with the Internet, culture itself becomes a technology, hence, the absolute necessity to allow differing cultures the chance to co-exist. In the new context of digitization, everything hard turns soft, everything static starts to move, the virtual takes over from the real, the local moves to global and back, and time becomes more critical than space. Very soon, not to say inevitably, the cultural should indeed become the dominant form of all technologies. The meaning of design, in terms of cultural rather than strictly industrial or scientific technology, is a form of cognition. We get to know things with the help of design. Thinking will sooner or later become equivalent to doing. When that happens, we will need every bit of long-term, multileveled cultural sophistication just to survive the speed of our own transformation.

SUSTAINABLE CULTURE

The McLuhan Program recently opened a "sustainable culture" unit. With all the talk about sustainable development and the blissful ignorance about the radical impact of technology on culture, we felt that there was a need to investigate what was durable and resilient about culture invaded by technology, especially foreign technology. While there is no evidence of a concept of "culture" anywhere but in Western tradition, the evidence of stubborn stability in even profoundly disturbed cultural ecologies is very much in evidence. For example, in Australia, aboriginal peoples have survived decimation by white settlers, after having managed through the strength of their culture to live through 50,000 years of radical technological penury. The fascinating aspect of aboriginal people, not only in Australia but also in Canada, the U.S., and of course in Africa, is that these are cultures that survive with minimal media and maximum language input.

Now a new cultural question has arisen beyond the issue of Western cultural imperialism. For how long, we must now ask, can the developed countries themselves maintain their distinct identities even in a tenuous form? In many countries, including Canada and France, voices have been raised in opposition to multicultural influences which threaten to tip the balance of white supremacy. While I do not share that kind of anxiety, I am curious to know how the Greco-Roman heritage will fare on the Internet.

What Westerners call culture—when they don't mean the opera—is what is left of the content of the Greco-Roman heritage and its consequences, principally the legacy of literacy as sustained by the written and the printed word. Literacy allowed the storage and transmission of the thought of officially recognized great persons of the past; they stood as models for emulation long after most other remnants of the culture were gone. The Renaissance was not merely a high point in the rebirth of humanism, it was a monumental double take on the culture of literacy. Born-again literates.

It will be interesting to study how much of that heritage survives on the Internet. We find the Greco-Roman legacy being transformed in postmodernism, of course, and we find the new cultural standards in the blending of all traditions in media and entertainment. What delights me about the film *Blade Runner*, for example, and makes me trust it as a believable forecast of what's coming, is not the idea of the replicants, sophisticated organic robots programmed for short-duration perfection, it is that the English language spoken in Los Angeles in 2019 is almost unrecognizable, so laden is it with contraction, slang, and foreign words. William Gibson's perceptive novels also capture the sense of otherness that can undermine cultural continuity, given enough time.

Popular culture does for most people what art does for the specialist, that is, it provides a multisensorial decor and collective icons. The advantage of popular culture is that it is popular. It spreads far and wide instantly, without stopping at local cultural barriers. It may also be a marketing racket, but it is a racket that works only because it finds an avid market. People subjected to rapid sociotechnological change need popular culture. Pop culture adjusts the rhythms, the palette, and the feel of the hidden effects of new technologies on the individual sensorium. Rock videos bring the senses together in a coherent synergy, involving a physical response on the part of the viewers or dancers. The sounds and rhythms of the times fill the airwaves and the supermarkets, trickle into gyms and restaurants, run along the highways and generally saturate the environment to set our biological clocks to the new beat of the computer or nanotechnology.

Pop culture icons, myths, public figures, and paraphernalia provide a content to anchor the floating shreds of meaning left over from previous eras. Like medieval heroes once were, presidents, entertainers, and sport idols are endowed with superhuman mental and physical attributes, not without a little help from marketing experts. We can absentmindedly pin our desires to them. They also give tangible shapes to the amorphous desires and unformed identity yearnings of millions of people in search of reflections. Like Madonna, they rise and they fall according to symbolic needs, rather than historical reality. A Michael Jackson and a J. F. Kennedy can remain "good symbolic value" until they are not needed anymore, at which point they are executed on a symbolical level, usually through the revelation of some scandalous episode. It isn't that the behavior is new or that no one knew about it, it is that now the behavior and the obsolescence of the public figure coincide. *Sic transit gloria mundi.*

The pathways followed by the relentless pressure for global cultural standardization are varied. Creeping uniformity can arise out of amplification (television is louder than books), reach (shortwave radio penetrates further than FM), and speed (fax is faster than mail). Oral media tend to homogenize cultures while written media often tolerate high levels of diversification.

Computers, of course, colonize their users before they go out and colonize anybody else, in a process that might be called psychotechnological colonialism. And I am not just talking about the tweaking of the user's mental habits; I am talking about language. English is the dominant language of the Internet. This is a significant issue at every level, not only in terms of the communication and/or violation of local sensibilities, but also in terms of ordinary training. It has become almost axiomatic that you have to learn English in order to learn computers.

Our perception of language is warped by literacy. Language is much more than a vehicle for meaning.* Language is the first mass medium. It is an environment, both within and without the body. The body speaks and is spoken; words result from networks of nervous impulses that reflect and affect both the physical and the social body. That is why language is so closely tied to identity, both private and collective. Communications media extend and prolong language by moving it out of bodies and manifesting it in the environment. In this context, many kinds of nonverbal artifacts should be treated as linguistic forms as well: images and services coming from a specific community and contributing to the social construction of meaning; money; networks which allow for the circulation of meaning such as highways (land-based or electronic), the telephone, satellites. The sum total of these technological infrastructures creates huge linguistic environments which sometime threaten to wipe out local customs and identities. Technological colonialism may seem to be more radical than the military, political, and economic varieties, but it may also be part of a largely unconscious, self-organizing system. Violence results when cultures are rushed, but the new order insinuates itself inexorably, of its own accord.

Will English become a global language? The question may be moot, because the global networks, in seeking uniformity, can tolerate linguistic differences that will be gradually perceived as indispensable. New technologies may help to emphasize the value of local cultures by allowing people to explore the subtleties of nonverbal differences in languages. In the short term, however, the issue for many languages and cultures is survival. Strategies differ: former French president François Mitterand proposed that every Francophone be granted French citizenship (thus continuing a great tradition begun

---

* The key to this issue is in John Austin's assertion: "Words don't mean anything, people do."

by the Capetians). Native Canadian artist Lawrence Paul Yuxwelup-
tun has created a completely original and self-contained virtual reality environment called *Vision Rights, Inherent Rights,* where instead
of trying to tell the story of his people with words, he has chosen to
show it and make his audience live in it.

The worldwide evolution of networked communication is a
revolution of such historic importance that it demands humane
management and timely human intervention to correct market defi-
ciencies and correct injustices. It is important either to require from
industry that it develop a statesmanlike sense of responsibility, or to
insist on effective, morally informed oversight from responsible government. There may be, as cyber-utopians believe, a largely self-
organizing system at work, but, for the moment, it is primarily
self-serving. While some businesses are beginning to show a measure
of social responsibility, if only in their advertising campaigns, most
are still focused intently on the bottom line. There are good reasons
to fear a future where purely economic pressures could drive the
have-nots into permanent exclusion and misery.

At the same time it must be noted that, because of the implosive
tendencies of communication media, we are developing forms of
sensitivity that might be incompatible with the old dog-eat-dog
approach to society. A true sensitivity to the plight of peoples in the
emerging nations may overwhelm connected people and move them
to concerted action. The Berlin Wall fell as a result of such a wave of
emotional release. There is still time to turn things around and start
collaborating on the common welfare instead of forever competing
for shreds of our own flesh. The thought we have to connect with is
that the health of the whole body depends on the health of all its
parts and vice versa.

CHAPTER TWELVE

THINKING
THE EARTH

A SATELLITE gives people omniscience for a penny. The view from above, even if mediated by much interpretative technology, is comprehensive, to say the least. No matter what amount of technology intervenes, the end result is a reliable representation of what there is, and the biases of the computer data-rendering are known, adjusted, tested, and corrected to get as precisely factual a rendering of reality as possible. All the technological instruments and transformations required to make satellite images visible on a Web site, for example, amount to the equivalent of a pair of glasses. Nobody ever complained that spectacles distort reality; rather, they enhance access to it for those whose natural faculties are impaired. Let us then assume that a satellite image is as faithful a representation as what we might see with our own eyes.

The satellite vantage point is also becoming a personal one. Not too long ago, satellite images were accessible only to experts who could muster the considerable technological support necessary to interpret the data. Today, anybody on-line can access a weather site and obtain an image that was computed a few minutes earlier, straight from the satellite. The basic image will be continuously refreshed with new data, showing, for example, the minute-by-minute progress of a hurricane. Though it's getting to be a commonplace of on-line experience, I still marvel at the fact that I have personal access to this godlike view of my basic life-support system. Mine and everybody else's.

If we were to internalize the consequences of our technological innovations, especially those which extend our sensory reach well beyond our natural body's abilities, we would soon conclude that the standard psychology we have learned at home and in school, our everyday self-image, simply does not fit the scale that is now becoming the norm. If, for two thousand years, man was "the measure of all things," today the planet is the measure of all things. The change of scale brought to the content of our technology needs to be accompanied by a comparable change of scale in our psychological makeup.

We might say that satellites globalize the Earth for the common man. They make the planet whole again. Psychologically speaking, this situation is not entirely unprecedented, insofar as most ancient cosmogonies and most aboriginal religions did and do cultivate a sense of the world's unity. This point of view was arrived at, of course, without recourse to advanced technology, and one might argue that it is precisely because so much technology intervenes "between ourselves and our roots," as Philippe Boissonnet would say, that our fundamentally important relationship to the Earth is not immediately intuitive. To grasp it requires a leap to a higher order of perception, and to achieve this, people need to internalize the Earth.

If survival dictates priorities for the individual, it should dictate them too for the new kind of connected consciousness that our technologies are building around us. The new priority of a much-enlarged world population, more or less in touch and in sync via global communications but threatened with dissension and the depletion of vital resources, is to achieve a new self-image. This self-image will have to go beyond the skin, beyond the single point of view we carry within as a permanent reference for our position in space. From the earliest stirrings of the child's consciousness to the last thoughts of the dying, people need to "think the Earth." By this I mean we need to capture the whole planet within the realm of our consciousness, and beyond that, to add the image of the earth to the list of core constituents of selfhood.

A self-image that would include the Earth would have to transcend local differences and individual agendas without eradicating them. It would also have to be anchored in tactile as well as visual perceptions. It is not enough to see the Earth differently; we must also feel it differently. Some of this tactile contact may not be altogether pleasant, but that may be part of the bargain we strike for survival. The sensation of pain is not a punishment but a survival mechanism. If the Earth's body is the totality that is connected as a life source to my body, then, in a subtle way, I have to be able to feel its areas of friction and inflammation, I have to sense its fever. Indeed, whether I like it or not, the world has now become my backyard. Personally, I may not approve of the vertical integration of communication media or of huge corporate conglomerates which have profit more than our well-being or our enlightenment in mind, but I have to recognize that I benefit from them to a certain extent and that I share in the responsibility for their existence. I may balk at the dependence of wealthy industrialized countries upon the arms trade, which makes the world less safe to live in, but I can exercise the option not to invest in funds that might go to support that trade, even at a great remove. I may very well be against fundamentalism or the deforestation of the Amazon, or child labor, but in order to be in a position to overcome their negative influence on the health of the Earth, I have to first make them mine; that is, to recognize that they are a part of the total destiny of this planet of which I am a responsible and dependent part.

Media bring us to the world just as much as they bring the world to us. They make each one of us commensurate with the planet. Just as we are responsible for our own welfare and happiness, we are becoming responsible—whether we are willing to recognize this or not—for that part of us which now extends far into and around the Earth. The self-centered ego is now seeking a counterpart in the world perceived as an extension of self. Furthermore, our minds are being extended far and wide and accelerated by our computerized technology. Ecological consciousness is not only a matter of global hygiene, it is also the best metaphor for the expansion of our minds to global dimensions. Media technology is approximating the mind and enabling it to command material change in real time.

Nowadays so much of our technology is geared to information processing rather than industrial production that perhaps a quarter of the world's population is engaged in activities more closely related to mind than to matter. While such activities do not necessarily interconnect, more and more they are evolving in ways that will make interconnection a purpose, not just a consequence. New technologies are now promoted by popular metaphors such as "virtual reality," "information highway," "personal digital assistant," which have a way of turning into self-fulfilling prophecies. This implies that the way we think and the way we shape thoughts with language, now more than ever, is endowed with transforming power. When you can do anything you want (at least in simulation), the question ceases to be what you can do, but becomes what you want to do.

As we move from a culture of archiving (oriented to the past) to one of programming (oriented to the future), the right metaphor becomes an important issue. It may be more urgent than ever to practice connected positive thinking when global mood changes can go either way. The word is not out yet on the fall of the Wall, the crumbling of all walls, for that matter. Getting rid of guilt, paying increased attention to other people's voices, staying open, expanding one's mental scale to planetary proportions, consulting one's body and the body politic for proprioceptive information about the state of things generally, are some suggestions for grounding personal ethics in a democratic and sustainable development.

In principle, it is a good idea not to jump to conclusions, especially ethical conclusions, in times of great social and cultural transformation. We are in such a time, and yet an ethical imperative can be seen developing in various guises, whether in political correctness, fundamentalist attitudes, antismoking campaigns, recycling crusades, or other behavioral groupware. Some trends, such as talk about collaborative rather than competitive ventures, new gender relationships and attitudes, political correctness, multiculturalism, social responsibility movements in professional societies and even in free enterprise, are indicative of a general orientation to a radical mood change. Part of this phenomenon can be attributed to "population implosion": thanks to media, people are exposed to each other in greater numbers, with greater frequency, greater intimacy, and greater impact. We are routinely thrown into situations that do not, at first, seem to concern us. So the correlative psychological issue is one of processing speed, that is, the power of integration a mind needs in order to make sense of such a huge and incompletely accessed realm.

What if spirituality were not metaphysical after all, but just a faster processing of all connections? Spiritual dimensions do exist, there's no question about that. Whether they stay attached to the forms that we give them is another question. Spirituality, for me, is an issue of processing speed, not of theology. The mind goes at certain speed and beyond the speed of the mind there is a spiritual realm which is very much faster. As an integrator of complex orders of eventfulness, spirituality is akin to information processing taking place at such a speed that everything becomes limpid and contradictions seem to work themselves out on their own.

With this argument based on processing speed I am trying to connect spirituality with physics, even if it were only through superluminal speeds. There is no reason, it seems to me, why spirituality shouldn't belong to physics. Light, after all, is a physical phenomenon whose existence no one would question in the name of some fanatical theory. Light, by reaching and stabilizing the speed at which all the other rhythms of matter are synchronized, functions like a very fast integrator of even the most baffling and conflicting jumble of heterogeneous entities. We should perhaps start exploring the possibility that spirituality is an emergent property resulting from the concentration of human, material, and life forms, and from the convergence of apparently contradictory agendas.

Spirituality is something that becomes more and more necessary because what is needed now is a form of guidance at levels of integration that were hidden or uninteresting to the mechanistic, literate mind of the West. The world is unfolding for us now in a very deep, fundamental way. As humans, as a species, we are coming to terms with the fundamentals of life and matter. We've gotten to the core of matter, or are getting there. We've uncovered the code of life, or are getting there. And we can turn information into matter: indeed, at the subatomic level there now seems little to distinguish between them. And so these three master codes—the subatomic code, the genetic code, and the information-manipulating digital code—are the keys to the given.

The consequence of possessing such powers is that brute survival strategy is simply not precise enough to tell us what to do. Survival was our previous guiding principle, but we do not have a teacher or a rule book anymore to instruct us in how to behave. As a species we have reached a point which is quite beyond that. You can explore the new territory yourself quite easily. Anybody can toy with a fantasy. Just try to imagine that you had the power to control all of nature. What would you do with it? What would be your next job? Merely by thinking along those lines, you get to the point where a fundamental integrating principle, including everything and everybody's agenda, becomes indispensable. When you get to that point, you realize that, yes, it's all in your mind; that is, the average of whatever you and the rest of humanity think of doing with these powers is precisely what is going to happen. And so your thinking and your feeling and your total sense of being become much more involved as an indicator of what it is you ought to do. At that speed, you either crash or integrate.

TEST CASES IN CONNECTED INTELLIGENCE:

HOW TO RUN A PRODUCTIVE WORKSHOP

I HAVE COME to workshop organization rather late, and almost by accident. I used to hold a rather jaundiced opinion of workshops in general, having been a participant in so many that didn't amount to much.* I find that I have now become deeply involved in their development and leadership. I apply workshop strategy in my

---

* Workshops are often no more than an excuse for professionals to engage in a talkathon with their peers. Think tanks end up as piles of chart paper scribbled with red and green and blue felt-pen ink. Some brainstorming sessions are better than others and leave you at least with a sense that your mind was active, almost in the manner it is when exposed to a very good movie. The end result, however, is like all oral promises or contracts: "not worth the paper it's written on." The conclusion that I draw from most of my experiences with group thinking is that it can be a lot of fun, but seldom even remotely practical in its outcomes. When there is a record, it often comes out as either terse and desiccated minutes or as a lame manifesto of some description. Rushing to consensus laminates individual input and brings the best ideas down to the level of the smallest common notions. In its results, if not in the process itself, group thinking tends to have a homogenizing, limiting, and downsizing effect on the individual intelligence, however brilliant.

teaching and I practice it around the world. This new vocation developed in two stages: first, I was invited to participate in a really good workshop on ecological issues in the tourism industry in Australia, where I learned the basics by observation; later I was asked to lead a workshop in Cologne, at the Design Institute run by Michael Erloff and Uta Brandes.

HOW TO RUN AN EFFECTIVE WORKSHOP

What first opened my eyes to the true potential of workshopping was taking part in the Winter School Collaboratorium at the Royal Melbourne Institute of Technology (RMIT).* The immediate task at hand was to serve as one of the media experts in several groups of workshops on eco-tourism. My own agenda was complementary: at the outset, I had announced that one of my principal goals in the session at RMIT was to identify forms of connected intelligence among people in small groups addressing a very new issue, and working under a certain degree of pressure. My question was: Is it possible to manage human intelligence in groups to achieve results unattainable by individuals?

The term "collaboratorium" was well chosen as, for me, the experience resembled being involved in a top-drawer research group looking into collaborative processes. I met and worked with about forty people from all over the world who, like me, didn't know much about tourism or about information technology's connections with ecological issues. But, in the end, we came up with real proposals supported by exceptional presentation material, all within one week. It was exhilarating, and it produced authentic results. The process

---

* This week-long workshop (July 9-15, 1995) at the Royal Melbourne Institute of Technology followed a keynote conference on "Where Worlds Converge: Travels Around the Info-Eco Future." The workshop addressed the issue of tourism and its connections with information technologies and ecological concerns.

rekindled my interest in workshop structure and provided me with a superb example of group thinking in action.

Because it is an organic process and because it unfolds over time, connected intelligence, whether computer-assisted or not, goes through different stages. Periods such as the conception of the idea, its birth in a decision to act, its growth in organization, the first signs of true innovation, patterns of expansion and contraction, followed by tentative projections, contradictions, verifications, reassessments, and final delivery, can all be seen at work in human gatherings. To observe such intelligence at work, that is, to try to imagine such separate moments in a continuum, is to see a single current of mind supported by words and gestures, at some moments self-organizing and at others being guided to connect to the overall purpose. I have identified twelve such elements, each of which describes an aspect of applied connected intelligence.

1. A sense of urgency

Why, how, and where does something like applied connected intelligence begin? A need must be felt and expressed eloquently by someone. In the case of the RMIT workshops, the urgency derived from the need to protect the natural environment in a sustainable economy, and it is interesting to see how this need was communicated. Sustainable development is one of Ezio Manzini's prime concerns. Manzini is a director at Domus Academy, the famous design institute in Milan. He developed the notion of "Factor 20," the idea that if our way of life and development is to be sustained at all, our whole society, and especially business and government, must achieve a ratio of 20 to 1 in reducing the present consumption of natural, social, and industrial resources. Ezio talked about this at the International Congress for the Societies of Industrial Design (ICSID 93) in Glasgow, and again at several meetings in Toronto in preparation for ICSID 97, but the idea really caught fire at a meeting in February 1995 at the Netherlands Design Institute in Amsterdam (NDI).

For many professionals, ecology and the environment are not exceptionally sexy issues and it takes some persuasion to get them stirred up. The notion of "sustained development" has more of the dull ring of a UNESCO project than the zing of a cutting-edge business proposal. The problem of tackling the whole planetary economy in a responsible way is enormous, disarming, and not immediately urgent to most. What was needed was new food for new thought.

2. A new connection

The novelty of the NDI meeting was in putting together "info" and "eco," information technologies and ecological considerations. Somewhere in the back of people's minds and smoothly moving to the fore was the corresponding idea that information technologies are themselves organizing along the lines of an ecosystem. It was also readily apparent that much of the data monitoring and retrieval that was enabling us to newly perceive the interdependence of a global ecosystem was provided by information technologies. However, what the first meeting revealed was that no one knew of any formal attempt at making a direct, conscious, and sustained connection between the two. Our job was to make one. That new connection would be akin to a giant synaptic contact between two largely self-organizing realms of human experience.

3. A focused and easily accessible area of investigation

While tourism is obviously very familiar in most regions of the world, it is not something that comes readily to mind in considering the priorities in ecological prudence. Tourism, however, is perhaps the most natural—physically experienced—connection between local and global sensibilities. It affects people everywhere personally, even those who are not fortunate enough to travel.

4. A task-oriented approach

Even more than a focused theme, we needed an exciting professional challenge.

The chosen strategy was to set up and conduct workshops, but not let them evaporate in mere talk. The key to the whole process would reveal itself to be the organizers' insistence that the workshops develop concrete presentation materials to support their proposals. Designers could be expected to excel in this area, but it was the principle that was important: it isn't the product but the process that really counts here.

The kind of attention people give to creating objects is quite different from that which they give to talking, or even writing. The product is a pretext to improve the quality of the process. The need to produce objects forces the connected intelligence to include *connected imagination* in its process, something that rarely occurs in a standard workshop.

In fact, the real problem for the organizers would be how to manage the timing of the various phases of the workshops. While nothing could be rushed at the beginning, there would be great haste towards the end because of the very concrete demands of the production of objects. The focus of mind, too, would be affected by the search for elegant and meaningful ways to express what turned out to be rather complex issues.

5. A broad mix of people

In a good workshop, everybody brings more to the process than just "something to contribute." Each participant is a specific being with a presence and a behavior that affects the whole process. Personal intelligence or expertise are only fragments of a whole person. One of the pitfalls cleverly avoided by the Melbourne workshops was the assumption that only qualified experts can contribute effectively to connected problem-solving. Crowding together the best and the brightest rarely produces success. The majority of the workshop members in this case were students, artists, designers, and generalist thinkers.

In a way, a workshop is not so much a meeting of minds, as a meeting of persons, and that means bodies, too, and gestures, tone of voice, and attitudes. The space of the minds' unfolding is that of the bodies meeting in colloquium. Confrontations between individuals create useful—or disastrous—imbalances in the group. All of that has to be managed somehow, worked into the mélange that will produce a truly connected, unified creation. And the mix, of course, includes not only the participants in the workshops, but everybody involved in the planning and the executing of the process.

6. A multi-tasking structure

The collaboratorium had more than forty registered participants, who were organized in five teams with a view to avoiding duplication of energies. The main workshop theme was "Where the Worlds Converge": this poetic turn of phrase actually translated as, "How does the convergence of information technology and ecology affect tourism?" That general theme was redistributed in five different subthemes. The five complementary sections bore the following names:

The Virtual Explorer (touring virtual reality/visiting virtually)
Travels to the Edge (discovering limits as a form of tourism)
The Virtual Museum (space-time data retrieval in cyberspace)
Techno-Touro (ecologically sensitive itinerant shows on demand)
@Home (how far can we go without leaving home)

What is effective and worth noting about these themes is that they all demand the use of imagination. They demand mental projections, just as design does. Each represents the frontier of today's technology, of today's levels of skills and expectations. They imply, at their center, the role of networks and virtual experiences, but they adopt different positions.

7. Managing mental energy

Motivating group intelligence is a complex affair. It is a problem of mental energy, which is why workshops are successful only to the extent that they have a manageable number of participants. You can neither teach nor learn very well in large groups because mental energy scatters easily, like incandescent light. But it bounces and ricochets extremely productively when it is confined within small, seminar-like groups. The big hurdle in connected-intelligence management is priming. Mental energy, like the other kind, has to be produced, pumped up out of its reservoirs. There is a need for a great initial stimulation and a few repeats during the early phases.

Phase one at RMIT was the briefing. A series of lectures and performances, packed with energy and passion and disguised as a public conference, set the tone and hinted at the content of what would follow. These were not really pep talks, but rather a series of insights to whet the mental appetite and challenge further thinking. As the performances concluded, the organizers reminded everyone that the work was only beginning, and those among the audience who would not be taking part in the workshops were invited to return to see the results at the end of the week. Throughout the week, the workshops would be fed with more input coming from a variety of sources: guest speakers, slide shows, demonstrations, short visits to a gallery or a museum, a busy schedule with healthy disruptive effects, especially at the beginning and in the middle of the week. If the priming is successful, connected intelligence will run on its own energy supply through to the end of the project. It could be a sort of "synaptic thermonuclear effect": if there are enough connections made at the priming stage, then momentum will come from the exponentially multiplying interconnections that follow. Mental energy can therefore be made to grow in groups and to flow.*

8. A hormonal strategy of management

The complementarity of the subthemes ensured that any participant could go from one workshop to another without losing the thread of discussion. The novelty of the collaboratorium was to place not one but two facilitators in each workshop section. One, the "shaker," was permanently assigned to the same group for the week; the other, the "mover," was assigned to a single group as well, but was also expected

---

* An analysis of the flow of mental energy is easily done, and can be documented and properly tested. It can be carried down to the individual group and should address the various levels of transistence (resistance and transparency ratios) each individual participant carries into the common task.

to move about during the afternoon sessions from one group to another, listening and making suggestions. Movers and shakers behaved like hormones in a biological system, working at different speeds in different mental and social territories.

As a mover, I remember dropping in to different groups as if I were visiting family. The hormonal function here is that the presence of a person whose job it is to connect patterns from group to group is enough to change the balance within a group and unblock energy. The fascinating thing is that you couldn't push your way in just anywhere. You pretty well had to wait to be invited. The effect was magnetic, both on me and on the new group. Sometimes, it felt as if I were an incarnation of the previous group's experience.

9. The huddle

Another successful innovation in the process was that all the movers and shakers, along with the workshop organizers and support staff, were required to huddle every morning for about an hour to discuss the progress and the problems of the sections. The huddle presented a perfect opportunity to compare notes and find solutions to problems of any of the groups. It was also a way for the shaker to assess and monitor the relevance of the work done in his or her assigned workshop. At these morning sessions, a certain lucidity would establish itself, even if critical problems were raised and disagreement arose. The huddle was also the place from where a change of direction in management could be made, if need be. It was classically democratic, in the sense that each workshop section—the constituency—was represented by two voices. In return, the clarity gained at the huddles would feed back into the workshops and establish useful continuity.

The huddles were where the workshops really came together, repeatedly, as if to measure themselves in the context of the larger goals of the whole process. The process of weighing possibilities, playing out scenarios, testing simulations, and coming up with decisions is called "thinking" when it is practiced in an individual's mind, and it precisely happened each time the group met for huddle time. Behind the talk, something like a total shape of the relationship between information technologies and ecological concerns in tourism was being discovered and acted upon. We were working in real time, taking on responsibilities that, initially, we wouldn't have thought we could manage.

10. Work-in-progress reports

Once a reasonable amount of time has been allowed for themes, ideas, and scenarios to be discussed, the process must be crystallized into decisive action of some sort. This decision cannot be left to a self-organizing outcome. It has to be taken consciously and some pressure has to be applied, otherwise, the process will go on without ripening and bearing fruit.* At the collaboratorium, the teams were asked at mid-week to present their work in progress and their plans. This turned out to be a kind of dry run for the work to be developed later. It was also the first time that each of the groups could really find out and appreciate what the others were doing.

With a final presentation in prospect, a certain level of rivalry between the groups was inevitable, and the spirit of competition really began to set in at that time. In fact the whole collaboratorium shifted gears. On the following morning, you could see mental energy rippling in more animated talk, more and better suggestions and insights, even improved memory, as if the connections had awakened useful recollections from each individual. Competition also brought the groups closer together as teams.

11. Final production

Two days before show time, you could feel another change of atmosphere. Bodies began to move faster, change places, look for materials, sit up in front of screens: the focus and self-absorption of each group was riveting. At that point, any pressure coming from outside a group was found to be rather unwelcome. Ideas, mined from a rich

---

* To overcome the proverbial "writer's block," one solution is to write something, anything, down on paper.

lode, were being quickly forged into presentation projects. Designers, programmers, presentation software gurus were coming forward. Doors were now more often closed than opened; people whispered, or conversed in enigmatic codes.* The free-ranging discussion and argument of the first three days had yielded to a period of intense contraction with rapid distillation of ideas and execution plans. There was energy enough to sustain some until late into the night.

12. Delivery

When we all assembled on the final Saturday, it felt like an end-of-the-year high school valedictory and prize distribution. Coming from adult professionals, there was a distinctively youthful kind of excitement in the air. Interestingly enough, while hardly any technology (except for pens and paper and chalkboards) had been used to develop and multiply the connected-thinking process itself, the end products benefited greatly from the skilled use of available high technology. The teams produced two CD-ROMs, a Web site, and two slide shows, all of exceptional quality. Two or three are themselves potential accelerators of connected intelligence.** There is no doubt that fortunes could and will be made on a dozen of the concrete ideas that came out of that process.

For me, the message of the Winter School Collaboratorium in Melbourne is that there is such a thing as connected intelligence and that it doesn't have to be machine-based. Connected intelligence is all

---

* One idea developed in my team, but not exploited there, found its way via another mover to another group and became one of the foundations of their proposal (much to the mock dismay of our team).

** In recognition of the privilege of having shared this experience with them, I would like to name the people who were part of the @Home team: the moderator (shaker) Dimity Reed, the documenters, Niels Peter Flint (designer), Patricia Picinnini (visualizer), Kevin Murray (writer), Peter Hennessey (photographer), and the participants, Nick Beams, Malcolm Enright, Richard James, Vasilije Kokotovich, Jesse Reynolds, Michael Sheridan, and Nancy Spanbroek.

around us. We have known it in different guises since childhood, but we have rarely recognized it for what it is because we thought that, as individual people, we are pretty well impermeable to each other. Connected intelligence can be gauged in a classroom, in a city, or in a culture. However, it cannot easily be perceived in such groups because it works both faster and slower than the individual human minds, over a different scale of time than that to which we are accustomed. It works in real time, and changes from second to second, like the thought in your own mind, so that it is next to impossible to get a single overview of it. However, it is clearly and demonstrably susceptible to significant improvement when it is purposely managed. Indeed, the real breakthrough in the developing human and technological networks of connected intelligence is not only that they promise new avenues to the solution of urgent human problems, but also that they reveal natural, organic connected intelligence as an age-old resource heretofore unexploited—like electricity, the airwaves and the atom once were.

TEST CASE #1: MADEIRA

Uta Brandes, one of the stars of German design, teaching, and criticism, had asked me to conduct a week-long seminar with a small group of design students at the Institute of Design of Cologne. The choice of date and of theme was up to me. As I was still mulling over the idea, I happened to give a talk in Funchal, on the island of Madeira, about "Madeira in the Age of Information." My approach to this theme was inspired by reading about efforts made by the island government of Majorca to develop an offshore consulting and development industry for networked services and system integration. I was particularly interested in the fact that while there are only 270,000 people living on Madeira, there are more than a million Madeirans living all over the world and most of them still consider themselves as Madeirans first and nationals of their adopted country second. I talked about the growing networking industry in Majorca and suggested that in the age of information, no island is an island anymore. I showed a few Web sites already existing on and about Madeira. I also showed a video of T-Vision. At the end of the conference, Pedro Ventura, the organizer, asked me if I would like to help him with plans for contents and directions of the Madeira Tecnopolo, the high technology scientific research park then under construction.

At first, I was rather daunted by the proposal, having never tackled a project of that scale. Then the idea of making that the theme of my workshop in Cologne occurred to me. A few weeks later, I was in Cologne showing a promotional videotape of the plans for Madeira's Tecnopolo to seventeen baffled design students. Only two of them could locate Madeira on the map. We started to work on ideas right away.

My method, which I call "Connected Intelligence Workshops" (CIW), is to work on such projects with teams usually made up of a combination of students, designers, experts and nonexperts, and whoever is interested in participating. Here is a shortened version of the text I sent to the participants:

The object of the CIW is to produce one or more presentation materials to support the development of a cultural, social, or business project.

Project Description: The project is to find and develop ideas appropriate for the orientation of the Madeira Tecnopolo, the high technology research and development center of Madeira, and to design materials to support presentations to Madeirans and European Community authorities for evaluation and assessment.

Objectives: The task of the CIW is to provide suggestions for contents, displays, multimedia interactive, Web sites, perhaps virtual reality, and other audiovisual displays. The final project presentation materials should be either on video or digital supports (CD-ROM, Web site, video, PowerPoint, or other presentation). The overall aim of the workshop is to train the participants in handling complex and ambitious projects with a team constituted with available local resources in personnel and equipment.

Method: The method of the CIW is inspired from common practice in industrial design and project management and involves both experts and nonexperts in a structured working association over a period of four days.

Process: Participants will be distributed in groups of no less than five, and no more than ten persons. Each group will be working—under my direction—on a different theme:

1. The global/local connection between Madeira and expatriate Madeirans.
2. The establishment of an experimental information delivery free zone.
3. The development of an experimental art and technology research center (two different groups are working on that theme, one devoted specifically to giving a characteristic Madeiran identity to art and technology on the Internet, and the other, developing a locally based research and design center).

These themes are just examples, not prescriptive suggestions; the finalizing of the thematic selection will be up to each individual group.

In each group, there is a facilitator, one or more travelers, and an implementer. These positions are to be decided at the first meeting of each group. The rest of each group is composed of experts on different pertinent subjects and nonexperts whose presence and active participation are considered and treated as contributions of equal importance to those of everyone else. A general coordinator, assistants, and technical support personnel are always available on the site of the workshops.

The specific task of the facilitator is leadership. The facilitator takes charge and responsibility for the sustained presence, participation, and active involvement of each member of a

group. The facilitator stays with the same group from the beginning to the end.

The task of the traveler(s) is to spend the first half of each day
with the original group, but the second half sessions with
another group of his or her choice. Every morning, the trav-
eler(s) must return to the original group to share what has been
learned elsewhere.

The implementer has the responsibility to keep records of
applicable strategies that have been explored and make sure that
they have real-life potential in the local context of the project.

Every morning, all facilitators, travelers, and implementers
meet with the coordinator to discuss the previous day's progress
and to plan for the present day's work.

Four days later, we had four elegant and polished presentation
materials on the following themes:

1. How to use networks to tighten the connections between
    Madeira and expatriate Madeirans. (The group conducted
    an Internet search and asked contacts on the island for infor-
    mation regarding Madeiran associations in the world, and
    created a PowerPoint presentation on how to develop com-
    munity networks on the Internet and with Web sites.)
2. How to stimulate multimedia production. The project was to
    establish an experimental information broadcast free zone,
    using the resources of Madeira's existing cable infrastructure
    and testing a wireless video transmission system invented by
    radio engineer Leonidas Ferreira (a four-minute video).
3. How to shape and develop an experimental art and technol-
    ogy research center. Two different groups worked on that
    theme, one, devoted specifically to giving a characteristic
    Madeiran identity to art and technology on the Internet (they
    created a Web site mock-up), and the other, developing a
    locally based research and design center (this group made a
    superb multimedia presentation integrating environment,

marine biology, and technological art to reflect some of the natural and human resources of Madeira).

The seminar ran from December 12–19, 1995. Taking advantage of the interruption of my teaching duties at the University of Toronto during Reading Week, I chose to conduct the second workshop between February 15 and 21, on location with the principals of the Madeira Tecnopolo. It happened to be right at the time of Madeira's wild and woolly Carnival. Seven of the original seventeen design students came along, invited by the Tecnopolo. In four days, we designed and developed three new presentations for the local Madeiran authorities and media. To do this, we reworked the original material completely to fit the actual local context as we found it, covering all the bases required of a feasibility study.

We discovered, for example, that perhaps more than anything else, we needed to find strategies to encourage a greater number of Madeirans both on and off the island to take advantage of new technologies that the majority (85 percent) either feared or ignored. To that end, we developed two simple concepts for projects. The first one was to open a continuous video-conferencing link over two switched telephone lines between a public area in Funchal and another one in Lisbon and later in other cities such as Toronto, for example, where there are many expatriate Madeirans. The proposal would be an experiment in market stimulation. The basic idea was to invite the islanders to hear, see, and talk to their relatives at the other end of the link. Our (as yet unverified) supposition was that people having this unexpected personal contact via the new technologies might be better disposed to requests from their own children for modest computer equipment. A second research goal of this project was more specific: it was to monitor and evaluate the communications traffic between Funchal and Lisbon before, during, and after the establishment of the video-conferencing link. Our guess during the workshop was that while many people would want to take advantage of free communications between Funchal and Lisbon, many more would prefer to go to the phone for privacy. The question then would be: Does the availability of free communication in public surroundings stimulate or decrease standard telephone usage?

The second project was called the "Madeiran Sea Lions Club." The object here was to use networks, and especially the Internet, to establish or reinforce connections between local and expatriate Madeirans and their communities. There are four, small desert islands (*Desiertas*) within sight of Madeira that are home to the last survivors of a once vast population of Monachus seals, popularly known as sea lions. The animals congregate on tiny, inaccessible beaches where they are protected by nature, and now also by law, from the merciless hunting they were subjected to twenty years ago. The workshop project proposed setting up a solar-powered camera trained permanently on beaches likely to be visited by sea lions. The slow-scan video source would be connected to a Madeira Sea Lions Web site open to all Madeirans, and anybody else interested in Madeira, anywhere in the world. The idea was to provide an incentive for people to join the club and return to the Web site frequently, if only to check the local weather, since they would never know whether this might be the day they would be treated to a rare view of a sea lion basking on one of the *Desiertas* beaches.

Today, work continues on the next steps involving the actual implementation of workshop projects. What I learned from this experience was that the CIW concept could withstand reality checks and also that there is tremendous value in doing this sort of research in two stages: one far from the real site so as to allow maximum freedom for imagination and conceptualization; the other on location, to adjust the dreams to local reality.

TEST CASE #2: FLORENCE

I tested the CIW formula again with MediARTech, a high technology and culture trade show at the Fortezza da Basso in Florence, this time with students from the European American Institute of Sophia

Antipolis in France. With these students, the format was completely different because the work was to be done over a longer period, rather than in a concentrated fashion as in Madeira. I also had to take advantage of short trips to Europe for other purposes because of my duties in Toronto. So, as is often the case in French academic institutions, the workshop was distributed in irregular periods of two to five hours, separated by long stretches of time. This made concentration more tentative. What surprised me is how committed the students showed themselves to be both before and after the workshops despite the elongation. Here is the syllabus for the workshop in Sophia Antipolis:

Objective: In the new economy, many people will soon have to invent or create their own job. And that will more often than not involve a good knowledge of the new powering technologies available to them for that purpose. The course is geared to help the students to understand the opportunities that lay ahead and to develop strategies to take advantage of them. So there is first a theoretical side to it, followed by hands-on practice in a real project.

Format: The first six lectures address the development of psychotechnologies, that is, technologies that support and modify the use of language—and thus affect the mind—from the alphabet to the Internet via radio, TV, and computers. Then next six-hour-long lectures address the effects of the recent convergent and networked technologies on business and the economy.

Workshops: The last eighteen hours are devoted to workshops to learn how to approach and develop real projects involving technology, culture, and business. This year's project (Spring 1996) is to run a professional development workshop on the social, industrial, and economical opportunities afforded by the new technologies at MediARTech, the high technology and cultural goods trade show in Florence (May 28-June 3, 1996). The task at hand in Florence is to find ways and means of implementing four major policies:

1. Wiring and networking the schools and generally the educational system of Tuscany
2. Connecting the Tuscany Regional area to the larger Mediterranean technopoles such as Barcelona, Montpellier, Sophia Antipolis, and Athens
3. Promoting the cultural heritage and the artistic tradition of Tuscany with the new technologies such as multimedia, virtual reality, and the World Wide Web
4. Persuading the larger segments of the Tuscan population to begin addressing their attention to these new technologies

The students will be redistributed in four groups, each addressing one of these themes. Midterm, each group will show a pre-project to the rest of the class. At the end of the course, each group is required to propose a final project presented in one or more of the following media: video, PowerPoint presentation, multimedia, CD-ROM, or Web site. The projects are evaluated according to whether they are good enough to present to Medi-ARTech a month later. It is hoped that some, if not all, of the students, will be able to also repeat their workshops in a concentrated fashion in Florence, using their presentation as starting point. Some of the lectures will be conducted by video conferencing from Toronto.

To tell the story of Florence—the exquisite charms and refined frustrations of working in three languages with more than seventy participants in the midst of a maddeningly noisy trade show, interrupted by eager and impatient journalists and/or technical breakdowns every four and a half minutes (I timed it)—would require another book. Suffice it to say that of the six projects developed in Florence, one is in progress at this time, one is being adapted for another region in Italy, and three more are undergoing feasibility studies for implementation in Tuscany. The work in progress is a Virtual University in Sherwood Towne created by Alpha World

expert, Bruce Damer, with my students from Sophia Antipolis.*
Here are some of its goals and principles established by our connected-intelligence group as formulated by Elselien Smit, a Dutch
educational technology consultant who took part in that workshop:

The Virtual Reality University (VRU)

The VRU is based in the Alpha Worlds, a virtual world in which
75,000 registered users live. The VRU is located in Sherwood
Towne which is a virtual city which served as the basis of social
experiments on human behaviors in virtual worlds. The VRU is a
multinational university constructed by the world twenty-four
hours a day in all time zones and where users can be everywhere
and nowhere and are not restricted with being somewhere in
particular. In this environment, an exhaustive database of people
and documents will be constantly updated by the publishing
and reading of documents in the Virtual Library.

Objectives

In general terms, the project aims at distributing knowledge in
multimedia technology and networks among university students and professors in order to prepare them for tomorrow's
electronic world and to practice "connected intelligence" in a
structured virtual environment.

More precisely, the VRU has the following aims:

1. To create a transnational university. A university in which
   students and professors from the whole world could interact,
   and therefore bring together their cultural differences in the
   purpose of connected intelligence.
2. To support lifelong learning. Today technologies are evolving
   so fast that people constantly need to update their knowledge

---

* The students who created VRU under the direction of Bruce Damer and consulting with Marc Pesce are Sébastien Canus, Eric Busch, David Villechaise, and
Patrice Arnera.

in a certain field in order to keep up to date and avoid becoming obsolete. This implies that people should not have to go to university for five years and then never come back anymore, but rather that they go through different phases of training at different periods in their professional lives.

3. To enhance the cooperation between students and professionals. Through workshops run by professionals, databases, using real-life simulations, students will get a better insight of what their future professional career will look like if they follow such or such kind of studies. The above also implies an improvement in connected intelligence by sharing and exchanging information and expertise and an enhancement of the cooperation between the academic world and the actual market.

4. To teach multimedia by using multimedia.

Principles

1. Just-in-time education. This principle is the engine to achieve our aim of providing lifelong learning. The VRU will in fact supply what people will be asking for, at the time they'll be asking for it.

2. Learning is exchange, not broadcast. The end of mass communication also implies the end of mass education. VRU's mission is to bring back the old model of mentors and followers and transforms the lecture to a journey of initiation through the virtual world and towards connected knowledge. Different from the academic system, virtual university has a flat hierarchy, there is not a single person with all the knowledge but every person has the same status. Exchange of information is the main rule of the virtual university. Learning is sharing and not only receiving information or knowledge. In this perspective, the VRU rejects the broadcast model of education to replace it with a networked model of education.

3. Enviromorphing according to user profile. Enviromorphing is the fact that the whole environment is shaped by the user's

own characteristics. By defining a profile on their first log-in, users will state their field of interests, and during their journey, the environment will be constantly reshaped to match his/her profile. Users will therefore have access only to what they are really looking for. When people come to the virtual university, they can choose, very precisely, their own information. They can also consult and contact the persons that they want, following their interests of the moment. This is feasible by letting the user define his/her profile at anytime as well as the system recognizing the user's evolution. Default keywords or criteria can be customized and contain as much as is needed to levels specified by the need, or remain at a basic level.

Registration

To register, people give their names, e-mail addresses, working qualifications, field of interests, and also workshop participation. People are selected in this register by their profiles. The register is the key to find contacts and people in a specific field of knowledge. In the register, you put out the people which you are interested for formation of new workshops. In this way, the register creates a real database.

There are many more details in our original plans that can be found on the site itself. The work on the VRU started by our group in Florence continues today on the Web. The name has been changed to The U and it is the object of intensive study, observation, international collaboration, and improvements.

The upshot of all of this experience is that connected intelligence works and that it can emigrate from its locus of origin to go on affecting the lives and minds of people you might never meet.

NOTES

Prologue

1 Derrick de Kerckhove, *The Skin of Culture* (Toronto: Somerville House Publishing, 1995), 63-64.

2 See "Cyberspace and the American Dream, A Magna Carta for the Knowledge Age," a position paper by Esther Dyson, George Gilder, George Keyworth, and Alvin Toffler, release 1.2 posted on the Net, August 22, 1994. For updates and further information, e-mail to pff@aol.com.

3 Marshall McLuhan, *Understanding Media: The Extensions of Man* (New York: McGraw-Hill, 1964), 66.

Chapter One

1 For those who would like to pursue this matter further, I recommend Chapter 2 of my previous book, *The Skin of Culture* (Toronto: Somerville House Publishing, 1995), 7–18.

2 Op. cit., 49–50.

3 Stephen Talbot, *The Future Does Not Compute: Transcending the Machines in Our Midst* (Sebastopol, California: O'Reilly, 1995), 17.

4 Jerry Mander, *Four Arguments for the Elimination of TV,* (New York: Vintage Books, 1986).

5 Nicholas Negroponte, *Being Digital* (New York:Vintage Books, 1995),102.

6 Peter Weibel, "New Space in the Electronic Age," Boek voor Instabiele Media, Stichting v2 Organizatie, 's-Hertogenbosch, 1992, 72.

Chapter Two

1 Don Tapscott, *The Digital Economy, Promise and Peril in the Age of Networked Intelligence* (Toronto: McGraw-Hill, 1996), 20. One-third of Canadian homes have PCs.

2 Douglas Rushkoff, *Playing the Future* (New York: Harper Collins, 1996), 181. In this very funny, but seriously researched book, Rushkoff calls teenagers "screen-agers."

3 Allucquère Rosanne Stone, "Cyberdämmerung at Wellsprings Systems," *Immersed in Technology, Art and Virtual Environments* (Cambridge, Mass.: MIT Press, 1996), 115.

Chapter Three

1 Katherine N. Hayles, "Embodied Virtuality or How to Put Bodies Back into the Picture," *Immersed in Technology, Art and Virtual Environments* (Cambridge, Mass.: MIT Press, 1996), 1.

2 Ibid., 2.

3 Further information on "ALIVE" and "Hamsterdamer" can be found on the Net at <<http://lcs.www.media.mit.edu/projects/alive>>.

4 Sandra Farran, "Virtual Spaces," *Maclean's,* June 17, 1996, 46.

5 Turkle, op. cit., 268.

6 "Technosphere" can be found at <<http://lcp20.lond.inst.ac.uk/technosphere>>.

7 Mark D. Pesce, "Final Amputation: Pathogenic Ontology in Cyberspace," published on-line at <http://www.hyperreal.com~mpesce.Fa.html>(1994): 27.

8 Turkle, op. cit., 170.

Chapter Four

1 Susan Kozel, "Virtual Reality: Choreographing Cyberspace," *Dance Theatre Journal,* vol. 11, (1994).

2 http://www.dds.hl

Chapter Five

1 Gary Wolf, "The Curse of Xanadu," *Wired,* June 1995, 140.

2 T. H. Nelson, *Literary Machines, 9.3.1* (Sausalito: Mindful Press, 1965), 15.

3 Raymond Hammond, *Digital Business, Surviving and Thriving in an Online World* (London: Hodder and Stoughton, 1996), 14.

4 Steve Steinberg, "Seek and Ye Shall Find (Maybe)," *Wired,* May 1996, 113.

5 Ibid.

6 Howard Besser, "From Internet to Information Superhighway," *Resisting the Virtual Life, the Culture and Politics of Information,* eds. James Brook and Iain Boal (San Francisco: City Lights, 1995), 67.

7 Idem, 156–57.

8 Steinberg, ibid., 113.

9 Op. cit., 180.

10 Ibid.

11 Ira Sager, "The Race Is on to Simplify," *Business Week,* June 24, 1966, 45.

12 Pierre Lévy, *Qu'est-ce que le virtuel?* (Paris: La découverte, 1995), 41.

13 Stephen L. Talbot, *The Future Does Not Compute: Transcending the Machines in Our Midst* (Sebastopol, California: O'Reilly, 1995), 360.

14 Plato, *The Phaedrus,* par. 256.

15 Op. cit., p. 210.

16 Michel Bernard, *"Hypertexte: la troisième dimension du language,"* TEXTE, 13/14 (1993): 5.

Chapter Six

1 Thomas de Quincey, *Confessions of an English Opium Eater* (*New York*: Everyman, 1962), 145.

2 Nicholas Negroponte, "Products and Services for Computer Networks," *Scientific American,* September 1991, 111.

3 George Gilder, Life After Television (*New York*: W. W. Norton and Co., 1994), 23.

4 Warren Caragata, "News, One Byte at a Time," *Maclean's,* January 29, 1996, 34.

5 James Fallows, "Navigating the Galaxies," *The Atlantic Monthly,* April 1996, 105.

Chapter Seven

1 B. W. Powe, *The Solitary Outlaw* (Toronto: Lester & Orpen Dennys, 1987), 16.

2 Robert Cook, co-director of Technology, Education Commons, OISE, University of Toronto, quoted in "End of Chapter?" *The University of Toronto Bulletin,* (August 19, 1996): 8.

3 *The Economist,* October 16, 1993, 105.

4 Joost Kist, "The Role of Print on Paper in the Publishing House of the Future," Incidental paper, Program on Information Resources Policy, Harvard University (December 1993).

5 Robert Bothwell, "End of Chapter?" *The University of Toronto Bulletin* (August 19, 1996): 8. Allegedly, the argument of one sultan who ordered the torching of the Library of Alexandria around the eighth century A.D. was : "If it's in the Koran, then we have the Koran; if it's not in the Koran, we don't need it, so burn it." Noah Kennedy (*the Industrialization of Intelligence*) suggests that we take this legend with a grain of salt and that "a competing theory ascribes the same crime to fanatical Christians centuries before."

6 G. M. van Trier, "Information 2000: A Dutch View," *The Electronic Library,* vol. 10, no. 3 (June, 1992).

7 James Larue, "The Library of Tomorrow: A Virtual Certainty," *Computers in Libraries,* vol. 13, no. 2 (February, 1993): 16.

8 Kenneth Dowlin, "Public Libraries in 2001," *Information Technology and Libraries* (December 1991): 318 and 320–21.

9 Colin Steele, "Millennial Libraries: Management Changes in an Electronic Environment," *The Electronic Library,* vol. 11, no. 6 (December, 1993).

10 John Corþin, "Technology and Organizational Change in Libraries," *Library Acquisitions,* vol. 16, 349-353.

11 Speech to the U.S. Senate, as quoted by Colin Steele, op. cit., 394.

12 John Blegen, "Beyond Access: Implications of the Information Age for the Public Library," *The Future of Books* (1993): 459.

13 Mark Surman, "From VTR to Cyberspace: Jefferson, Gramsci and the Electronic Commons" (May 1994). For more information e-mail to msurman@io.org.

Chapter Eight

1 Helen Searing, quoted in "Old Images, New Metaphors: The Museum in the Modern World" (part 3), "Ideas," CBC Transcripts, 1982, 20.

2 Marjorie Halpin, idem, 22.

3 Thierry de Duve, "La condition Beaubourg," reprint from *Critique*, no. 426, quoted in *L'époque, la mode, la morale, la passion, aspects de l'art d'aujourd'hui, 1977–1987* (Paris: Publications du Centre Georges Pompidou, 1987), 401.

4 Paul Virilio, *"Images publiques,"* in *"Théatres de la mémoire,"* *Traverses*, no. 40 (April 1987): 38–53.

5 From the catalogue *"Les Immatériaux,"* Paris, Centre de Création Industrielle, Centre Georges Pompidou, Paris (March–July 1985).

6 Jean Baudrillard, *L'echange symbolique el la mort* (Paris: Gallimard, 1976), 176.

7 Liz Addison, quoted by John Bentley Mays in "Getting in Touch," *Globe and Mail* (Toronto), April 9, 1987, section C.

8 Marjorie Halpin, op. cit., 23. In his *Psychoanalysis of Artistic Vision and Hearing*, Anton Ehrenzweig supported the thesis that the creation and the acceptance by the consumers of new harmonies of color and sound were not due solely to biological or mathematical laws but to people's tendencies to reorder their sensory responses according to the experiences they had been exposed to over time. Thus, what was once deemed to be discordant would eventually become pleasurable after some repetition.

9 Marshall McLuhan, op. cit., 78.

10 Marjorie Halpin, ibid., 23.

Chapter Nine

1 David Kline, "The Embedded Internet," *Wired*, October 1996, 98.

2 <http://www.ffly.com>

3 <http://www.ideosphere.com>

4 Kevin Kelly, *Out of Control: The New Biology of Machines, Social Systems and the Economic World* (Addison-Wesley, 1994), 26.

5 Kelly, op.cit., 20.

6 MIT's Media Lab Web site <http://www.media.mit.edu> Autonomous Agent Group, posting May 24, 1996.

Chapter Ten

1 Robert McIlwraith, "The Feelings Economy," unpublished paper, a personal communication, August 1996.

2 Noah Kennedy, *The Industrialization of Intelligence* (Unwin, 1989), 6.

3 W. Brian Arthur, "Increasing Returns and the New World of Business," *Harvard Business Review*, July-August 1996, 101. (I am grateful to Tom Strong for bringing this article to my attention.)

4 Ibid.

5 *Out of Control*, op. cit., 201.

6 Op.cit., 104.

7 Walter S. Baer, 1973. "Cable Television: A Summary Overview for Local Decision Making." National Science Foundation Research Applied to National Needs Program, 134-NSF. Santa Monica: Rand, quoted by Howard Besser in "From Internet to Information Superhighway," *Resisting the Virtual Life, The Culture and Politics of Information*, eds. James Brook and Iain Boal (San Francisco: City Lights, 1995), 60.

Chapter Eleven

1 W. Wayt Gibbs, "Lost Science in the Third World," *Scientific American* (August 1995): 92.